D1626825

ADOLESCENT GIRLS AND THEIR FRIENDS

For my friend Marguerite and my daughter Sara

Adolescent Girls and
Their Friends

A feminist ethnography

VIVIENNE GRIFFITHS

HAVERING COLLEGE
OF FURTHER & HIGHER EDUCATION
LEARNING RESOURCES
CENTRE

Avebury

Aldershot • Brookfield USA • Hong Kong • Singapore • Sydney

302.314   Q   144729

© V. Griffiths 1995

All rights reserved. No part of this publication may be reproduced, stored in a retrieval system, or transmitted in any form or by any means, electronic, mechanical, photocopying, recording or otherwise without the prior permission of the publisher.

Published by
Avebury
Ashgate Publishing Limited
Gower House
Croft Road
Aldershot
Hants GU11 3HR
England

Ashgate Publishing Company
Old Post Road
Brookfield
Vermont 05036
USA
Reprinted 1996

British Library Cataloguing in Publication Data

Griffiths, Vivienne
    Adolescent Girls and Their Friends:
    Feminist Ethnography

ISBN 1 85972 019 6

Library of Congress Catalog Card Number: 95-77824

Printed and bound in Great Britain by
Athenaeum Press Ltd, Gateshead, Tyne & Wear

Contents

Figures and tables

Acknowledgements

There are many people who have helped this book come about. Firstly, I should like to thank Alison Kelly and David Morgan, who supervised the research at Manchester University, for all their advice and positive support over several years. Many thanks also to Liz Stanley for continually encouraging my ethnographic work and for first suggesting that I turn the research into a book.

At Sussex University, the Institute of Education women's group have been most supportive, especially Lisa Dart who made positive comments on the revised chapters, and encouraged me to keep going. Thanks also to Barry Cooper for his constructive criticisms of draft extracts. Special thanks to those who have helped in the production of the book: Albert Noronha for preparing the tables and diagrams, and Geoff Hockney for technical advice and printing. Their time and expertise have been much appreciated.

Help of a different but equally important kind has been given by my sister Angela Butterfield, who gave me much valuable advice on publishing, and by my women friends, who have helped talk through the ideas and shared their interest and experiences. Many thanks to Jenny Sessions, who helped revive my creativity during the last stretch. A big thank you to my family: my partner Peter Johnson, who has lived with the project at all its different stages, and our children Chris and Sara, who have grown up with the book.

I am most grateful to the Head and staff of Barnsdale High School for allowing me into their midst; in particular, to Lesley Green who so generously let me share her class for a while. Last but not least I should like to thank all the young women who participated so fully in the research, and without whose contributions this book would not have been possible.

Original versions of chapters 2, 7 and 8 were previously published in the following books and journals: 'Working with adolescent girls: making the research process feminist', in Vivienne Griffiths, Maggie Humm, Rebecca O'Rourke & Janet Batsleer, Fiona Poland, & Sue Wise (eds.), *Writing Feminist Biography 2, Studies in Sexual Politics* No.19, University of Manchester Sociology Department (1987). Thanks to Liz Stanley, the series editor.

'From playing out to dossing out: young women and leisure', first appeared in Erica Wimbush & Margaret Talbot (eds.), *Relative Freedoms: Women and Leisure*, Milton Keynes: Open University Press (1988). A small part of 'Stepping out: the importance of dancing for young women', (ibid.) can also be found in chapter 7. My thanks to the editors and publishers.

'Adolescent girls: transition from girlfriends to boyfriends?' was first published in Patricia Allatt, Teresa Keil, Alan Bryman & Bill Bytheway (eds.), *Women and the Life Cycle: Transitions and Turning -Points*, London: Macmillan, and appears by kind permission of the British Sociological Association and the publishers.

Notes on transcripts and classification

(1) ... indicates that some words have been omitted.
   eg.'You don't use your proper name though ... I'm Queen Bee'.
(2) Single round parentheses give clarificatory information.
   eg. 'And you just go like that' (gesturing).
(3) - represents a pause or hesitation.
   eg. 'You see we - in an afternoon'.
(4) Certain words or ways of speaking common in West Yorkshire
   have been included.
   eg.   all t'time = all the time.
         tek = take.
         mek = make.
         nowt = nothing.
         owt = anything.
         summat   = something.
         me friend = my friend.
         she goes = she says.
         right close = very close.

Social class classification, e.g. Classes I and II: Government Census 1991.
Ethnic classification, e.g. Black-Caribbean, Indian, Pakistani: Commission for Racial Equality.
School year group classification; old system, e.g. third year, fifth year; recent system in brackets, e.g. (Year 8): Education Reform Act 1988.

All the names of the young women and their teachers, the school and district, have been changed to protect anonymity.

1 Girls and friendship: An introduction

Looking through family albums and holiday snapshots, I came across two photographs. In the first, two girls in early adolescence pose for the camera in dance positions, balancing each other in a double arabesque. One looks straight ahead with a confident grin, while the other looks down, smiling shyly. In the second, four thirteen year-old girls in shiny dance dresses make a tableau, arms outstretched, hands clasped. All four smile broadly, but self-consciously, hardly able to contain their laughter.

These two photographs were taken thirty years apart, but they have some remarkable similarities. The first is myself (the shy one), photographed with my best friend at a dancing summer school; the second a group of friends from the same youth club, about to take part in a disco-dancing competition. They are all at that in-between stage, no longer little girls but not yet young women. In spite of the awkwardness expressed by some because of the intrusion of the camera, both photographs capture the physical closeness between the girlfriends, their love of dancing, and their enjoyment in each others' company.

There are differences too. The first photograph, in black and white, shows two middle class girls in the South of England in the fifties; the second, in colour, a group of working class Yorkshire girls in the eighties, whom I got to know whilst researching this book. I have many other photographs of girlfriends, then and now, but the shared elements are more striking than differences in time or place, ethnicity or class.

This book is a celebration of such friendships, based in adolescence and young womanhood. For adolescent girls, the transition to adulthood is a time of major development and change: in physical

1

appearance, sexuality, relationships with parents and friends, interests, attitudes and feelings. Small wonder that girls' friendships between the ages of eleven and eighteen are so important, so close but turbulent, and so potentially long-lasting.

In this opening chapter, I introduce the main aims and themes of the book, summarise previous research in this area, and briefly describe the fieldwork which forms the basis of the findings.

Negative images or strong friendships?

Whilst images of strong friendships between men are commonplace, from David and Jonathan to Starsky and Hutch, the popular view is that women are incapable of such attachments, as Anne Seiden and Pauline Bart (1975) report:

> There has been a popular cultural stereotype that women do not really like each other very much. It has been said that women do not really trust women friends, do not have grounds for trusting them......and are inherently in competition for the available men. This competition is said to override the possibility of genuine friendships. (Seiden & Bart 1975 p.192)

One argument is that women are seen in this way because of their subordinate position in a patriarchal society. Simone de Beauvoir describes women friends as 'rarely rising to genuine friendship......as they face together the masculine world' (1952 p.607).

This picture starts early, perpetuated by magazines such as *Jackie* (McRobbie 1981 & 1991), and more recently *Just Seventeen*. In these girls are shown as bitchy, catty, jealous and divided in competition over boys. This stereotype is all too often carried over into schools, where it is still common to hear both men and women teachers talk about girls' friendships as shallow and shortlived, characterised by cliques and quarrels, in contrast to the closer, more long-lasting friendships between boys. On the other hand, even when girls are clearly enjoying themselves together, they are often described as giggling and silly, for ever chattering about pop stars or boys, and distracting each other from work. Girls themselves will often use the same negative terms to describe their friendships.

Such a picture does not accord with either my own memories of adolescent friendships, or my experience over many years of working with young women through teaching, drama and research. There are certainly some recognisable elements in the stereotype, but presented

2

in a superficial and incomplete way, which essentially undermines the real value and everyday nature of girls' relationships with each other. It is easy to see this trivialising of friendships between girls as part of the wider subordination of women, which has been analysed in detail by feminists in recent years.

What I aim to do in this ethnographic study is move below the surface of a general theory, and look closely at young women's lives and relationships, to see how they make sense of their experiences and friendships. I do not want simply to jettison negative ideas as false, but to offer an alternative, more positive interpretation, grounded in the rich data that I collected during my research. Although there is a strong emphasis on the young women's own accounts, they are set within social, cultural and institutional frameworks, thus hopefully avoiding the one-sidedness of some ethnographies which Ann-Marie Wolpe criticises (1988). Nevertheless, the girls emerge as active agents in their own lives, finding positive strategies and forms of resistance to cope with and surmount difficulties and constraints, rather than as passive victims of oppression.

The book examines the nature of girls' friendships, and aims to show how important these are in providing them with positive self-identity and self-esteem. Friendships between girls are deep, intense and long-lasting, and often continue alongside relationships with boys. Compared to boys, girls experience considerable restrictions on their lives (such as where and when they can go out), and the strength of their friendships with other girls enables them to keep some measure of power and control, not to mention fun, in their lives.

Talking is at the heart of this, ranging from the everyday exchange of ideas and events, to the confiding of secrets and sharing of problems. It is often observed how good women are at relationships and communication in general, and how they almost inhabit a different world from men in the way they relate to others (Tannen 1991). Another aim of the book is to show how this develops through years of girls relating to each other in a close and meaningful way.

A particularly interesting aspect of the friendship theme is its dual nature: friendships between girls are close and supportive, but also liable to cause jealousy and emotional tension, as Susie Orbach and Luise Eichenbaum (1987) describe in relation to women friends in their book *Bittersweet*. There is fun and laughter, but there can also be hurt and pain; as in any close relationship, these aspects are inextricably linked. Reasons why girls fall out, such as one girl rejecting another or breaking a trust, will be explored in detail in the book.

Pressures on girls to move away from female friendships are strong, especially as they get older and begin to go out with boys. In contrast to many other studies, the book stresses the ways in which young women resist these pressures, and return again and again to the secure base of the girls' group.

Why girls?

The last fifteen years have seen a vast number of studies of women's experience, but still relatively little research on young women's lives, except in the area of education. As long ago as 1976, Angela McRobbie and Jenny Garber pointed out the omission of girls in books about youth culture. Boys' interests such as football, trends such as skinheads or punks, and even popular music which has always been of great interest to girls, have all been written about from a male perspective (Clarke 1978, Frith 1978, Hebdige 1979). These youth cultural studies not only largely ignore the experience of young women, the (male) writers often show a 'marked antipathy to feminist critiques' (Griffin 1987 p.83).

As a counterbalance to this 'academic machismo', as David Morgan calls it (1981 p.101), feminist researchers set out to provide a female equivalent to the 'gangs of lads' model (Griffin 1987 p.84), particularly exemplified by Paul Willis's influential study of boys' anti-school culture (1977). For example, Lynn Davies focused on gender and deviance in school (1984), whilst Christine Griffin studied the transition from school to work for young working class women (1985a). Neither study found a direct equivalent to the boys' subcultural groupings identified by Willis. Davies describes a group of bottom stream girls who to some extent acted supportively together in school, but did not display the same kind of collective solidarity as Willis's lads. The girls in Griffin's study spent most of their time in female friendship groups, but these were smaller than male equivalents.

There have now been many studies of gender and schooling, in which girls' experiences and girls' groups have been analysed, ranging from Audrey Lambart's 'The Sisterhood' (1976), to Barrie Thorne's *Gender Play* (1993), but a detailed look at the way in which girls' friendships in school relate to those outside school is still lacking. This was an important reason for undertaking the research on which this book is based.

Angela McRobbie's work on girls' subcultures still stands out as one of the strongest investigations of girls' friendships and the 'culture of femininity' (McRobbie 1977 & 1978a). Unusual in being based in a youth club rather than a school, McRobbie's study found 'strong supportive networks of friends' (1977 p.30) and 'a real sense of solidarity' (ibid p.143) between girls and their friends. McRobbie's work is important in putting young women's experience centre stage and delineating aspects of their private culture, as well as stressing the value of friendships as at least in part providing girls with a means of challenging their subordinate position.

Reading these earlier studies is like piecing a jigsaw together, a jigsaw with some pieces missing or which can be put together in a variety of ways. The main findings which emerge from both sociological and psychological research (Duck 1983, Kutnick 1988) are that close friendships between girls are based on trust, loyalty and the confiding of secrets or problems. These friendships can be intense and stormy, and the breaking of friends seen as a betrayal of trust. More recent studies start to build a different picture from McRobbie's, notably in showing that girls may go round in groups as well as pairs, and that their culture can be accommodated on the streets as well as in the home. Rather than assuming that girls' friendship disappear as they go out with boys, more recent research (Griffin 1985a, Lees 1986 & 1993) also demonstrates that young women show resistance to the break up of their friendships.

It is not surprising that different findings have started to emerge. As more research is carried out in this area, so a broader spread of information becomes available. Also, young women's daily lives and experiences might be expected to have changed over the last fifteen years, especially in the light of the women's movement and its widespread influence. In *Adolescent Girls and Their Friends*, I aim to bring these threads together, recognising that one book in itself can only present a partial account, and that since the research was carried out in the 1980s, aspects of girls' experiences may have changed yet again.

The book has been written to make young women's experience visible, to fill the gaps left by previous studies and question some of their findings, and to look at girls' distinctive and different cultures, both in and out of school. It sets out to document, in the manner of life histories or oral history, to explain, and in some respects, to put the record straight. Because the emphasis in previous work has so often been on boys' lives, the focus in this book is on girls, rather than a comparison of girls' and boys' friendships. However, boys will be included in terms of their relationships with girls, where relevant, and when it helps to explain some aspect of girls' experience.

Affirmation of female friendships

This book has also been written in the context of a recent revaluing by feminists of friendships between women, in contrast to the popular view that women are incapable of deep attachments. In 1938, Virginia Woolf expressed surprise and pleasure at reading a novel by a woman writer depicting women as close friends. Now such novels are becoming commonplace; contemporary women writers such as Marge Piercy, Margaret Atwood and Michele Roberts make friendships between women the focus or central thread of some of their novels, and portray the strength, intensity and lasting power of close relationships between women. Children's writers such as Rosa Guy and Ann Fine write powerful stories about girls' friendships too.

'Sisterhood is powerful', one of the central tenets of the women's movement, is a strong statement of the belief that women working together can be strong, that the personal can become the political. Women's collectives, or women-only spaces, have been one manifestation of the mutual support that women can provide. For many feminists, sisterhood has been taken further in a rejection of heterosexuality, and a positive affirmation of lesbian relationships.

However, the existence of strong female friendships is nothing new, even if the emphasis on them is more recent. In a fascinating and scholarly account, Lilian Faderman (1981) traces romantic friendship between women from the sixteenth century to the present day:

> Passionate romantic friendship between women was a widely recognised, tolerated social institution before our century. Women were, in fact, expected to seek out kindred spirits and form strong bonds......It was not unusual for a woman to seek in her romantic friendship the centre of her life, quite apart from the demands of marriage and family. (Faderman 1981 p.411)

As well as being close and supportive, many of these friendships were 'charged with conflict, jealousy, ambivalence, all the emotions which normally accompany an intense sexual relationship' (ibid p.71), even if the women's intimacy did not in fact find sexual expression.

Faderman argues that the context for and social construction of close friendships between women has changed dramatically in the twentieth century. She suggests that the toleration of these friendships ceased at the turn of the century because women's roles were changing and women were beginning to demand more power, for instance through the women's suffrage movement. Friendships between women came to be seen as deviant as men's dominant position in society was threatened; in the 1920s and 30s, lesbianism was seen as a particular threat to 'normal' feminine sexuality. This change is also clearly charted in the schoolgirl fiction over this period (Anderson 1994).

Although the second wave of feminism, as Faderman calls it, has presented a general challenge to patriarchal culture, Faderman argues that lesbian-feminists at best co-exist with heterosexual society, rather than operating within it as the women friends of earlier centuries were able to do. This has considerable implications for any investigation of friendships between young women who, as I shall describe, still experience strong cultural pressures towards heterosexuality. At the same time, there is an increasing awareness among adolescent girls of the women's movement and struggles by women to take a more equal place in society, which affects their views and their relationships.

Starting points and fieldwork

What sparked off my particular interest in this area, and provided the impetus for the book, was a drama project which I set up at a school in West Yorkshire, in which girls were exploring aspects of their experience through role play. The strength and value of friendships between girls came through as a dominant theme. This was particularly exciting because it was an unexpected finding, introduced and developed by the girls themselves, and the one positive feature of their lives stressed by the girls in their improvisations. The picture of friendships between young women presented in the drama whetted my appetite to take the subject further and make friendship the focus of a more detailed investigation.

In order to carry out the research, I spent a year from 1983 to 1984 in a mixed-sex comprehensive school in West Yorkshire, gaining access through a friend who was a former teacher there, and then formally through the Head. Barnsdale High School is situated in a council estate on the outskirts of Millbrook, an industrial town close to the Pennines. The area was described by the Head as 'very socially deprived', and there was and is high unemployment. The population was largely working class, a mixture of white, and some Black-Caribbean, Indian and Pakistani, and mainly stable in nature. In many ways this was a traditional, close-knit community typical of the region.

7

The Headteacher Miss Jones chose the classes with whom I was to work, perhaps as Helen Simons suggests 'to reflect credit on the school' (1981 p.31), although through 'snowball' sampling (Burgess 1984 p.55) the original groups soon expanded to include friends from other classes. I spent most of the time with sixteen girls, all but one working class, following them from their second to third year of secondary schooling (Years 8 & 9). Within the class, G2, there were three distinct girls' friendship groups: a large group of eight white girls, and two smaller groups, one of four white girls and the other four girls of mixed ethnic background (two Black-Caribbean, one Indian and one white). A detailed picture of these groups will be built up during the book, as well as of other groups and of parallel friendships which existed both in and out of school.

At first I spent most of the time observing lessons, but over the year more and more time was spent with the girls at break, lunchtime and after school. I was also in contact with the girls for a further year afterwards. Apart from the girls and their immediate friends, I also got to know the boys in the class, and through the school's setting arrangements for different subjects, girls and boys in other classes, bringing the total of pupils with whom I had regular contact to over a hundred.

As well as these, I also worked with sixteen school leavers (all white), interviewing fifteen of the girls just before they left school in the fifth year (now known as Year 11), and ten whom I met again nine months after they had left school. These young women also had a variety of friendship group sizes, including a large group of eight, a group of four, a pair of friends and two loners who spent some of their time together in school.

What I found constantly when investigating girls' friendships was how eager the young women themselves were to talk about themselves and their friends, to share their experiences with me, and show me the places they went together. One reason for this may have been that it is unusual for girls to be asked their opinions, or made to feel important; the young women were certainly surprised but pleased by my interest, and often said that it made them feel special. However, this eagerness to talk also seemed to reflect their interest in the subject itself, as well as the importance of talking which formed a key aspect of their own friendships. So 'interviews about friendship' were more often conversations between friends, which carried on their normal interaction.

More widely, I have found this kind of interest expressed by women whom I talked to whilst writing and researching the book. Even casual mention that I was writing a book about girls' friendships has sparked off memories of their own adolescence, or a discussion of their teenage daughter's current group of friends. Great excitement is often generated in these accounts of past exploits with friends, recalling both pleasure and pain.

This introduction ends, as it began, on a personal note. Like the women I talked to while writing this book, thinking about girls' friendships has helped me to recall my own relationships, and look at my experiences in a different light. I realise that at school, girlfriends were important to me, but in a taken for granted way; I am now better able to assess just how important they were. In more recent years, particularly since my involvement with the women's movement, I have been far more conscious of the importance of female friendships. This is the perspective which I have brought to writing the book.

2 Making the research process feminist

In this chapter I shall explore some of the research processes involved in working with young women, how my role as 'researcher' changed during the fieldwork, and ways in which I tried to make the research process feminist. I shall discuss how I tried to involve my own experience, both past and present, in the research process, and the impact which writing up the research had on re-thinking that experience.

Feminist research

> Essentially feminism is a perspective rather than a particular set of prescriptive values. (Oakley 1974 p.3)

The feminist critique of sociology has largely focused on positivist research (Bernard 1973, Oakley 1974, Spender 1980). Writers have highlighted the dominance of male models of society and the invisibility of women at all stages of the research process (Griffiths 1984). Dorothy Smith writes:

> In almost every area of work, we have had to resort to women's experiences as yet unformulated and unformed; lacking means of expression; lacking symbolic forms, images, concepts, conceptual frameworks, methods of analysis; more straightforwardly, lacking self-information and self-knowledge. (Smith 1979 p.144)

Positivist methods have been particularly criticised for their masculine bias (Bernard 1973, Spender 1978) in favouring qualities like reason and 'objectivity' and methods that yield 'hard' data. Jessie Bernard called this the 'MACHISMO factor in research' (Bernard 1973 p.73).

Other feminists have criticised the objectification of the subjects of research (Graham 1982, Oakley 1981). For example, Ann Oakley wrote a detailed critique of text book models for 'correct' interviewing procedures which she regarded as a 'rationalisation of inequality' (Oakley 1981 p.40) and inappropriate for her own research on women and childbirth.

However, such criticisms are not solely levelled at positivist methods. Feminists have also pointed out the exclusion of women and masculine bias in qualitative research (McRobbie 1979, Griffin 1980). I have already mentioned the relative invisibility of young women in research into peer groups and subcultures, which was one of my reasons for wanting to study this area. In an earlier article I suggested:

> A certain romanticising of, and identification with, oppressive aspects of masculinity, may almost be a prerequisite for this kind of ethnographic account, where white working class males are the subjects. (Griffiths 1984 p.512)

In looking at textbooks on educational ethnography, there is also an emphasis on objectivity, detachment and minimum 'interference' in the field alongside a stress on building rapport and trust between researcher and researched (Denscombe 1983, Burgess 1984, Woods 1986).

In the light of the above, it is obviously not possible simply to equate feminist research with all ethnographic research. Moreover, some feminists use quantitative methods, either in isolation or in conjunction with qualitative methods, and argue that positivism can be made feminist if a feminist perspective is used (Kelly 1978, Jayaratne 1981). Thus, it is not sufficient to define feminist research by looking at the methods (ie. *techniques* of research) alone.

In thinking about my own research I found it helpful to identify factors which might make up a feminist approach or perspective, or might be called a feminist methodology in the broader sense of the research *process* being used. I have identified three main areas: starting from the perspective of women, breaking down researcher-researched divisions, and creating a sociology for women, and these will be used as a framework for the chapter through which I shall analyse the processes of working with young women. In many ways the research methods used followed standard educational ethnographic practices which I have detailed elsewhere (Griffiths 1991). But at times there were some tensions between these and feminist approaches which I shall also describe.

Starting from the perspective of women

A feminist approach makes women's concerns of central importance; women's everyday lives become the starting point (Smith 1974, Spender 1978). Janet Finch calls for a 'sociology *for* women - that is a sociology which articulates women's experience of their lives' (Finch 1984 p.86). However, feminist research does not necessarily have to be *about* women, as Liz Stanley and Sue Wise point out (1983). A sociological approach which, in Dorothy Smith's words, 'starts from the perspective of women' (Smith 1977 p.15), would adequately encompass a diversity of research topics under a feminist umbrella.

In my own research on girls' friendships, starting from the young women's perspective was a central aim, and I tried to achieve this both by working with the girls on their own, and by making their experience the focus. As a feminist it seemed to me crucial to make the experience of the young women central, rather than peripheral or invisible as many previous studies of young people had done. Because I was working in a mixed-sex school, I obviously needed to take into account the relationships between the girls and the boys. Nevertheless, I wanted my main focus to be on the friendships between the girls. In order to do this, and to make the experience of the young women I worked with my starting point, I decided to work with girls on their own. I had worked with girls-only groups in a previous research project (Griffiths 1984 & 1986). In this situation I had found the girls extremely responsive and felt it had been a valuable experience for them. This was an additional reason for choosing a girls-only approach again.

I was interested in the responses which my decision to work with girls on their own seemed to provoke in others. It seemed to worry the boys tremendously. Boys frequently accosted me with the question 'Why aren't you working with us?' or comments like, 'You shouldn't be working with the girls. They're boring' or 'Girls are stupid. We're much more interesting' . The boys obviously felt they were missing out, and this was an interesting and amusing reversal of the normal pattern in mixed-sex schools, where boys demand, and get, much more attention than girls (Spender 1982, Whyld 1983).

Some of the men teachers also seemed quite worried by my girls-only approach. One of them accused me of being sexist because I was not including the boys. I responded by explaining that most previous studies had excluded girls so I was really only redressing the balance a little. As other feminist researchers have pointed out (Davies 1985,

Griffin 1985b), male-only studies are accepted as normal whereas women-only research is perceived as unusual or strange.

On the other hand, my decision was understood and supported by the woman Head of the school, and was never questioned by the women teachers. My 'attachment' to the girls was welcomed by the girls themselves who would proudly introduce me to friends or teachers as someone 'doing a study of us' or 'interested in the girls in our class'. Girls in other classes seemed to accept quite readily when I explained to them that I could only spend a long time with a small number of girls, as if the attention given to those other girls nevertheless made all the girls in the school more important. I also noticed that, as I got to be a familiar sight around the school, young women whom I did not know would come up to me and start a conversation. It seemed as though I had become known as 'the woman who was there to talk to the girls'.

Creating space for girls (and women) to be together in single-sex situations is widely recognised as valuable by feminists. In mixed-sex schools where such occasions are rare, it makes the girls seem special and important. As Lynn Davies writes about the girls she worked with, 'they were singled out as special, perhaps for the first time in their school career' (in Ball 1985 p.29).

Focusing on the young women's experience was a crucial factor in building up that feeling of being special and in emphasising the positive importance of friendships between girls. The general attitude in the school towards girls' friendships held by boys, teachers, and to some extent the girls themselves, was a negative one. A typical comment from a (female) teacher was, 'Girls aren't as loyal as boys. They're always falling out. Boys stick together more'. As I got to know the girls, I found this kind of stereotyped attitude to be a gross misinterpretation as I shall describe later in the book.

Talking about their friendships was something the girls had not been asked to do before, and they enjoyed the opportunity to do this. I feel that using their experience as the focus of my research made that experience seem much more important and positive, rather than the negative light in which adolescent girls were often viewed, for example as bitchy or silly. Girls in other classes got to know that I was asking about girls and their friends, and would come up in the playground to tell me about their own friendships.

Breaking down researcher-researched divisions

Many feminists argue that researchers must aim for a more equal relationship between those carrying out research and the subjects of that research (Oakley 1981, Acker, Barry & Esseveld 1983, Stanley & Wise 1983). While ethical issues are widely discussed in the social sciences generally (Barnes 1977, Bulmer 1982), they are a particularly prominent concern in feminist research (Finch 1984, Poland 1987, Wise 1987).

As well as stressing the importance of the type of relationship between researcher and researched, and being aware of the power differential in that relationship, feminists also stress the need for researchers to 'invest his or her own identity in the relationship' (Oakley 1981 p.41), and to make explicit their own involvement in the research process (Stanley & Wise 1983). As Angela McRobbie writes:

> Feminism forces us to locate our own autobiographies and our experience inside the questions we might want to ask, so that we continually do *feel* with the women we are studying. (McRobbie 1982 p.52)

This may be a difficult and in fact questionable activity if, as McRobbie goes on to argue, one assumes a basis of 'shared femininity' (ibid p.52). The complexity of the process and tensions inherent within it are widely recognised and discussed by other feminists too (Acker, Barry & Esseveld 1983, Finch 1984, Williams 1987, Wise 1987), and were certainly experienced in my own research.

The ways in which I tried to encompass these aims within my fieldwork on young women's friendships are best illustrated by describing how my role as researcher changed during the time I spent with the girls. Also linked are the ways in which I tried to involve the girls in the research process, and the extent to which I brought my own experience into the research. I do not feel that I was altogether successful in breaking down researcher-researched relationships; however, I did so as far as I was able or as far as I felt appropriate or ethical, as I shall explain.

From outsider to class pet?

What my role would be was a major consideration in setting up the research. I wanted to develop a friendly relationship with the girls, which would enable me to understand their friendships from their point of view rather than by imposing my own version of events from outside. I recognised that both my account and theirs would be a construction of events partly dependent on the kind of relationship we had (Campbell 1984), rather than that I would magically uncover a 'true' account unrelated to my presence in their groups.

I started off as a non-participant observer, sitting at the back of classes and writing notes. This was very much an 'outsider' role. Both pupils and teachers regarded me at first with a mixture of curiosity and suspicion. Some of the girls were keen for me to sit near them in lessons, but once I was in position, usually at the back of the class, they seemed to forget about me. In between lessons, I usually tagged on to a group of girls as we went to the next room. I often felt like a spare part, trailing round the corridors after a group of friends who were busy ignoring me. At this stage, I was uneasy in my relationships with both the girls and their teachers.

Although I was not intentionally taking on the role of a pupil, I often felt like one sitting with the class and seeing lessons from their viewpoint. With the stricter teachers, who often harangued the class about behaviour, I sometimes felt as though rebukes were addressed to me as much as pupils. Barrie Thorne reports a similar response in her fieldwork at American elementary schools (1993). This was useful in terms of understanding how the girls experienced lessons and, like Thorne, it reminded me of my own schooldays and the particular terror which some teachers could invoke. On these occasions I would, like the pupils, sit with head lowered, wanting to sink into the desk. I certainly experienced the 'ethnographer fatigue' (Wolcott 1975 p.118) mentioned by many educational researchers (Beynon 1983, Griffin 1985b, Woods 1986), both from the emotional and mental exhaustion induced by long school days, and the physical exhaustion of constant note taking.

After four weeks of observing lessons, I went on a week's field trip with the second year class, G2 (Year 8). This was like going from one extreme to another. From having had little contact with the girls up to this point, I was suddenly with them day and night. This made a great deal of difference in getting to know them informally, seeing them in their own clothes in an out of school context. Rather than being the detached observer, I was very much joining in here, sharing the same activities of walking, swimming, caving. In this way I was on an equal basis to them, rather than having the superior status that being an adult in school conferred. There were plenty of opportunities for us to talk to each other naturally, and I felt pleased to have had this chance, not only for me to get to know the girls better, but for them to get to know me.

After that week, returning to the school in an observer's role definitely seemed wrong. I was much more friendly with the girls now and felt odd going into lessons in the same way as before. At the same time, some reactions from teachers made me feel that I was being forced the other way, into a teacher's role. I had used the fact that I had been a teacher myself to overcome some of the teachers' initial suspicions of me, and now this rebounded on me. On several occasions teachers asked me to 'keep an eye on the class' whilst they went to fetch something or see somebody, as other researchers have also found (Hargreaves 1967, Burgess 1984). I found this extremely uncomfortable, as I did not want to destroy the good relationships I was beginning to build up with the girls by suddenly acting in an authoritative manner.

In order to avoid this, I gradually stopped going into lessons altogether, unless the girls especially asked me, and then only saw the girls in out-of-lesson time, i.e., form time, break and lunchtime. These changes gave me a totally different perspective on the girls' experience and enabled me to get to know them much more fully. As on the field trip, the range of things we talked about now extended beyond school topics to family relationships, boys, clothes, records, and what they did out of school.

The girls began to show a certain possessiveness and pride in having me around. They enjoyed showing me off, introducing me to their other friends, sometimes dragging people up to meet me. Was I becoming the class pet? Other researchers working in schools have noted this process of being 'adopted' by the pupils they worked with (Measor, Davies & Ball in Ball 1985). Lynn Davies describes it in a very similar way to how I perceived it: 'They treated me as a sort of pet gerbil really' (Davies in Ball 1985 p.29).

Part of the enjoyment the girls were showing in my new role was to do with my being an adult acting in some ways like a pupil. The fact that I was joining in with them at school seemed crucial. For instance, I joined in games at break with some of the girls which caused great amusement at first. I started to line up with the girls before lessons and on several occasions got told off for talking by the teachers along with the others, before they realised who it was.

There was no question of me trying to 'pass as' a pupil, as Mandy Llewellyn had done (1980), but I was now clearly in a different category from the teachers, more like an 'honorary pupil' as Mary Fuller puts it (1980). Stephen Ball has mentioned researchers being accepted by pupils once they were regarded as not quite like a 'proper adult' (Ball 1985 p.36). This certainly seemed true in my case: I was clearly departing from what was regarded as normal adult behaviour at school. Nancy Mandell (1988) calls it the 'least-adult role in studying children', and other ethnographers describe similar attempts to lessen their adult authority and status, both in order to see things from children's perspective, and in order to gain their trust (Davies 1989, Fine & Glassner 1989, Thorne 1993).

Once I had established this new pattern, the girls accepted it readily. For the rest of my time at the school my role ceased to be problematic. I now felt much happier that I was at least partly achieving my original aims. The emphasis shifted away from school altogether as I started to go to clubs and other activities the young women went to in the evenings. During the following school year I was still coming into school to do interviews and make arrangements to see the girls out of school, but the time I actually spent in school gradually diminished. In some ways then, I became an 'outsider' again in terms of the school, but in terms of my relationship with the girls I was much closer and friendlier.

Some of the most enjoyable times I spent with the young women were the informal chats at break and lunch, and my visits to their clubs and groups. These occasions were to some extent unrecordable; there was no question of standing outside events and making notes as I had done in lessons (although I did make notes afterwards). The whole point was that I was joining in whatever the young women were doing. It was through this kind of participation that I became most accepted by the girls and they learned to trust me as a kind of friend.

There is a noticeable difference between my first interviews with the girls, and later ones when I was joining in the girls' out of lesson or out of school activities. The early ones are somewhat stilted on both sides, whereas the later ones are generally more relaxed and friendly, and include more self-revelation from the girls and myself, reflecting the mutual trust we had now built up.

Involving the girls in the research process

Many school-based ethnographers comment on the fact that pupils are not usually asked for their consent in taking part in a research project (Simons 1981, Davies 1982, Ball 1985); a researcher usually just appears in the classroom. As far as I was able to do so, I did seek agreement to the participation of the young women in my project. This was easier for the older girls who were about to leave school, because I was concentrating on interviewing rather than classroom observation, so opting out of the research was a feasible proposition.

With the younger girls in the second year class G2 (Year 8), it was not practical to give them the choice of opting out of the lessons I observed, although I am sure this would have proved popular. Nevertheless, I felt it was important to give the pupils who were to have me imposed on them as full an explanation of what I was doing as possible. This I did at the start of fieldwork and at various points during the year.

Most of these formal explanations took place at the beginning of a term or half term, or when the research was about to enter a new phase. However, I also engaged in many informal exchanges with pupils throughout the fieldwork, usually answering questions about what I was writing down, or what I was 'looking for'. These mainly came from girls and boys in other classes (ie. not G2) who had not received an introduction. In this way I hoped to counter the pupils' lack of choice, at least to some extent.

I explained to the girls that I was like a reporter, writing down 'what happens, what seems important, who works with whom, who talks to whom'. I also stressed that I was not looking for good or bad behaviour, a concern which exercised some of the pupils at first, particularly the boys, as Barrie Thorne also found (1993). When I explained that I hoped that what I found would be turned into a book one day, the girls were understandably pleased and excited, and could not wait their turn to be interviewed. I had to bear in mind Janet Finch's caveat (1984) that women who do not normally have a voice may be over-eager to become involved, and may be particularly vulnerable to exploitation by researchers anxious to collect 'good data'.

At the same time, I found that the young women were more than ready to remind me of my stated intentions if I appeared to forget them. For instance, one girl challenged me about what I was writing down: 'Are you going to tell us like you said or are you going to just going away without telling us?' Another asked, 'You said you were going to come with us at break and you haven't.' With these reminders about my best feminist intentions, I tried to talk to the girls more openly about my research, showing them my notebooks if they were interested.

Later, when I started going round with the young women in the evenings, I always made a point of asking them if it was all right for me to visit their club or disco, and if they expressed reluctance at the idea (as a few did) then I did not push it any further. This seemed absolutely crucial in terms of the ethics of the research. After all, the younger girls had not initially had any choice as to whether I observed their lessons, so I thought they should have the right of veto when it came to their own time, both in and out of school. Lynda Measor expresses similar reservations about stepping into the private sphere of adolescents:

> I took the view that I had no right in it. I would go to the school disco but it wasn't comfortable, they didn't want me there. I didn't go often ... I think it was because I respected certain areas of their privacy that they were prepared to talk to me. (Measor in Ball 1985 p.43)

Like Measor, I felt that some of the girls were more prepared to talk about themseves, their friends and where they went in the evenings because I did not push myself into their out of school life.

In some ways the move from a non-participant observer to a more closely participating role based on trust and confidentiality followed the progression which other ethnographers working with young people have noted (Simons 1981, Measor 1985, Ball 1985). However, as I mentioned earlier, there is a tension between this and the emphasis in some of the literature on ethnography in schools on keeping some measure of detachment and lack of bias. For example, Peter Woods stresses the danger of 'according primacy to the views of a particular group' (1986 p.38), and the risk of 'going native' (ibid p.34):

> that is, identifying so strongly with members that defending their values comes to take precedence over *actually studying them* . (ibid. p.34, my emphasis)

In some ways, this kind of view clashes with the basic tenets of feminist research. As a feminist researcher, I wanted to 'accord primacy' to the girls' views, rather than seeing it as a danger. I felt that I was getting closer to understanding them by getting more involved (as Woods himself suggests) and to a certain extent re-living adolescence with them. I was also averse to the notion that I was 'actually studying' them, because I felt that this turned the girls into the objects of research rather than the subjects.

However, it is important to distinguish between 'according primacy' to a group by seeking to understand their perspective, and necessarily agreeing with or 'defending their values'. In my own research this was not particularly problematic, but in other cases it might be. For instance, in Anne Campbell's research on female gangs (1984 & 1993), there are inherent tensions between getting close to and understanding the young women concerned, and appearing to endorse their often highly violent behaviour. Looking at research on young men, it is the apparently uncritical endorsement of some aspects of sexist or racist behaviour, and 'romanticising the activities and beliefs of the privilged group' (Woods 1986 p.38) that I and other feminists have criticised. In these kinds of cases, then, I could certainly agree with Woods' view.

There are complex ethical issues involved here, and the researcher's stance can be a difficult one to balance. In my own research, although I did break down certain barriers between myself and the girls, perhaps as far as I could in the circumstances, by virtue of the age difference alone I could never have become 'one of them'. I actually set my own boundaries in recognition of this fact, as I have described, by not intruding too far into the girls' private lives. To some extent, then, I had decided that 'going native' was both inappropriate and unethical, not for the reasons Woods gives, but in relation to my own feminist aims and concerns. As Joan Acker, Kate Barry and Joke Esseveld also acknowledge:

> Our commitment to bringing our subjects into the research process as active participants....strengthened our critique of research methods, and forced us to realise that it is impossible to create a research process that completely erases the contradictions between researcher and researched. (Acker et al 1983 p.134)

Other ethical issues arose around trust, which was fundamental to building a more equal relationship with the young women. When I started interviewing, I always promised confidentiality, assuring the girls that I would not play the tapes to any of the teachers or to other girls, and I certainly kept to that. But trust takes time to be established, and there was a certain testing out period while the girls made sure I would not report back what they said to the teachers or break confidence to other girls. Then girls started confiding in me about family, school or friendship problems, so that for some I moved into a semi-counselling role. Other researchers report a similar aspect to their work with girls: for example, Lynda Measor became someone 'that they could talk to' (Measor in Ball 1985, p.22); Lynn Davies became 'a sort of spring board, a sounding board for their ideas' (Davies in Ball 1985, p.22).

At times the role of confidante created real dilemmas for me about whether to pass on information or not, as other ethnographers have found (Davies 1982, Burgess 1985, Ball 1985, Thorne 1993), particularly when teachers saw me as a potential source of inside information, for instance over whether girls were 'bunking off' school or not. The most difficult decision arose around a possible case of sexual abuse, and in this instance I sought outside advice, and also went back to the young woman concerned to see if she wanted to take it further. In general, it was important for the continuing trust of the young women not to divulge their secrets, as this would have seemed a kind of betrayal.

Bringing in my own experience

The other main way in which I tried to equalise the research relationships a little was by bringing in my own experience. At first I did this in a rather unnatural way, self-consciously 'injecting' something of myself into an interview in order to encourage the girls to talk. For example, I would tell them that I had been to an all-girls' school so I was interested in finding out what it was like to go to a mixed-sex school. However, I was aware of the falsity of forcing anecdotes into the conversation in order to generate 'good data' in response. The more at ease the girls and I were with each other, the more the interviews became conversations rather than question and answer sessions, and this made it easier for both them and me to talk about our experiences. What the girls talked about started to remind me of aspects of my own adolescence, which I was able to share with them in a much more natural way.

This was a somewhat unexpected aspect of the research for me. Whilst several educational ethnographers mention the problem of 'making the familiar strange' (Becker 1971, Delamont 1981), because everyone has at some time been a pupil, I have never entirely shared this perception. Even though I have spent most of my working life in schools, the fact that I went to an all-girls' direct grant school in the 1960s in the South of England provided me with plenty of contrasting experiences to those of the girls in the Northern mixed-sex comprehensive where I carried out my research. Although there were moments of horrible familiarity, such as the Geography lesson on rubber planting in Malaysia which could have been taken straight out of my own schooling twenty years before, in general I expected to see differences. The possibility of 'being surprised' (Willis 1980 p.92), which Paul Willis argues comes at moments when perceptions are *not* shared, was in my own case more likely to occur when I discovered a *shared* experience with the girls.

At first there was one particular girl, Janette, with whom I found it easiest to share experiences. This may have been partly because she was the closest to me in background, being the only middle class girl in the group. She was highly confident and articulate, and found it easier than most of the others to talk about her own experience. Her experience at school also reminded me strongly of my own: Janette was having problems because her high academic ability made her unpopular, and this brought back painful memories for me of having a hard time at school when I was always top of the class and other girls resented it. In the light of this, Janette and I were able to talk about what she could do in the circumstances.

At the other extreme, Dawn was a quiet, shy girl who was nearly a loner, being only marginally attached to the large group of friends in G2. She reminded me painfully of myself at that age, because she was so withdrawn and, in contrast to Janette and other key-informants, reticent about her own views and experience. During fieldwork, I never felt able to break through her strong defensive shield, and gain her trust; indeed, remembering how I felt at her age, I never pushed too hard. However, I did feel for her unhappiness and tried to be as friendly as possible. Interestingly, Dawn was one of the young women who corresponded with me most frequently after the fieldwork was over, and kept in touch even after she left school. Perhaps, like me during adolescence, she found it easier to express her feelings in writing.

As I got to know the girls better, I realised that there were many others whose experience reminded me of my own adolescence, regardless of the difference in class or race, and the fact that my adolescence had been twenty years earlier. For example, when I met some of the older girls six months after they had left school, they started to tell me about going out at night to forbidden places:

Sarah   We're not supposed to go round town on a night but sometimes on a weekend we go.
Jenny   We say that we're going to t'pictures and then we end up going round town (laughs) ...
VG   I can remember I used to say I'd go round to a friend's or something, and in fact we might go out somewhere rather than go - stay in the house.
Jenny   That's what we do!

Rather than me starting with a leading question or anecdote in order to draw the girls out, what they said sparked off vivid memories for me. We then proceeded to swop stories with much hilarity about when we had been caught out by our parents after such escapades. The pleasure of tapping into my own memories was as great as the enjoyment at hearing about the young women's experiences. Examples

22

such as these, where interviews became transformed into conversations about shared experience, were the high spots of the research.

At other times, however, I was aware of how different my experience had been as an adolescent from many of these girls. This was particularly in the area of domestic responsibilities. Most of the young women had some childcare or domestic duties which took up a considerable amount of their 'leisure' time. Several girls were virtually running large households single-handed at the age of 13 or 14, looking after the younger children, cooking and cleaning, whilst their mothers were at work. My own experience as a middle class teenager in the 1960s was very different. Apart from washing up, the only responsibilities I had to discharge in the evenings were homework not housework. Having no younger sisters or brothers I had no contact with babies or small children.

The difference between my experience and some of the girls I was working with was brought home to me in a striking way when I took my four month-old son to show the girls (after the fieldwork was officially over). Being a mother was still very new: I had just about got myself and Christopher ready and into the school before morning registration finished. The first to hold Christopher was Charleen, a Black-Caribbean girl who looked after three sisters, one mentally handicapped, and ran the house generally while her mother was at work. I was struck by the ease with which she took Christopher from me - I still held him like a piece of bone china - and the matter of fact way she 'neatened his clothes, pulling down his tracksuit top'. At 14 years old Charleen was already an old hand with babies whilst I, as a first-time mother at the age of 35, was totally inexperienced. The contrast was enormous.

The fact that I was pregnant during fieldwork was actually the most direct way my own life was brought into the research. I had mixed feelings abut the possible effect it might have on the girls. On the one hand, it gave them something about me which many of them were interested in and wanted to ask about. I was pleased that they had a chance to ask me questions for a change. On the other hand, I was worried that myself and the class teacher Lesley Green, both pregnant at the same time, were providing negative role-models; that is, placing undue emphasis on having children, and thus reinforcing the traditionally feminine interest that many of the girls already expressed in babies and childcare. Looked at another way, however, you could say that we were providing positive role-models: we were both having our first child in our mid-30s, having followed careers up to that point; Lesley returned to work after the minimum maternity leave and I resumed my research.

Creating a sociology for women

The third aspect of a feminist approach concerns the means and purpose whereby research data are interpreted and transmitted. There is much discussion in feminist literature about how best to create an 'emancipatory' sociology (Acker et al 1983 p.424); that is, one which will have a consciousness raising effect on the women taking part, both researcher and researched (Wise 1987), create an understanding of the conditions which oppress women (Griffin 1980), and produce knowledge that can be used by women themselves (Acker et al 1983). These are grand claims and inevitably problematic to achieve. For example, Janet Finch discusses the difficulties in 'ensuring that information given so readily in interviews will not be used ultimately against the collective interests of women' (1984 p.83).

However, in spite of the problems and dilemmas, there are also many positive outcomes from the kind of feminist ethnographic approach I developed. Christine Griffin (1980) sees talking and shared experience as a central part of the process. She argues that this approach is empowering because women's experiences, usually unspoken and unacknowledged, are expressed and exchanged in the research process. Enabling the young women to find a voice in my research was certainly central in importance, as well as generating the feeling that their experience was special and important. The sharing of experience was a crucial part in this, as Griffin and other feminist researchers have found (Oakley 1981, Finch 1984). Although there may be some benefits in what Lynn Davies calls 'cross-sex ethnography' (1985 p.85), I would suggest, as Janet Finch does in relation to her research (1984), that the same responses or process of identification would not have occurred if a man had been interviewing the girls.

Both Christine Griffin and Lynn Davies stress the importance of feminist ethnography, not just in making women's experience visible and important but also, to use Dale Spender's words, in creating 'new models of the female' (Spender 1978 p.11). Griffin and Davies both point out the danger in trying to fit girls' experience into existing subcultural theory because it may be inadequate to explain young women's experiences. In doing feminist ethnography, then, one must also be reformulating theory. Christine Griffin stresses that this is not grand or abstract Theory (with a capital T), far removed from the subjects of the research, but theory actually generated in the research process, and 'similar to consciousness raising' (Griffin 1980 p.3). The idea of theory as everyday practice, arising out of experience, has been central to my own way of working as a feminist researcher.

3 Getting to know you

This chapter looks at how and why girls make friends, and analyses some of the factors which are important in this process.

Why friends?

> You wouldn't enjoy yourself as much on your own. (Vicky)

In my collection of photographs of friends, there is a series taken at a school Sports Day, where girlfriends talk and laugh, arms round each other; pictures of closeness. One of these snapshots is of Pam and Suzanne, who were in different friendship groups, and hardly ever talked to each other or showed signs of friendliness. Yet as I went round the sports field with my camera, they happened to be standing near each other, and immediately posed with their arms round each other, as though they were the closest of friends. Proximity provided a means of being seen together with someone rather than on their own.

This photograph visually demonstrates one of the essential reasons why people in general make friends at all: that is, to alleviate loneliness. Being with a friend, and being seen with a friend, is extremely important, especially during the vulnerability of adolescence. More than this, friends seem to be essential for our social development, helping to form our self-identity. As Bronwyn Davies stresses:

> Friends not only alleviate the uncertainty which stems from being alone, but via companionship and cooperativeness go on providing the means for warding off the vulnerability which attends being

26

alone. Being with your friend, then is important. (Davies 1982 p.70)

The psychologist Steve Duck, in his book *Friends for Life* (1983), argues that we need friends to give us a sense of self-worth and belonging, and to provide us with both physical and psychological support. These ideas throw light on some of the important reasons why we make friends. Peter Kutnick (1988) identifies the following factors as important in the formation of friendship: proximity or nearness, continuity, and similarities. These factors emerged as crucial in my own research.

How girls make friends: proximity

Most young women find it easy to recall how long they have been friends and how they met. Many friendships seem to have a somewhat arbitrary origin, because girls happen to live next door, or to sit next to each other in lessons. Proximity is certainly a vital starting point.

Living near: friends at home

At home, girls often become friends because they live next door or in the same street, and can easily 'play out' or hang around together. As Pat said, 'Go around with everyone that lives round here, there's loads of us'. In Barnsdale, friends at home included whoever happened to be around and were not so rigidly demarcated as school in terms of age, gender or ethnic origin. For example, friends in the neighbourhood often included boys, unlike school, where girls and boys rarely mixed. Whereas the Black-Caribbean and Indian girls mixed almost exclusively with each other at school, at home they often had white friends; for example, Charleen (Black-Caribbean) was friendly with Paulette (white) who lived nearby. Helena Wulff (1988) found very similar differences in friendship groupings between home and school in her study of a mixed ethnic community in London.

Unlike school, where girls only mixed with other girls of the same age, at home girls of different ages often became close friends. For example, there was a year's difference between Suzanne and her friend Dot, and two years' difference between Marilyn and Shona. Although these friends often saw each other every day after school, once at school they did not meet but mixed with other friends their own age. When I arranged interviews with these girls together, I often had to go to great lengths so that the girls in their own classes did not find out.

Barrie Thorne (1993), who also found age and gender separation at school but not in the local neighbourhood, argues that this occurs for several reasons. Firstly, school provides more potential friends than home, and the crowded nature of school means that there are more witnesses to 'unusual' friendships. Schools also institutionalise age separation by organising children in year groups. Organisationally and ideologically, schools also separate girls and boys in many ways, even though they are in the same classes, a finding replicated in numerous studies (Spender 1982, Whyld 1983, Wolpe 1988, Measor & Sikes 1992) and certainly the case at Barnsdale High School.

For friends in the neighbourhood, other factors predominate. In Barnsdale, the frequency and informality of contact between girls who lived near made them in some cases almost part of each other's families. For example, Pat went to Tina's house every day to help her make the tea and look after her younger brothers and sisters. Such friendships were also often strengthened by ties betweeen other members of the families, reinforcing the close-knit nature of the community. For instance, Lorraine and Elaine lived on the same road, and often went camping together with their families at the weekend. June's and Joanne's parents were friendly, and both families sometimes went away together for weekends to Blackpool.

Being in the same class or lessons: friends at school

At school, girls often become friends with other girls in the same class. This happens particularly when they start secondary school and find themselves with girls they do not know. Surinder, Charleen and Marilyn provide a typical example when they describe how June came to be part of their group:

> Surinder Well you see, June were on her own and she just sat
> next to us cos there were a spare seat and -
> Marilyn - and she were talking to us.
> Charleen So we made friends.

Even in this account of the beginning of a friendship, other elements vital to the continuation of that friendship are evident: the sensitivity to June being on her own, and the importance of talking. Proximity seemed to be the key factor, coupled with the continuity of daily contact. As Kim, one of the Year 11 girls, described, 'We just met 'er

28

(Tricia) cos she were in our form'; Janette (also Year 11) met Marie 'because we both used to hang around the back at break'.

At Barnsdale, some girls had been friendly for a long time already, since infants or junior school, and simply continued those friendships into secondary school. For example, Vicky, Penny, Pam and Karen had all been to the same junior school. They ended up in the same class at Barnsdale High, and formed the nucleus of the big group of eight white girls, very like Audrey Lambart's 'sisterhood' (1976) who had also been to junior school together.

Prior acquaintance frequently triggered a relationship once girls found themselves in the same class, even if the previous circumstances had been inauspicious, as Surinder described about Manjeet whom she 'used to hate':

My Mum and her mother used to walk up to temple (Sikh) and she......and her brother used to call me names an' all that. And then when we came to this school we were in t'same English group and, I don't know, we sat together......and then we were friends.'

In this case, the girls' ethnic background was probably an important factor in bringing them together at school: both girls' familes came from India and their mothers were friends.

Some girls saw going to secondary school as a time for making new friends, even when previous close friends were already at the same school, as Jackie described:

It's when you come to senior school that you start to drift away don't you?......Like me and Marilyn and Charleen and this other girl used to be really really close, we used to be going everywhere together......and when we came to seniors and been in different classes we just sort of drifted away and we found new friends.

The initial organisation of classes and sets at secondary school seems to be a crucial factor in strengthening or changing friends at this stage. This would appear to confirm the fears of the middle school girls in Robert Meyenn's study (1980) that they would lose touch with their friends when they moved to the senior school and were split into different classes.

However, in some cases at least, moving to secondary school may simply confirm a change in friendship already taking place. For example, Pam told me:

Kathleen Underwood used to be our best friend all through infants to third year o'juniors......but in fourth year o'juniors she started going off with Michelle Hutchinson and then we fell out......then we changed school, went into different classes.

In this case, changing school provided an opportunity to make new friends. Other girls did retain their friends from juniors, even when they were in different classes, so there was no one single pattern.

New opportunities for making friends are also provided when young women leave school, and go to college or start a job. As with girls at school, the context dependent nature of how these friendships start is evident. Anne, who went to art college after leaving school, and soon made new friends with other young women on the course, summed it up succinctly by saying, 'You make new friends where you go don't you really?'

In a new situation, relationships are formed quickly because people are at their most vulnerable, and need to feel that they are with somebody else. At its most extreme, this kind of coming together under traumatic circumstances was evident on a school field trip in the Yorkshire Dales when a group of thirteen year-olds from Barnsdale went potholing. Interestingly, only two boys out of thirty opted to go; perhaps they did not want to put themselves in a vulnerable position. The rest of the party of fifteen were girls.

To give them a real taste of potholing, the group leader took them through narrow, wet tunnels where they had to crawl on their stomachs. Two of the girls, Janice and Annette, not previously friends, found themselves next to each other in the dark. Although they were both scared, they urged each other on and Janice (in front) helped pull Annette through. When they came out into the daylight again, they hugged, through relief at getting out in one piece, pleasure at having accomplished the challenge, and a closeness forged by the circumstances.

How girls stay friends: continuity

Friendships made under such extreme conditions are not likely to last unless there are other reasons to reinforce them. The most obvious of these is continuity of contact. Pat and Tina were close because they saw each other every day, even though they did not go to the same school, and shared the routines and responsibilities of their daily lives.

Frequency and informality of contact help strengthen and sustain such friendships.

Where young women live nearby and go to the same school, friendships are particularly strong and long lasting, as shown in Audrey Lambart's classic study of a girls' group in the 1960s, 'The sisterhood' (1976). In my own research, Jenny and Sarah lived in the same road and were always 'popping round' to each others' houses, as they put it. They were also in the same class at school, and always walked to school together. Their friendship was constantly being consolidated by this frequent contact. The daily rituals of calling for each other in the morning and again at night occur frequently in young women's friendships, and are vital in strengthening and renewing their relationships.

In contrast, when girls live further away, they do not have the same opportunities to meet on a regular basis. Jenny and Sarah only saw another friend, Sue, at school or occasionally at weekends, because she lived too far away to meet at night. This became a crucial factor later when the young women left school and did not have the daily contact with Sue, making it far harder to keep in touch.

The friendship between Jenny and Sarah was also strengthened further because they had known each other since junior school, and had gone right through secondary school in the same class. A similar interweaving of several factors is shown in Raphaela Best's study of girls in the USA (1983), where the closest friendships were formed between girls who went to the same school, lived near each other, and had played together for years.

Long-standing friendships between girls are particularly strong because they have a basis of shared memories. If early discoveries and developments are made together from infancy or even babyhood, then friends have a long history to draw on which can override any temporary differences later. For example, Charleen and Paulette had known each other since babyhood 'when I first came over to England' from the Caribbean (Charleen), and they remembered playing together in each others' gardens as toddlers. Surinder and Alison, who had been friends since Junior school, recalled with much laughter how they used to 'play princesses' together.

In talking to young women, friendships which go back this far are recalled with particular fondness, clarity and often great amusement too. Like shared family histories, small events are remembered and repeated, and idiosyncracies accepted. Marge Piercy vividly describes such a friendship in *Braided Lives*, the story of Jill and her cousin Donna who is also her best friend. Jill and Donna share childhood experiences, early physical closeness and sexual explorations, their lives closely intertwined:

> My thirteenth summer, Donna and I were in Cold Springs together. We climbed the mountain over town. We slept upstairs in an attic room and giggled all night... Donna was small and blonde with skin that burned in half an hour and seemed to tear on every fence we scaled, on every blackberry bush we picked from. I was always leading her into temptation, but I remember that she always went. (Piercy 1982 p.37)

Elaine and Lorraine reminded me in some ways of Jill and Donna; they had been friends since the age of two, and kept up their friendship even though they were in different classes at secondary school. Elaine felt that she would stay friends with Lorraine 'for ever' because she had known her so long, whereas more recent friendships might be more easily broken. The two girls sometimes quarrelled fiercely, and fell out for quite a long time during the third year (Year 9), but they always came back together eventually. They were still friends when I last had contact with them, six months after they left school.

Why girls make friends: similarities

Apart from the more arbitrary reasons for making friends already discussed, friendship choices between young women are based on factors such as appearance, ability and interests, class and ethnicity. A combination of these factors usually exists within a pair or group of girlfriends, without any one necessarily predominating. In fact, shared interests may be developed later, after an initial link is established, rather than the other way round. Harriet Bjerrum Nielsen and Monica Rudberg (1982), in a study of gender and schooling in Norway and Denmark, suggest that this may be a gender difference in friendship formation:

> For the girls, it seems, a relationship is the prerequisite of common activity, whilst the opposite is the case for the boys: for them joint activity is a way of establishing a relationship. (Bjerrum Nielsen & Rudberg 1992 p.8)

Bjerrum Nielsen and Rudberg found that what is most important in identifying and reinforcing friendships between adolescent girls is that they look and dress the same, and 'have exactly the same views on everything' (ibid p.10). In the following sections, I shall explore this aspect first, before discussing maturity, academic attainment, social class and ethnicity. All these aspects will be followed up in more detail later in the book. Young women's interests and leisure activities are discussed in detail in chapter 7.

Sameness and difference

The need to identify themselves as the same as their friends stood out in my own research. If I asked the young women at Barnsdale why they were friends with their particular group, sameness was almost inevitably mentioned before the specific factor which made them the same. For example, Mandy, one of a large group of nine white girls in the second year (Year 8) told me : 'We all do t'same things, we all act t'same way'. Carol, from another big group of eight white girls, had a very similar answer: 'We're like all t'same. We all like - I don't know really.' She and her friends then had to think hard about exactly what was the same about them, and added, 'cos we talk about dancing and that', 'and boys', identifying some adolescent interests that they had in common.

Older girls were readier to home in on what made them close straight away, being more self aware by the age of sixteen, and more able to articulate reasons for friendship. For instance Jenny, from the large group of seven white girls in the fifth year (Year 11) said, 'We all like a joke......we're all silly!' Claire, from the same group, thought it was because they all came from the 'same background, same upbringing, same interests'. This was brought home to them more clearly when three of this group went to the same sixth form college and for the first time met young people from different class backgrounds. However, Claire's definition of sameness was structurally determined by the social class background of the school, whereas Jenny's delineation was about an area of similarity over which the girls had more control.

Sometimes girls picked on a curious factor to delineate their sameness. For instance, Suzanne (Year 8) explained the friendship between her group of four white girls by saying, 'We're all nasty'. In some ways this was an apt description, because the most obvious characteristic of this group was that they were mutually abusive, calling each other names and generally hurling insults at one another.

However, as I got to know the group better, I realised that the 'nasty' veneer actually hid quite a degree of closeness and supportiveness, and that they also shared a strong sense of humour. Calling themselves 'nasty' was a typical example of a tongue in cheek attitude evident in the group, which made them amusing company. It was also a reflection of how other girls saw them, so it was quite an accurate self-labelling.

This leads on to the other main way in which groups of friends define themselves, by mentioning other girls or groups and how different they are from themselves. Anne Campbell (1984, 1992) argues that young women find their identity in defining or rejecting what they are not, and that talking about other young women in a negative way is a means of self-affirmation. This is not only true for deviant groups such as the female gangs which Campbell studied, but for other young women too, as Bjerrum Nielsen and Rudberg found in their study:

> The content of girls' friendships with each other is often built up around agreements and rules - secret ones more often than not - and these are often to do with who is in them and who is out. The exclusion is the means employed by girls to confirm their mutual alliance. (ibid p. 8)

This process certainly emerged as a strong means of group definition and reinforcement at Barnsdale. For example, Penny told me that Dawn was not part of their group for a while because 'she wouldn't do things we wanted to do you know, mess around and that'. In a similar way, Mandy and Elaine described a girl who used to be part of their group:

Mandy   She's too snobby......she don't fit in......When you get older you just change and you get more, you know, more mischievous, but she didn't you see -

Elaine   She used to stop us doing things......she used to try and stop us and that's when we fell out with her.

These examples illustrate how the girls maintained their sameness quite consciously by excluding girls who did not conform to group norms. This is one way in which the exclusivity mentioned by other researchers (McRobbie & Garber 1976, Llewellyn 1980) was demonstrated. In both the above cases, girls were considered different because they did not 'mess around' or join in 'mischievous' behaviour.

The defining and redefining of attitudes and behaviour within a group was a complicated and shifting process, indicated by Mandy's comment 'when you get older you just change.'

Maturity

For adolescent girls, the transition from girlhood to adolescence is a central reason for such changes. The question of maturity is seen as crucial, and is often one of the defining characteristics of girls' friendships, as previous studies have found (Delamont 1976, Meyenn 1980). Within the second and third years at Barnsdale (Years 8 and 9), the transition between childhood and adolescence was evident both in terms of the girls' physical appearance and their interests. Some still looked very much like little girls: they were physically immature, and were not interested in fashionable clothes or hairstyles. These girls tended to spend breaktime playing ball games or hopscotch. Two of the main friendship groups in the class in which I was based, G2, consisted of such younger-seeming girls.

In contrast, other girls of the same age (12-13) already looked like young women. They were taller and fully developed physically. Some of them tried to make themselves look even older by means of modern short haircuts, dyeing their hair, or by wearing make up, jewellery, and the then fashionable straight slit skirts, all strictly speaking against the school rules. These girls, such as the large group in G2, stood around at breaktime talking in pairs or groups, and often referred to themselves as 'mature'.

However, 'mature' is an inadequate term for a quite complex and complicated process which takes place among girls anywhere between 9 and 15 years old. Firstly, as Barrie Thorne points out in her study of American elementary school children (1993), girls who have not reached puberty often adopt the clothes, language, props and symbols of adolescence. This was not evident in the cultural and regional context of Millbrook where, ten years ago at least, there was a traditional, quite formal approach to transitions (such as courting which I shall describe later). However, it is reported in other American studies (Best 1983, Canaan 1987), and in the 1990s I have become very aware of this trend among pre-teenage girls and boys in the South of England. Conversely, pubescent girls do not always take on the social practices of adolescence. At Barnsdale, this was particularly noticeable among some Black-Caribbean girls who, though physically mature, deliberately avoided teenage interests, and looked down on some of the white girls who 'mooned around after boys'. As Thorne sums it up:

> In short, being a child or a teenager is not dictated by the degree of one's physical maturity or the state of one's hormones; social practices shape the transition. (Thorne 1993 p.147)

The second way in which maturity is a problematic term is that it is not static or fixed. At Barnsdale, girls who saw themselves as mature felt that they were poles apart from others whom they dismissed as 'babyish'. In front of their peers they would not admit to anything which might be regarded as childish or old-fashioned. However, in reality, the division between the younger-seeming and 'mature' girls was not so clearcut. Like Barrie Thorne (1993), I found that the category 'adolescent' continually 'dissolves' (p.136) into 'child'. As I got to know the girls, I realised that many of them were at an in-between stage, combining both childlike and adolescent interests. This was most evident in the large group in G2, who amongst themselves were often very childlike in their actions, like the mixed-ethnic group in Helena Wulff's study (1988), who swung between teenage and childish behaviour.

At times, the transition between childhood and adolescence gave rise to some changes in friendship as girls shifted between one stage and the other. For instance, when Lizzy became interested in fashion and boys, she started to move away from the younger seeming girls in her group and to form friendships with more 'mature' girls in other classes; although she kept her original group of friends as a 'home base', and this was important when she wanted to behave in a more childlike way. For the sake of shorthand later in the book, I shall use the terms 'younger-seeming' and 'mature', but this assumes and contains an implicit understanding of the problematic and incomplete nature of the terms.

For older girls, the question of relative physical maturity is less crucial, as they all clearly move into and through puberty, although self-defining and the labelling of others in terms of behaviour and attitudes is still important. At Barnsdale, by the fifth year (Year 11), the girls were clearly young adults and regarded themselves as such. The question of relative maturity did not loom so large for them, so other factors affecting friendship choices then became more prominent, such as common interests.

Academic attainment is another factor which may give rise to or help to strengthen friendships between girls, but it often intersects with other factors such as 'maturity', class and race, and is highly context dependent (Walker & Barton 1983, Wolpe 1988, Bjerrum Nielsen & Rudberg 1992). School intake and organisation, curriculum differentiation, teacher expectations, and pupils' orientations to school, all interweave and affect friendship choices and forms of interaction (Pollard 1984, Grant 1992, Mickelson 1992). As Linda Grant wrote:

> The process by which this occurs is multi-layered and involves the cumulative, sometimes contradictory, influences of many forces. (Grant 1992 p.91)

For example, in a school which streams heavily by ability, and has a highly differentiated curriculum between top and bottom streams, girls' friendships are likely to be formed from within their respective streams (Llewellyn 1980, Davies 1984). This may occur in all-girls' or mixed-sex schools, and in some ways is close to the pattern found in studies of boys in similarly organised schools (Hargreaves 1967, Lacey 1970, Willis 1977). However, a major gender difference is that low stream girls exhibit less solidarity and collective resistance than equivalent groups of boys.

In other schools, with less differentiated forms of school structure and organisation, the variations in friendship pattern and orientations to school among girls are more marked (Lambart 1976, Meyenn 1980, Fuller 1980, Pollard 1984, Lees 1986). Audrey Lambart's study (1976) in an unstreamed grammar school was one of the first to indicate that there is no simple correlation between academic attainment and attitude to school within girls' friendships, which most of the later studies confirm, including those in schools with unrestricted attainment.

Sue Lees (1986) found four main orientations to school in her study of 14-16 year-old girls at three London comprehensive schools. Academic, pro-school groups are more likely to be middle class girls from a single-sex comprehensive, who do not have to cope with boys' disruptive behaviour or demands for teachers' attention (Deem 1984, Mahony 1985). Lees argues that the school ethos is also an important factor in girls' positive, career oriented attitudes. Many other girls, from whatever class background, want to learn and have a career, but are alienated from school by factors such as boring lessons, teachers' attitudes and, in the case of girls from mixed-sex schools, boys' behaviour. Some girls are not interested in work but value school life because of the social contact with friends. Other girls are doubly alienated from school, and cannot wait to leave and get a job.

It is important to stress here that even within the same school context, not all pupils receive the same message (Connell 1987, Wolpe 1988), so different groups of friends may develop quite different orientations to school as they rework and reconstruct the range of gender or ability codes to which they are exposed. Rather than seeing pupils as passive recipients of a single pattern of socialisation, research findings show that they are active in shaping their own responses and resistances to ideological pressures (Arnot 1983, Measor & Sikes 1992).

This was certainly the case at Barnsdale, where attitudes to ability and orientations to school were important in differentiating groups of friends. Academic attainment by itself was by no means the most important factor in any group of friends. For example, the close-knit group in G2 contained four girls of mixed academic ability, ranging from Marilyn who was in high sets for most subjects, to Charleen, who was in so-called remedial groups for English and Maths (Table 6.1). Among the older girls, friendships were sustained even when they were divided into different sets or options for many subjects. The school culture and organisation was important here: setting was done subject by subject, which meant that some pupils could be in high sets for some subjects and low for others, rather than in high or low streams for all subjects. There was certainly not evidence of the deep divisions by ability found in schools which are heavily streamed (Willis 1977, Llewellyn 1980, Davies 1984).

The nearest to an ability grouping was the big group in G2 who were all considered bright, some above average in academic ability (Table 6.1). However, perceived ability rather than academic attainment was the important factor to the girls themselves; it was an important group norm that they were not seen as too bright. As Penny said, 'We're not dunces and we're not brainies, we're just all right.' Interestingly, the perception of a group from the outside and the inside could be quite different, as I have already mentioned in relation to the self styled 'nasty' group. One of these girls, Annette, defined the big group as different from themselves in this way: 'They think they're better than us......cos there's Janette with them and she's - she's brainy'. What Annette was unaware of was the internal resentment within the big group towards Janette because of her high ability and, perhaps more important, the fact that she showed off about her academic success. This was another example of the fine distinctions which were so

38

important in defining the 'sameness' of groups of friends. Perceived ability was part of a group's general attitude to school, which will be discussed further in chapter 6.

A final important point has to be made here. Most previous studies of girls and education (Spender & Sarah 1980, Whyld 1983, Measor & Sikes 1992) have concentrated on girls' underachievement at school, particularly in secondary education. Recent findings in the U.K. and U.S.A. (Measor & Sikes 1992, Mickelson 1992, Grant 1994) have shown that girls are achieving better than boys overall at both school and university, so this changing pattern may have a major effect on girls' friendship groups and their attitudes to school.

Social class

Social class can be an important factor in friendships, and like ability is both dependent on the context, and one of many overlapping factors, as Bjerrum Nielsen and Rudberg (1992) indicate:

> A combination of class and gender is a prerequisite to understand either of them in a school context: in the classroom social class is expressed in a gender specific way, and gender is expressed in a class specific way....The way gender and class are expressed also seems to be related to the age of the pupils, the socio-cultural mix of the particular school class and historical time. (Bjerrum Nielsen & Rudberg 1992 p.1)

I would add school ethos and teacher expectations to the above, as these can also make a large difference to friends' orientations to school in class specific terms (Wolpe 1988, Gardner et al 1992, Grant 1992).

In general, working class girls have been found to be more disadvantaged at school than middle class girls (Ball 1981, Measor & Sikes 1992, Mickelson 1992), whether in mixed or single-sex comprehensives, and also more likely to form anti-school groupings or exhibit deviant behaviour (Llewellyn 1980, Davies 1984, Bjerrum Nielsen & Rudberg 1992). In contrast middle class girls, even when they are alienated from school (Lees 1976), are more likely to use school instrumentally in order to achieve qualifications (Delamont 1976, Ball 1981, Bjerrum Nielsen & Rudberg 1992). There is growing evidence that some black girls, whether middle or working class, may respond in a similar way to white middle class girls (Fuller 1980, Mac an Ghaill 1988, Grant 1992), often in spite of less encouragement from teachers.

However, as with ability, there is no single reponse along class lines exhibited by pupils in the same school. As AnnMarie Wolpe argues (1988), 'a complex set of contradictory messages are simultaneously being generated' (1988 p.45) in any classroom, so a top down model of socialisation is inadequate to explain the variety of responses that children in the same school class, as well as the same social class, may exhibit. Although schools do play an important part in the constructions of gender and class, young people themselves can be seen actively to rework and reshape the various ideological messages they receive (Anyon 1983, Connell 1987).

Most of the studies cited above are of schools with comprehensive, i.e. mixed social class, intakes, and class differences are often focused on in the presentation of findings, leading to a polarised and incomplete view. Studies of schools with a more limited class intake are rarer, but are interesting in showing the variety of responses evident among groups of friends. For example, Sara Delamont's study of 14-15 year-old girls in a private school in Scotland (1976) found that, in spite of the highly selective intake both academically and socially (Classes I & II only), different groups of friends had quite different sets of interests and attitudes to school. For instance, one group was both interested in adolescent culture and had high ambitions; they were 'academic but alienated' in Lees' terms (1976), and objected to the teachers who 'treat us like babies' (ibid. p.38). In contrast, another group, who called themselves the 'academic set', were unashamedly studious, and not interested in teenage pursuits; however, they did often challenge the teachers' definitions of knowledge, and disliked certain authoritarian aspects of school life. Delamont found fine but important distinctions between all the groups and, as in my research, interesting discrepancies in the perceptions of the groups from inside and outside.

Barnsdale also had a restricted social class intake, though largely working class (Classes III, IV & V), rather than predominantly middle class as in Delamont's study. This meant that broad divisions along class lines were rarely evident. There were a few middle class pupils, who were generally integrated into friendship groups, but who could sometimes be ostracised because of perceived affluence. However, even these did not fall into a general category. For instance, in G2 Janette stood out not only because of her ability but because of her middle class background (her father and mother were in professional and managerial occupations respectively). This caused her some difficulties. She told me, 'They call me names cos we don't have a TV'. I heard girls and boys being rude about her clothes, which her mother made for her and were considered old-fashioned. These differences could have been seen as a sign of poverty; in Janette's case they were part of her family's rejection of material values, rather than a lack of money.

Most of the time, Janette was accepted by the large group in G2, which was a very diverse group in terms of fathers' occupation (Table 3.1), ranging from professional (Janette) to unskilled (Dawn), with a mixture of skilled and unskilled manual workers in between (the girls' term 'engineer' was listed in school records as skilled factory workers). The other groups in G2 were both more materially deprived overall, both including two one-parent families and a high level of unemployment. Even amongst these groups, distinctions were made according to perceived affluence, but these were generally used by girls outside particular friendship groups as one indicator of difference, rather than as a reason for sameness from within a group. For instance, Annette was regarded as 'posh' by girls in other groups because she lived in an owner-occupied house rather than a council house. However, within her group it was recognised that she was hard up; as Lizzy explained, 'If she can't afford to buy her clothes it's not her fault....And we've got two parents, Annette's only got one - father'.

Among the older girls, there was a growing realisation that class differences could also be to do with culture, life style and atttitudes as much as possessions. For example, when Jenny, Sarah and Jacky went to sixth form college, they met young people from different class backgrounds for the first time. Although they made friends with some middle class students, they were very aware of the differences between them:

Jenny I mean look at us compared to Fiona.

Sarah She's not really one of us is she?

Jenny She's kind of different to us you see. She doesn't fit in as well....She's sort of a snob really.

Sarah But she's nice with it. But some o't'things you say she says, 'Oh I wouldn't do that'.

Jenny And she says, 'I wouldn't be seen dead working in the Coop'.

Jacky I mean she has, what um, breakfast, lunch and dinner, whereas we have breakfast, dinner and tea.

Table 3.1
G2 Family details
(Girls' own questionnaire answers)

NAME	MOTHER'S OCCUPATION	FATHER'S OCCUPATION
Suzanne	Unemployed	Builder
Pat	Unemployed	-
Lizzy	Cleaner	Night supervisor at mill
Annette	-	Engineer
Marilyn	Nurse	Don't know
Charleen	Unemployed	-
Surinder	Bedclothes factory	Pipe-making factory
June	Unemployed (cleans house for friend)	Knife grinder
Carol	Cleaner (at school)	Textile engineer
Vicky	Unemployed	Stepfather: drinks factory
Penny	Housewife	Father: factory
Karen	Mending	Engineer
Pam	National Westminster Bank	Engineer
Janette	Loans Officer	Sports firm
Elaine	Market Research	Stepfather: Senior accountant
Dawn	Chippy	Sales rep. (timber)
		Binman

Such differences in aspirations and everyday language set Fiona apart from the others, and meant that she did not 'fit in' even though she 'tried hard'. The way that class factors affected the young women's attitudes to school and leisure activities will be discussed further in chapters 6 and 7.

Race and ethnicity

As with other factors, race and ethnicity play an important but complex part in friendship formation, and like class, are largely context dependent. Many studies show the racist attitudes that black pupils may be subject to at school (Jamdagni 1980, Amos & Parmar 1981, Phoenix 1992), and the low expectations that teachers may have of black, particularly Black-Caribbean or Afro-American, pupils (Grant 1992, Wright 1993). This can be one factor in drawing black girls together into supportive friendship groups, sharing high (Fuller 1980) or low (Brah & Minas 1985) aspirations, though most likely to be alienated from school. However, shared ethnicity is not always the main reason for being friends; Ann Phoenix's study (1992) of black and white young people in London schools found that friendships were more likely to be formed within the same social class. Most had mixed-ethnic friendship groups, although middle class white girls were less likely to have black friends, perhaps because they mixed with fewer middle class black girls.

Other studies (Fuller 1980, Phoenix 1992) have found, as I did, that attitudes and aspirations differ among the Black-Caribbean, Indian and white girls. The black girls may experience less pressure to go out with boys or take part in adolescent culture generally than their white counterparts; they tend to have higher aspirations for the future and to consider remaining unmarried. These cultural factors could account for different friendship groups outside school as well as inside.

However, as with ability and class, there may be regional or school-specific differences in the way that ethnic differences are constructed. It became clear during this and previous research (Griffiths 1982) that, school intake and ethos could make a considerable difference here. For example at Barnsdale, there were comparatively few black pupils, and they tended to stick together in the playground, forming large groups containing both Black-Caribbean and Indian pupils. The usually rigid barriers of gender and age were not apparent, and the different ethnic groups mixed together with apparent ease. This overtly black grouping, which had a strong visual impact, may have been at least in part because of the small numbers of black pupils (about 5% of the

43

school population), and because of racism from white pupils, which the black (Black-Caribbean and Indian) girls in G2 told me was a frequent occurrence. 'Shut yer black mouth' was an insult often used by white pupils to black and white pupils in the school. To counter this prejudice, the Black-Caribbean girls in particular used the term 'black' positively about themselves, as Charleen (Black-Caribbean) told me: 'I say, when they say that, I go, I'm proud of me colour'.

In contrast, at Newton High School, in another part of Millbrook, where three quarters of the school population was black (Black-Caribbean, Indian and Pakistani), there was much more variety of groupings between and among both black and white young people, and exclusively black groupings were not so evident. In particular, Black-Caribbean and white pupils mixed easily together, as in the mixed ethnic American schools described by Barrie Thorne (1993). Perhaps because they were in the minority, white pupils did not exhibit open racism. The greatest tensions existed between different Asian groups, reflecting divisions in the community between Indian (Sikhs) and Pakistani (Moslem) families, based on religious and cultural differences.

At Barnsdale, the picture became more complex as I got to know the pupils. For instance, in G2, one of the closest friendship groups was between four girls: two Black-Caribbean, one Indian, and one white. Lesley Green, the class teacher thought that race was one factor in the friendship:

> I think race has a bearing on why they're friendly......They are the only non-whites in the class, Surinder and Marilyn and Charleen, so I think that's why they've stuck together. And then June because she hasn't had anybody else maybe.

Interestingly June, the only white girl in the group, identified herself at least to some extent as an 'honorary black' (Fuller 1980), which was strikingly exemplified when she drew a self-portrait in Art which was half white and half black. However, there were other factors, such as 'having fun' together, which drew these girls together, so ethnicity alone was not a sufficient explanation for their friendship. Also, all three black girls in the group had white friends at home as well, so their friendship choices were by no means restricted to other black girls.

On the other hand, different ethnic groups did retain a clear identity both in and out of school. For example, Surinder and Manjeet, both Sikhs, met each other at the local gurdvara (Sikh temple), and spent time with each others' families, as well as playing together at school. Both girls had lived in India during their early years, still had relatives there, and had strong links with India.

The Black-Caribbean girls, like those in Mary Fuller's research (1980), were conscious and proud of their West Indian origins, and still had close ties with the Caribbean. There was evidence of the influence of Rastafarian culture, particularly in the girls' long beaded hairstyles, which were often done at home in extended family groups. Marilyn and Charleen told me that this used not to be allowed at school:

Maril. They (teachers) used to say we couldn't wear them before.
Charl. Yeah, cos last - when my sister were in this school, right, 'er friend wore beads in 'er hair, and of t'teachers told 'er to tek 'em out, and she said no, she 'adn't to tek 'em out, so she (teacher) just got 'er hair and just took 'em out, and she (girl) just put 'em back in.
VG But now they let you wear them do they?
Maril. They don't say owt to me.

This incident was somewhat apocryphal, was often referred to, and was symbolic of the girls' Black-Caribbean identity and their triumph over school racism.

As a white researcher I am aware, like Linda Grant (1992) of having had greater access to the perspective of white girls; this inevitably limited the picture I obtained of the experience of black girls, and must be taken into account in any reading that I make of events or the girls' own accounts.

Friendship groups

From the above, it is clear that a complex interaction of factors is involved in the formation of friendships. Girls who share a cluster of similarities form friendship groups, a term which I have so far used unproblematically. Sara Delamont (1980) defined friendship groups or peer groups as an association of a number of girls who consistently get together outside lessons or outside school, and who share interests and attitudes. Previous studies (Meyenn 1980, Pollard 1984, Griffin 1985a, Lees 1986) have found considerable variety in the size, structure, attitudes and interests of these peer groups, but agree that they are an important feature of young women's lives.

At Barnsdale, the variety in groupings was also evident, confirming that there is no single or simple picture of girls' groupings equivalent to the 'gangs of lads' model. There were some groups of three girls, although these threesomes seemed inherently unstable, and at least two that I was aware of disintegrated during the time I was in the school. In G2, there were three main friendship groups (see Fig. 3.1), two of which were small (four girls each), and the third large (eight girls). These stayed more or less constant throughout the two years I was in contact with the girls. Variations occurred within the groups as to who was closest to whom, or who sat together in lessons. Occasionally a girl would tag on to another group for a time if she had fallen out with the friends in her own group. Otherwise the group boundaries were never crossed, and there was little communication between the groups.

Parallel friendships

However, although this picture is accurate, it is incomplete, and gives a misleading impression of relatively static, self-contained groups based within individual classes. What was most striking about the friendships I gradually unravelled over the two years was that they often existed in parallel with other friendships, either in or out of school. Depending on the context, one or other set of friends might take precedence. I later describe this as a hierarchy of interaction in relation to lessons at school, but it also applied to out of school activities.

At Barnsdale, parallel friendships were often based round out of school activities; for instance, Vicky had friends at her dancing school and Janette at orchestra. These were quite distinct from their friends at school. Others went to clubs with school friends, so formed parallel friends together; for example, Penny, Pam and Dawn were all friends with Becky through the Girls Friendly Society; Elaine and Lorraine made other friends through the RAF cadets.

A strong description of parallel friendships is given by Sinikka Aapola in her research on Finnish young women (1992). She argues that this kind of arrangement enables young women to try out different roles, interests and personality traits. It also provides a safeguard if any particular friendship breaks down, and prevents too great a reliance on any one friend or group of friends. Aapola sees this as a move by young women towards greater equality in friendship, and a means of balancing the potentially conflicting ideals in adolescence of independence and closeness.

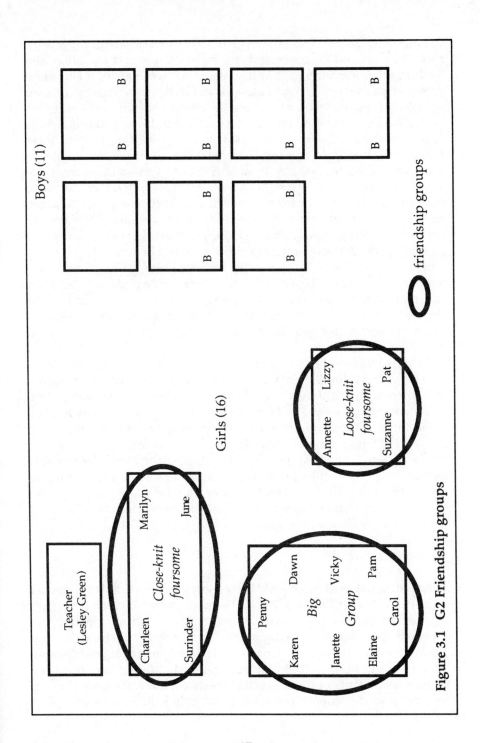

Figure 3.1 G2 Friendship groups

Parallel friendships also enable girls to ease the transition between childhood and adolescence, moving between one and the other and back again. For example, at Barnsdale, Lizzy was part of a close-knit group of younger-seeming white girls in G2, who spent much of their time out of lessons in a den behind the church, playing hide and seek and telling stories, in an unselfconscious, childlike way, using fantasy and humour. At the same time she was also part of a group of three white girls, two from another class, who shared 'mature' interests in adolescent culture, fashion, boys and music, and went to the same youth club in the evenings. As Aapola indicated, Lizzy could move between the two sets of friends, which was particularly useful when she fell out with Suzanne in the foursome for a while. This gave her more bargaining power, as well as enabling her to enjoy more childlike interests without fear of ridicule when she wanted.

In a similar way, Elaine moved between two large groups, one 'mainstream mature' based in G2, the other a subcultural group from two other classes with interests in punk and Citizens Band radio. She too could try out different interests, and attitudes to school, and have a refuge when at different times she fell out with members of each group for a while.

For girls who were part of more than one group at school, this was at times a difficult juggling act, particularly in the light of the emphasis on sameness and difference within groups. Inevitably, at times, there were tensions between sets of interests and group norms, which could sometimes lead to quarrels and temporary or more permanent breakups of friends, as I shall describe in chapter 5. However, for much of the time these parallel friendships coexisted remarkably easily. For girls who had one set of friends at school and another at home, the situation was usually easier, but for most of the young women in my research, there was usually some overlap (see Table 3.2 for a summary of other friends).

Size and structure

The traditional picture of girls' friendships is the close loyal pair of 'best friends' (McRobbie 1978a). The more recent picture is of girls interacting in groups as well as pairs, but in groups which are different from boys' by being smaller and non-hierarchical (Griffin 1985a), often consisting of pairs of friends put together (Bjerrum Nielsen & Rudberg 1992). In my own research, I found a more varied picture again. Pairs of friends certainly existed, but were more likely to interact outside school. In school, most girls belonged to groups of

Table 3.2
Parallel friends, 3G2

Girls in G2	Friends in other classes	Friends outside school
Suzanne	-	Janie (next door)
		Dot (2G1)
Pat	-	Tina (Pendleton High)
		Youth club
Annette	Kerry (3M2)	Cousins
Lizzy	Jill (3N1) ⟶	Youth club & St.
	Helen (3N1) ⟶	John's Cadets
Marilyn	Martine (3F2)	Shona (1N1)
	Manjeet (3F2)	Lesley (4M1)
		Jonie (4M1)
		St. John's Cadets
Charleen	Martine (3F2)	Paulette (2G1)
Surinder	Manjeet (3F2) ⟶	Gurdvara
June	Manjeet (3F2)	Sally (3G1)
	Jackie (3F2)	Joanne (1N2)
Carol	-	Guides, dancing,
		Air Cadets
Penny	-	Becky, Girls Friendly
		Society (GFS)
Pam	-	GFS
Dawn	-	GFS
Karen	-	Youth club
Vicky	-	Dancing classes
Janette	Marie (3M1)	Orchestra
	Samara (3M1)	Athletics
Elaine	Lorraine (3F2) ⟶	Air Cadets & CB
	Mandy (3F2) ⟶	CB radio
	Susan (3F2) ⟶	CB radio

different sizes. The larger groups tended to be non-hierarchical, with close but changing relationships between the members and, as Aapola found in her Finnish study (1992), with a clear allegiance to the group as a whole rather than to any individual within.

For example, Carol from the big group in G2 was most insistent that 'They're all good friends, don't really have a best friend', and other group members similarly resisted the notion of best friends. The girls were also keen to present themselves as a leaderless group. Karen explained that decision making was a joint process, 'cos we're sitting together, we all plan stuff......what we're going to do at night, where we're going'. This picture of equality in closeness and planning was emphasised by the way the group sat together in class, round one big table, forming a considerable presence within the room. Other girls often referred to them as 'the girls on the big table' or sometimes just 'the big table'.

A very similar kind of large, non-hierarchical group could be found among the seven young white women in 5N2 and 5F2 (Year 11). Although from the outside it looked as though there were two best friend pairs within the group, the girls themselves denied this. Jenny claimed, 'We're kind of all best friends', and Sue was also clear about the seven not having particular allegiances within the group, when she talked lucidly about them in retrospect six months after leaving school:

> We were just one big group, and you just went with who you wanted and it didn't matter. You didn't have to go with t'same people each time you know. We weren't possessive or owt - you know some people just stick together all t'time - we just went round in one big group.

In many ways, both these big groups reminded me of Lambart's description of the 'sisterhood' (1976). They all enjoyed 'having a laugh' together, and there was little major falling out between their members.

In contrast, the smaller groups at Barnsdale were far more hierarchical, revolving around clear leaders who exerted considerable power over the other group members, either overtly or more indirectly. In structure rather than size, the small groups appeared more like the popular picture of male friendship groups. Both the small groups in G2 were of this kind, but also had interesting differences in their structure and the dynamics of their relationships.

For example, the foursome which contained three black girls and a white girl was intensely close-knit, exemplified by their particular physical closeness. The girls were all small and very young looking; they always sat huddled together, laughing about something, and showed affection towards each other by hugging and holding. They never liked to be parted; in lessons where they had to sit in twos, the combination was always different. From my own observations, and what they said about each other, I have represented their group as a tight diamond or star-shape (Fig. 3.2), using categories derived from Button (1974). The dominance of Marilyn in the group only later became apparent, particularly when June fell out with her and the others. However, most of the time this was a stable foursome.

The other foursome was clearly led by Suzanne, an attractive girl who seemed to exert a powerful force over the others in the group. Lesley Green, G2's class teacher, summed up the dynamic well:

> She's the strongest personality of the four, and so because she's not a very strong personality within the rest of the form, she is a little bit of a dictator within her tiny group.

The other three girls in the group were not particularly friendly with each other, but were kept together by the mutual attraction to Suzanne. In some ways, it was hard to see why they maintained their friendship for so long, because of the cruel side of Suzanne's nature which was very apparent in their interaction, and which led to their self-labelling as 'nasty'. For instance, I noted early on in fieldwork:

> Pat said she'd lived here six months. Suzanne corrected her, 'A year you dummy'.......Suzannne did a 'thicky' sign (finger to head).

This was very much the external picture seen and disliked by other girls. Given that central elements of friendship are equality and reciprocity (Brain 1977, Allan 1979), the prognosis for this group was not good, and certainly the group structure was inherently less stable than that of the other foursome (Fig. 3.3.). However, as already mentioned, the group also had a close, supportive side, and enjoyed playing childlike games together, aspects which only became clear as I got to know the girls better, and must have provided more positive reasons for staying together. Both these small groups will be discussed further in chapter 5.

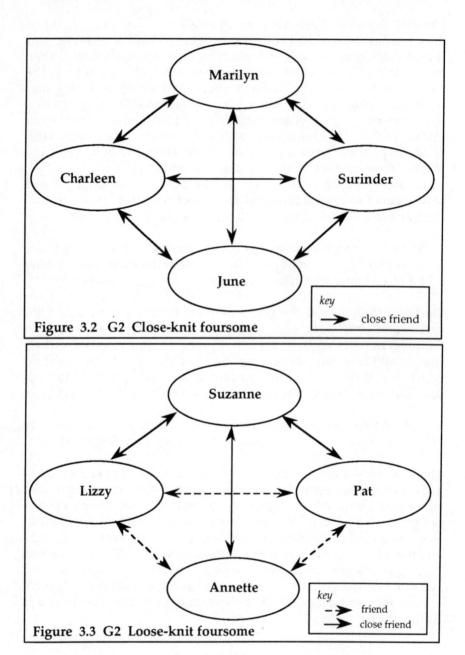

Figure 3.2 G2 Close-knit foursome

key
→ close friend

Figure 3.3 G2 Loose-knit foursome

key
--→ friend
→ close friend

physical closeness. The girls were all small and very young looking; they always sat huddled together, laughing about something, and showed affection towards each other by hugging and holding. They never liked to be parted; in lessons where they had to sit in twos, the combination was always different. From my own observations, and what they said about each other, I have represented their group as a tight diamond or star-shape (Fig. 3.2), using categories derived from Button (1974). The dominance of Marilyn in the group only later became apparent, particularly when June fell out with her and the others. However, most of the time this was a stable foursome.

The other foursome was clearly led by Suzanne, an attractive girl who seemed to exert a powerful force over the others in the group. Lesley Green, G2's class teacher, summed up the dynamic well:

> She's the strongest personality of the four, and so because she's not a very strong personality within the rest of the form, she is a little bit of a dictator within her tiny group.

The other three girls in the group were not particularly friendly with each other, but were kept together by the mutual attraction to Suzanne. In some ways, it was hard to see why they maintained their friendship for so long, because of the cruel side of Suzanne's nature which was very apparent in their interaction, and which led to their self-labelling as 'nasty'. For instance, I noted early on in fieldwork:

> Pat said she'd lived here six months. Suzanne corrected her, 'A year you dummy'.......Suzannne did a 'thicky' sign (finger to head).

This was very much the external picture seen and disliked by other girls. Given that central elements of friendship are equality and reciprocity (Brain 1977, Allan 1979), the prognosis for this group was not good, and certainly the group structure was inherently less stable than that of the other foursome (Fig. 3.3.). However, as already mentioned, the group also had a close, supportive side, and enjoyed playing childlike games together, aspects which only became clear as I got to know the girls better, and must have provided more positive reasons for staying together. Both these small groups will be discussed further in chapter 5.

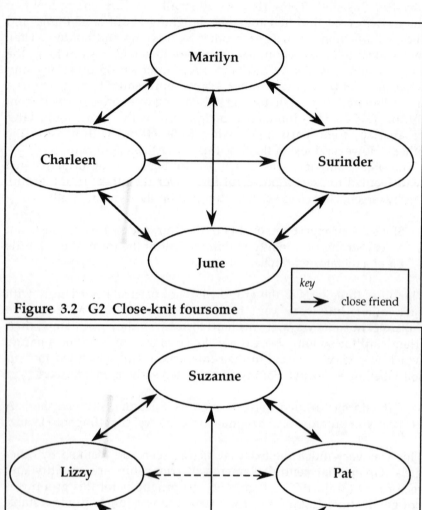

Figure 3.2 G2 Close-knit foursome

key
→ close friend

Figure 3.3 G2 Loose-knit foursome

key
--→ friend
→ close friend

Towards closeness

It is already becoming clear that there is no single pattern of girls' friendships, or girls' culture; rather, there is a richness and variety of interaction and possible perspectives. As Barrie Thorne stresses:

> We need...to develop concepts that will help us to grasp the diversity, overlap, contradictions, and ambiguities in the larger cultural fields in which gender relations, and the dynamics of power, are constructed. (Thorne 1993 p.108)

Looking at how girls make friends, a developmental picture of the friendships emerges, similar to that given in the psychological literature (Button 1974, Duck 1983, Kutnick 1988). Friendships progress from somewhat arbitary origins, depending on where girls live or who ends up in the same class, to relationships of closeness and intensity. If friendships have a pragmatic and selfish basis, in providing company and someone to enhance one's self identity, this does not preclude the existence of very real and deep feelings between friends, and a desire to give as well as receive help and support. These elements will be explored further in the next chapter.

4   What makes a good friend

> Callie was my best friend from seventh through ninth grades.
> ....We went round together arm in arm talking about boys and
> went to the movies and cut out pictures of singers and actors to
> worship. (Piercy 1982 p.24)

The main features of friendships between girls which stand out from
previous studies are physical closeness, 'having a laugh' together,
talking and sharing confidences (Ward 1976, McRobbie 1978a, Griffin
1985a, Lees 1986). Trust and loyalty are seen as particularly important,
as well as mutual support. Adolescent friendships in general are
usually characterised by 'intimate sharing, private knowledge, trust
and loyalty' (Duck 1983 p.123), but because of cultural pressures on
women to be more 'relationship-oriented' as Duck puts it (ibid p.76),
the pull towards intimacy and self-disclosure in friendships between
adolescent girls may be stronger than for boys. Elizabeth Douvan and
Joseph Adelson (1966) also report a strong emotional investment in
relationships between adolescent girls, and a stress on security. They
argue that close friendships are particularly important for young
women during adolescence because they may be experiencing similar
problems, and the process of identification is strong.

In my own research, I certainly found these features to be important
to friendships, not just between best friends as in the above quote from
Braided Lives, but between groups too. As with making friends, the
girls found it easier to tell me what they did and how they spent time
with each other than to answer the more abstract question of what
makes a good friend. From their answers and my own observations I
was able to pick out what I saw as behaviour characteristic of friends
(as opposed to acquaintances), and common to all the groups.

Togetherness

It was particularly noticeable how closely groups of friends kept together, seeing each other as frequently as possible during the school day. Where possible, friends would call for each other on the way to school and walk to school together. Breaks and lunchtimes were always spent together. If they were in the same tutor group, they would sit together during registration, and where possible in lessons too.

Some girls were reluctant to be separated for a minute. This was particularly true of the close-knit foursome in G2; for example, during an Art lesson:

> Mrs J. chose some (pupils) to go and help Mr H. with bunting for Fiesta tonight...Surinder wouldn't go unless Marilyn and Charleen could go too.

Teachers often acknowledged the inseparable nature of girls' friendships, although this was sometimes a source of sarcastic comment, such as, 'Can you bear to be split up for a few minutes?'

Even if friends were separated into different sets for certain subjects, (which happened more and more as they went up the school), friends would wait for each other outside the classrooms, ready to walk to the next lesson together or to walk home at the end of the day. This is also reported in Robert Meyenn's study of girls at a middle school (1980). When I was observing lessons, I often became aware of girls waiting outside the door, communicating with their friends in sign language through the glass partitions until the lesson was over. I never saw groups of boys waiting in this way for their friends; they seemed to gather at pre-ordained meeting places instead.

Togetherness was a highly ritualised procedure, in that the girls often followed exactly the same pattern each day. For example, the large group of seven fifth year girls described how they met on the way to school:

> Jenny Well we all walk together.
> Sarah We all meet more or less outside my house.
> Jenny Cos Marje goes for - Jacky goes for Marje .
> Jacky I go for Marje.
> Jenny They come up for Sarah and they come down for me and then we meet Sue as well, cos Sue lives at Raindley so she has to walk up....and we all walk up Hillside.
> Sarah And we all come up to school.

These young women also emphasised closeness by sitting together at dinner times in the fifth form common room, as Sue described, 'Same place every dinner time. Trying to cram on to one of t'tables (all laugh), about 24 of us round one table!' Like their older counterparts, the 'big' group of eight girls in G2 always demonstrated how inseparable they were by pushing the tables together in their classroom to form one large table during registration times. This visible manifestation of closeness was one way in which girls sometimes took over the physical space usually dominated by boys in lessons and the playground (Whyld 1983).

Physical closeness

As well as sitting together and generally keeping together as much as possible, girlfriends spent a lot of time showing physical affection by hugging or walking arm in arm. For example, girls often sat on each others' laps during form time, chatting and laughing. Penny in G2 was particularly demonstrative physically, and would often hug one of her friends spontaneously. During the field trip to the Yorkshire Dales, the girls posed for photographs with their arms round each other. This happened again when I took photographs of them on Sports Day; as though the closeness of friendship was represented in the photographic image by actual physical closeness.

As other researchers have also found (Schofield 1982, Thorne 1993), most of the girls also spent time engaged in what I called 'grooming', that is, doing each others' hair, and this was often combined with other forms of physical closeness. For example, after Karen had been away from school, all the 'big' group gathered round her: 'Penny hugs Karen...Vicky arm round Karen, combing her hair; Karen arranges Vicky's hair.' Although an interest in hairstyles was part of the 'mature' second and third years' (Years 8 and 9) growing involvement in the culture of femininity, doing each others' hair seemed to represent much more than this. On the one hand, it reinforced closeness between friends, as in the above example. Girls who were not interested in fashionable appearance spent as much time doing each others' hair. For instance, on one occasion June was stroking Surinder's long plaits and commented, 'It's that black hair, always looks as though you've just washed it - lovely and shiny.'

Fiddling with each others' hair was also one means of quiet resistance to lessons. Surinder explained that she and her friends often did it because lessons were 'so boring'. It was certainly a noticeable activity among the girls during lessons, but usually went unreprimanded. For example, during one Science lesson I noted:

> Janette and Vicky sit on same chair, Vicky fiddling with Janette's curls again. Dawn plaits Karen's long strand, Janette finding Vicky's split ends. Reminded of monkeys in zoo picking each others' fleas out!

This kind of observation was commonplace in lessons. Doing each others' hair was a fairly visible activity, as in the above example. Less obvious, but equally frequent, activities in lessons which involved physical closeness were things like playing with each others' fingers. Whereas grooming was often carried out with serious concentration, hand games were often a source of amusement, surreptitiously carried out under the tables.

To give an idea of the extent and frequency of this kind of physical interaction, I noted the following instances between two different groups of girlfriends during the course of three lessons on one day:

> (1) Surinder and co. slapping each others' hands, laughing.
> (2) Penny and Elaine slapping each others' hands and knees under table.
> (3) Dawn and Janette undoing Lizzy's skirt whilst she lay head on hands.
> (4) June and Marilyn painting nails with felt tip.
> (5) Surinder, Charleen and Marilyn piling up hands game.
> (6) Janette and Vicky in huddle...Vicky lying on Janette's shoulder, trying to lick her face as joke, rubbing noses etc.

As with grooming, these activities seemed to serve several purposes simultaneously. They were a means of reinforcing affection and closeness between the girls; they were a way in which girls managed to 'have a laugh' with each other even in lesson time; they helped to pass the time in lessons without being overly disruptive. AnnMarie Wolpe describes this kind of behaviour among girls as 'excessive use of body language' (1988 p.46), and notes, as I did, that it seemed an effective form of resistance because it largely went unnoticed.

Many of these examples of physical closeness would, if seen in another context, seem like expressions of sexual intimacy, or perhaps the first stages of a sexual relationship. There are different ways of interpreting this. Some researchers (Ward 1976, McRobbie 1978a) see physical and emotional intimacy between young women as analogous to and anticipating heterosexual relationships. For example, Raphaela Best (1983), in her study of girls in the U.S.A., describes such close relationships as 'prototypical of passionate love....a kind of apprenticeship for the mature male-female relationship of adulthood' (Best 1983 p.102). A heterosexual norm is clearly implied by her words: 'passionate love' is assumed to be between men and women, and seen as a 'mature' relationship, as opposed perhaps to the immature expressions of affection between young women. However unintended, these words undermine the importance of the girls' relationships, and present them merely as a practice-run ('apprenticeship') for the real thing, which will be between men and women. Homosexuality, however latent, is only a phase which girls will grow out of as they reach adulthood. I am taking a reading of these words to an extreme to make the point that, even among feminist researchers such as Best, there is an unspoken assumption of heterosexuality.

An alternative interpretation of girls' physical closeness would be that they are, indeed, 'prototypical of passionate love', but between women, that is, the first expressions of lesbian love. This reading is equally problematic, however, because of the context of 'compulsory heterosexuality' (Rich 1981) which still largely prevails. Many writers (Jones & Mahony 1989, Graham 1995), particularly lesbian feminist critics, have pointed out the lack of positive role models of gay women, especially in the school context, and the subsequent difficulty for young women in identifying themselves as lesbians. Section 28 of the Local Government Act of 1988 worsened the situation by introducing a 'prohibition on promoting the teaching in any maintained school of the acceptability of homosexuality as a pretended family relationship' (actual wording of Section 28), thus endorsing through discriminatory legislation a backlash against the growing campaign for gay rights (Sanders & Spraggs 1989 p.109).

However, well before section 28, girls had been very aware of the negative label of 'lezzie' as part of a more general abuse, both verbal and physical, by boys at school (Mahony 1985, Lees 1986). Certainly the young women in my own research tried to avoid this designation, and reacted to the slightest suggestion that their own relationships were lesbian by embarrassed laughter (to me) or vehement denial (to boys or other girls). This formed an interesting contrast to the proud rebuttals of negative labelling about race expressed by the black girls, and was, I would argue, located in the particular cultural and regional context at that time. I found a great difference in attitudes towards sexuality and gender, for example, between the young women at Barnsdale, and others with whom I worked at the same time in Manchester. In London and other large conurbations during the 1980s, positive action against homophobic attitudes was growing in prominence in schools and youth clubs (Cooper 1989, Dixon et al 1989, Gardner et al 1992), and thus young women could begin, albeit in a small way, to see positive images of lesbianism, but in Millbrook at the same time this was largely an uncharted and unchallenged area.

For the young women at Barnsdale then, openly to admit to a gay relationship or even lesbian inclinations would have been extremely brave, and it is hardly surprising that I did not hear anything directly about this. It is highly likely that some girls felt ambivalent about their sexuality, as I did during my own adolescent years, and were trying to come to terms with their feelings in an acceptable (i.e. heterosexual) way, or were hiding a lesbian relationship from even close friends, as Jill in *Braided Lives*, who 'seduced her (best friend) in 7A' (Piercy 1982 p.24):

> I was stuck on Callie. I could not touch her that often without attachment, without emotion, without love. Is she good enough for me? I asked myself when I was feeling smart. Am I good enough for her?......We were both running with the gang, but nobody knew of our secret attachment. What words did we have for it? It was as furtive as the fact that we both still sometimes played with our old dolls. (ibid p.24-5)

If imputations of lesbianism are, or were, so negative for girls, then how can they be so open in physical expressions of affection, as I have described? I shall end this section by taking a more positive line, that is, to argue that young women actually have a great deal more freedom to express physical closeness to each other than boys to each other. As with romantic friendships between women in previous centuries (Faderman 1981), adolescent girls are able to express their affection for each other physically without comment, as long as they do not overstep certain boundaries of acceptable physical contact. Unlike some women friends in Faderman's research who were able even to sleep together without any imputations of homosexuality, young women have a freedom within limits, but a degree of freedom none the less.

Boundaries and rituals surrounding the degree of acceptable expression are more visible in all-girls' schools, where the moral panic around possible lesbiansim was first raised by Havelock Ellis (1913). Although Ellis acknowledged that 'conventions allow girls more physical contact than boys' (Faraday 1989 p.33), he argued that this meant that 'lesbian passions can flourish freely under the guise of feminine friendship' (ibid.). The result of such fears gave rise to the tight circumscribing of passions in all-girls' schools, particularly around 'crushes' (Faraday 1989, Anderson 1994).

This was evident in the girls' grammar school I attended in the 1960s. Girls were allowed to have crushes, but only on girls at least three or four years older; the most common gap was between the first and sixth forms. A crush had to be overtly acknowledged by the younger girl writing to the subject of her admiration and asking if she would be her crush. If this was accepted, then the girl was allowed to walk with her crush at certain times, and even hold her hand occasionally. The situation is very similar in some girls' schools now; for instance, in some recent research at a girls' boarding school in Sussex (Griffiths unpublished), girls are allowed to have 'gone-ons', and the rituals and rules are almost identical to those from my own school experience.

The examples from all-girls' schools have relevance, I would argue, to the mixed-sex context, by indicating the boundaries of publicly acceptable closeness between girls, although in mixed-sex schools they are not so explicitly spelt out. Similar boundaries usually exist at school in relation to the expression of closeness between girls and boys, although these operate within a public recognition of heterosexual attraction, as opposed to the largely unspoken or unacknowledged context of lesbian attraction, as AnnMarie Wolpe points out in relation to crushes on teachers (1988 p.120). Finally, it is important to bear in mind Robert Brain's comment (1977) that the physical expression of affection between friends does not necessarily denote sexual attraction or intimacy.

Having a laugh

Celia Cowie and Sue Lees (1981) suggest that friendships between adolescent girls provide them with their 'major source of fun' (Cowie & Lees 1981 p.98). Having fun is mentioned as a central feature of girls' friendships in other research too (Meyenn 1980, Griffin 1985a). In my research, 'having a laugh' emerged as one of the key aspects of friendships, as I have already described in relation to the main groups of friends. It was a sign of closeness between friends, as Jackie put it so aptly:

> Well me and Lynn think - think alike you see... Me and her get on really really well, everyone says we get on well. We're always. well not messing about but we're always having a right good laugh.

'Having a laugh' often meant generally 'having fun' or friends enjoying themselves together. I observed or heard about many different instances of girls having a laugh or having fun together. Many of these are described in subsequent chapters. For the purposes of this chapter, I shall describe examples where girls literally had a laugh, that is, where laughing was the activity itself rather than a product of some other activity.

Although the girls themselves described 'having a laugh' in positive terms, it was one of the characteristics of friendships between girls which teachers often described negatively, as other researchers have also found (Spender & Sarah 1980, Stanworth 1981). Several male teachers mentioned that they found 'giggling girls' irritating, even out of lessons. I only found one teacher (Mrs Jebson who taught Art) who positively liked this aspect of teenage girls' behaviour. In lessons, giggling or laughing among girls gave rise to frequent rebukes from both male and female teachers, presumably because, unlike grooming, it was more openly disruptive. Usually a stern reprimand would be enough to quieten the girls, although they often continued to smile across at each other.

However, on several occasions which I observed, the laughing became completely unrestrained and dominated the lessons for a while until the girls were split up or sent out. I felt particularly sympathetic to the teacher during a Music lesson when the girls' laughter became uncontrollable:

> Mrs S. very fed up, getting angry and upset. Sent Pam out for giggling...Vicky and Carol almost hysterical with giggling. Surinder, Marilyn and Paulette (from another class) also giggling a lot. Really felt for Mrs S. - almost crying...felt awkward at being there, longing to help her out.

Although my sympathies lay with Mrs Sanderson on this occasion, looking at it from the girls' point of view, this was one of the few opportunities they had to have a really good time in a lesson. Other researchers (Davies 1984, Wolpe 1988, Thorne 1993) describe similar situations where the normal boundaries of prescribed behaviour in school are broken by girls having a laugh together in this kind of uncontrollable way.

Out of lessons, laughing and joking between girlfriends could continue unrestrained. I have a virtually untranscribable tape of a group of friends one lunchtime: whilst I try to talk to individual girls, there is a constant background of laughter from the others, ranging from quiet amusement to shrieks of hilarity. I remember girls, on this and other occasions, rolling around on the grass with tears of laughter pouring down their faces, sometimes set off by a single word. I have warm and vivid memories from my own adolescence of laughing with girlfriends in this way, often about nothing at all.

Having a laugh together was very much a sign both of intimacy between girlfriends and of exclusiveness. During form time I often watched one of the groups of girls huddled round a table, heads together, whispering and laughing, and felt it would be intruding on their closeness to interrupt. Whilst this seemed to be one of the positive means of reinforcing friendships for those in the group, for girls outside it could be a negative experience. Girls who wanted to become part of a group must have felt particularly excluded by this visual manifestation of friendship. For instance Dawn, who was not part of any group for a while during the second year (Year 8), used to hover uncertainly around the edges of the big group in G2, trying to catch somebody's eye so that she could be drawn into the circle. However, the girls in the group usually ignored her, apparently oblivious of her presence. I remember times from my own schooldays when I felt similarly shut out from a group of girls; their laughter would reinforce my own feeling of isolation and I would wonder if they were laughing about me.

At Barnsdale, I did not feel that the girlfriends' laughter was usually directed at or against anyone else, in the way that Paul Willis's lads were often 'having a laff' (1977) at the expense of teachers, girls or blacks. Nevertheless, although the girls in the big group were not being directly hostile or cruel to Dawn, she often looked tearful and was away from school for a few days during this time. As discussed in the previous chapter, exclusivity of this kind is a way in which girls reinforce group norms and define themselves in terms of sameness or difference, and has frequently been found in previous studies (McRobbie & Garber 1976, Llewellyn 1980, Bjerrum Nielsen & Rudberg 1992))

Having fun together did not seem to diminish as the girls got older. This was evident in talking to the young women who had left school from the way they interacted with each other, laughing and joking and obviously enjoying each others' company. I was particularly interested in the way that the three young women who had gone to sixth form college together talked about this aspect in a slightly self-denigrating way, as though it was incompatible with being mature:

VG   Do most people sort of seem to act more grown up now do you think?

Jenny Yeah, except for us! (All laugh)

VG   Except for you! (laughs)
Sarah Well, we can all be silly at times can't we?

They used the term 'silly' quite often to describe themselves and their friends. However, they also stressed the contrast between the way teachers at the college treated them as more mature than teachers at school had done, and the greater tolerance of so-called 'silly' behaviour shown by teachers at the college, who 'just laugh it off' (Sarah). An example of the kind of incident which college teachers tolerated also epitomises what sort of things these young women enjoyed:

Sarah Birthdays up here are great!
Jacky Oh it's great!
Jenny When it's your birthday everybody gets you and throws you in t'shower -
VG   Oh!
Jenny - and you get eggs all over you and flour (all laugh). I don't know, but if you did that at school you'd get done, yet everybody enjoys it, even the person that's having it done.

Talking

In his study of adolescent girls in Swansea, John Ward (1976) found that interaction between girlfriends was primarily verbal. Sue Lees also describes the 'centrality of talk' (Lees 1986 p.62) in girls' friendships. I certainly found this to be the case with the young women in my research. John Ward makes a useful distinction between 'ordinary verbal interaction with general acquaintances' (Ward 1976 p.49), and 'confiding' talk, usually with a best friend. I shall concentrate on talking between friends rather than acquaintances, but otherwise I shall use Ward's categories and divide this section into 'ordinary' talking and confiding talk. Although one type of talk often blurred into another (as also in Ward 1976), I did identify different levels of talk which seemed to serve different purposes and to represent different degrees of closeness between girls.

Negative Connotations

Janette   Sometimes we just walk around and sit on the swings and talk.
Charleen Sit down and talking and all.
Marilyn   Yeah we just talk.

Remarks about talking were often prefaced by the word 'just', which sounded somewhat apologetic and critical of the activity, as though the girls felt that they should have been doing something. As Deborah Cameron writes:

> Women's day to day language is undervalued even by women themselves, and...the disadvantaged doubt the strength and potential of their own language. (Cameron 1985 p.153)

This self-denigrating attitude was hardly surprising given the critical view taken of girls' talk in the school. Like laughing, talking was one of the most frequently reprimanded aspects of girls' behaviour in class, and seen as an aspect of teenage girls' general silliness in comparison to boys. Such criticisms of girls' talk are not isolated incidents, but part of a wider devaluation of talk between women which many feminist researchers have identified. Fern Johnson and Elizabeth Aries (1983) found talk to be the 'central feature' (Johnson & Aries 1983 p.354) of women's friendships, but argue that its value has usually been ignored or undermined:

> Folk wisdom has long denigrated women's talk as 'idle chatter', 'yackedy yack', 'hen cackling', 'gabbing' and 'gossip'. (ibid. p.354)

Dale Spender (1980) sees this as one way in which patriarchal order is maintained:

> It is not surprising to find that there are no terms for man talk that are equivalent to 'chatter', 'natter', 'prattle', 'nag', 'bitch', 'whine', and of course 'gossip'...No matter what women may say it fosters the conviction that you cannot trust the words of a woman and that it is permissible to dismiss anything she might say. By such means does the dominant group exert control over women talk. (Spender 1980 p.107)

The denigration of women's talk in everyday language is hard to avoid. My fieldnotes contain frequent references to girls 'chatting' or 'chattering' together, whereas the boys are always described as 'talking'. The girls themselves often referred to their own talking as 'nattering', 'gossiping' or 'bitching'. However, in spite of these derogatory connotations, the girls usually described their talking together in positive terms.

What the girls talked about varied according to their age and stage of adolescence. For some of the younger seeming girls, talking and playing were closely related; talk formed part of childlike games. For example, during a lunch hour spent with the loose-knit foursome in G2:

> Pat said, 'Five for gold', and they went through the magpie rhyme for me, all chanting just like young girls skipping. Then Suzanne started making up a story (said into the tape recorder)...'Well here we have Mrs Robinson. She has 105 children and lives in a castle. Why do you live in a castle Mrs Robinson?' Pat, 'Because I've got 105 children.'

This was typical of the kind of imaginative play which these girls enjoyed. The close-knit foursome found great amusement in talking about school, and often described events from lessons, as in the following example: 'Manjeet excitedly recounting how she fell flat on her back in Cookery, and Pam had one of her breads stolen'. They usually found enjoyment from incidents such as the above which were not directly related to learning, perhaps because these events kept their interest in lessons.

In contrast, 'mature' second and third years (Years 8 and 9) and older girls spent a lot of time talking about aspects of teenage culture: television, records and fashions. For example, the big group in G2 often spent breaktimes and formtimes looking at the latest copy of the pop magazine *Smash Hits* and talking about which new records they liked. On other occasions, they brought in catalogues and the girls decided what clothes they would order if they had the money.

Apart from shared interests, talking focused on the sharing of experience, either in anticipation or in retrospect. Marilyn and Charleen from the close-knit group told me they had spent one evening at Marilyn's house 'fixing about that party in Cooking', planning what each of them wanted to make and working out the ingredients. The big group tended to plan what they were going to do in the evenings, and spent a lot of time planning trips out which never materialised because they were not considered old enough by their parents. Nevertheless, the girls got a lot of enjoyment out of this fantasising, as I shall describe in relation to boys.

Reinforcing closeness through planning events was also mentioned by the fifth years (Year 11). The large group of friends kept in touch even at weekends as Sue described:

65

Jenny always...rings us all up one by one...she rings round, 'Do you
want to come to t'Monday market on Monday?' 'Oh yeah.' Then we
all meet at t'corner don't we?

As well as making arrangements for events in the future, the
importance of keeping up to date with events which had already
happened and talking them through afterwards was also stressed by
the fifth year girls:

Sue   We just catch up on all t'stuff that's been happening.
Kath All t'scandals.

For those young women who had left school, this kind of information
exchange was an important way of keeping in touch, as Michelle
explained; (Michelle worked in a bank and her friend Anne was at Art
college): 'Like we can both talk about what each of us has been doing,
diffferent like...different from what we used to talk about at school.'

'Boys and stuff like that' (Janette) were a favourite topic of
conversation among the older girls and the 'mature' second and third
years. As I found in my previous research (Griffiths 1986), the girls
spent a lot of time together talking about which boys they liked or
disliked, deciding who they would like to go out with, or comparing
notes about current boyfriends. I was never included in these
discussions, but either overheard snatches of conversation at break or
form time, or was sometimes told about them later. This was one area
where 'ordinary' talking moved into secret, confiding talk.

Confiding talk

Whilst both ordinary talking and confiding talk could involve a
sharing of interests and experience, confiding talk seemed to be
characterised by a deeper level of feeling, involving a sharing of
emotion and innermost feelings. Fern Johnson and Elizabeth Aries
(1983) argue that this is an important characteristic of friendships
between women generally:

Close female friends converse more frequently than close male
friends about personal and family problems, intimate relationships,
doubts and fears, daily activities. (Johnson & Aries 1983 p.356)

Ordinary talking reinforced friendship between groups of girls, but
confiding talk represented a level of intimacy which was more often
(though not exclusively) present between pairs of friends, as Jackie
described:

66

I had a very very good friend...and we got on really well and we never had an argument , never a fight, or never answered anything each other back...You see she told me everything about her, what had happened to her...and I told her everything.

Or as Pauline put it more briefly, 'I could tell Janie things'.

Secrecy was paramount if confidences were to be shared, as Janette explained: 'We just talk about anything that's happened really but that we don't want everybody else to know about.' For Janette and other girls, finding somewhere private to talk in this way was difficult. The girls were aware that sharing secrets made them vulnerable. As Jackie said, 'You know their weaknesses and know a bit about 'em'. Trust was therefore essential, as June explained:

We've shared all our secrets together haven't we? She's (Jackie) told me loads of secrets and I've never told anybody...I can trust Jackie not to go round and tell Marilyn all these things what I've said about her.

Betraying this trust by telling other girls these secrets was one of the worst things a friend could do, and a cause of particular hurt if close friends had fallen out, as June had reason to know: her falling out with Marilyn is referred to in the following chapter.

As with ordinary talking, the topics of confiding talk varied according to the girls' age and stage of maturity. As well as shared interests and the sharing of experience, relationships with family or friends, and in particular difficulties or problems at home or school, were discussed. For instance, Janette told me: 'We talk about what's happening at home and whether we don't like somebody at home cos summat's happened or not, and whether there's been a big argument.'

Similarly Anne (at art college) often went round to her best friend Michelle's house to talk about problems at home:

You see, half the time I don't get on with them (parents). It's just, they argue all t'time and that gets me...They're always at each other for some reason or another. You come in and they're arguing over nowt, it's stupid.

Anne wanted to leave home and get a flat, but she not only could not afford to pay rent on a student grant, but 'me Dad won't let me leave, he's told me that'. Seeing Michelle provided both a means of getting out of the house for a while, and a way of talking through the difficulties which made them easier to cope with afterwards.

67

Many of the young women mentioned how talking to their friends about problems helped them 'sort it out' (Jenny). For example, Pauline (Year 11) told me: 'Say I like a boy and I feel a bit distressed about it, I'd talk to them (friends) and they'd help me.' Talking of this kind was a way of making sense of experience and coping with problems, as Sue Lees also found among the girls in her research (1986). The young women also described how they could tell their friends about things that they would not be able to talk to their parents about. For instance, Sarah (6th form college) told me: 'If your school work's going badly, you're not likely to go and tell your Mum and Dad are you? They'll stop you going out!'

Relationships with boys were mentioned frequently as a subject that mature second and third years or older girls talked about with each other, rather than with their parents. For example, Sarah told me: 'I used to tell me Mum a lot but I don't tell her any more about boys.' Similarly, Helen confided: 'They'd (parents) play hell if they knew I went out with Ian'. Talking to friends about boys also included a certain amount of fantasising about boys they would like to go out with, which I remember from my own adolescence too. In particular, some of the younger seeming girls who were just beginning to get interested in boys engaged in this, as well as passing each other notes that said things like 'I love Andrew'. John Ward (1976) discusses this kind of fantasising talk in relation to the girls in his research:

> Our impression was that talk about boys and other things was not practised to the end that the content of the talk would get one anywhere in any significant way. *The talk was itself the medium of the interaction between girl and girl.* (Ward 1976 p.49, my emphasis)

Whilst agreeing wholeheartedly about the primacy of talk in relationships between girlfriends, I would argue that as girls got older the talk did actually have some practical benefits too, thus serving a dual purpose. For example, the girls could compare notes about boys they knew or had both gone out with; they could warn each other about which boys had 'wandering hands' or were not to be trusted. These aspects are discussed in more detail in chapter 8.

In contrast to Ward, who sees the value of talk between friends as an end in itself, Trisha McCabe comes to rather different conclusions. She describes how girls spend time:

> discussing boyfriends, or potential boyfriends, working out relationships with boys, each other or parents. That they share things with friends, dress up together and have a laugh is important...But the long term aim is looking good for boys,

handling boyfriends, commiserating over losing one, sussing out the next possibility. (McCabe 1980 p.130)

Whilst I have just noted that talking between friends could be instrumental as well as important in itself, the implication in McCabe's comment is that girls' talk about boys is only a means to an end, that is, not important in itself, and that ultimately the girls' friendships take second place to their relationship with boys, even when the girls are together. I would take issue with this, arguing that the sharing of experiences, 'working out relationships', 'commiserating', 'sussing out', are all vitally important in themselves. As with the talking through of problems at home, talking of this kind among the young women provides a great deal of emotional feedback and mutual support, enriching the girls' friendships rather than undermining them, and helping them to make sense of their experience, as Jill in Marge Piercy's *Braided Lives* describes:

> I begin to walk fast and then trot, wishing I was already in my dormitory room, transported instantly to Donna so I can spill out to her verbatim, gestures illustrated and pauses marked, the afternoon. Then it will be real for me, secured, understood. (Piercy 1982 p.77)

I shall just end this section by adding that some of the girls in my research commented that they thought girls were closer friends than boys because they talked things out more. As Jill said: 'They (boys) don't really know each other well as much as we know us.'

Loyalty and support

Just as close friends are trusted not to tell each others' secrets, so loyalty and support are evident between girlfriends. Much of the research on adolescent girls notes this aspect of reciprocal exchange between friends (Ward 1976, McRobbie 1978a, Meyenn 1980, Lees 1986).

In my research at Barnsdale, this kind of mutual support took many forms. Firstly, I observed many instances of girls sticking up for their friends in front of teachers or other girls. This might involve not telling on a friend rather than speaking up for her; it often involved putting blame on to another girl or group in order to protect one's own friends. For example, when Elaine from the big group in G2 started 'bunking off' school, the rest of the group covered for her by telling teachers that she was at the dentist, and remained silent even when teachers began to suspect the truth. They also rounded fiercely on girls from other groups who 'told on' Elaine. Other groups were similarly protective towards each other.

Active support for friends was mentioned by the Head, Miss Jones, who told me that 'West Indian' (her term) pupils in particular, both boys and girls, stuck up for each other if there was trouble with a teacher:

> If one's in trouble they'll say, 'If you don't believe me ask so and so', or a friend will come independently and put their side of the story to clear their friend: 'This is what really happened'.

I was interested that Miss Jones saw this in a negative light - she said, 'It's particularly bad at Barnsdale' - because she saw it making discipline more problematic, rather than as a positive aspect of friendship.

Girls also stuck up for their friends in front of other girls. This was particularly true if there was falling out within a group; the rest of the group closed ranks against the new outsider. For example, when Lizzy fell out with Suzanne, Annette acted as a go-between for Suzanne, delivering verbal messages or notes and adding her own insults, such as, 'Here you are, leader of the babies'. The rejected girl could also count on support from her 'contingency' friends (Davies 1982), as I shall explain in more detail in the next chapter. For example, When June fell out with Marilyn, Jackie (a friend of June's from another class) was ready to stick up for her when Marilyn and her other friends called June names, as Jackie told me in some detail:

> Cos she (Surinder) was talking about June at the time...and if she said it behind her back I wouldn't push her but she were saying it in front of her. And I'm right close to June and I just didn't like the way she goes on about her. So what, I pushed her (Surinder) and she went and told Marilyn that I slapped her across the face and pulled her hair.

Certain ritual aspects of falling out, such as distinguishing between overt or covert name calling, and the exaggerating of insults, are evident in the above example. Jackie, who liked a good fight, was ready to anticipate supporting June against her other former friends too: 'Now June don't like me sticking up for her, but if Charleen did ask her for a hand, she would have a fight, I'd - I would - er, kick Charleen in.'

As with sticking up for friends in front of teachers, support for friends often involved aggression towards other girls. June herself,

70

who would 'never have 'em a fight, never', saw Jackie's intervention on her behalf as a mixed blessing, partly because of the potential escalation of aggression which might result, and partly because she would not, or could not, take this sort of direct action herself:

Jackie She don't like me sticking up for her (June laughs) cos it makes her feel soft.

June And because when they think Jackie's sticking up for me they call me more names than anything you know.

It was ironic that supporting a friend, which was designed to help her, could in fact bring a girl more trouble rather than ending it or preventing it. I got the feeling that many girls operated according to a strict though unwritten code of practice, which they put into practice regardless of whether it was the best action in the circumstances. Support in this case upset the mutual exchange of favours which formed a frequent basis to friendships between the girls, and created an imbalance. Perhaps June did not want to be under any sort of obligation to Jackie which she could not reciprocate, particularly as Jackie was a 'contingency' friend.

However, this was not the only case where such an imbalance could be seen. I noticed that it was often those girls who were particularly vulnerable in some way, such as June who had a slight disability, or who had particular problems at home to face, who were supported most by their friends. For example, Annette was often made fun of by other girls because she was regarded as old-fashioned in her dress and manner. However, Annette was always strongly supported by her friends because of her personal circumstances, because her mother had left home. In spite of their reputation, I was always impressed by the support the rest of the so-called 'nasty' group showed to Annette. This was particularly evident on the field trip to the Yorkshire Dales, when Annette was scared and upset on several occasions, and her friends helped and comforted her.

There were other examples of support given to friends with difficult home circumstances. Pat helped her friend Tina who lived next door with her domestic responsibilities. In the big group, Karen supported Vicky after her parents separated by accompanying her on Sunday visits to her father, which Vicky found upsetting at first. Girlfriends also frequently gave each other support through talking about problems, as described in the previous section.

Although support and loyalty were particularly evident between close friends, I also noticed a general level of thoughtful kindness among the girls, which was shown to girls with short or long term

71

problems, regardless of whether they were close friends. For example, when Lizzy fell out with Suzanne, several girls from the other groups were kind to her: 'Penny called Lizzy over before History, talking about it. Lizzy wiping tears away. Penny half put her arm round Lizzy - kind.'After Suzanne and Annette made rude comments to Lizzy, June also went out of her way to be friendly towards her. In her turn, June was comforted by Karen and the rest of the big group when she fell out with Marilyn, allowing her to 'join' their group for a while so she would not be on her own.

Sinikka Aapola (1992) sees this kind of mutual support as one of the ideals girls share about friendship, and as one of the main features of girls' interaction. However, I do not want to paint too saintly a picture of the girls. This kind of general support may have had a pragmatic basis too, acting as a kind of insurance policy for when the girls showing support fell out with their friends. Acts of kindness also contrasted with hostility towards girls from other groups when the occasion arose, particularly if girls were acting in defence of their own group. Support, therefore, involves mixed motives and complex interaction, sometimes extending beyond girls' immediate friendship groups, but otherwise restricted to close friends.

Caring and sharing

Various strengthening factors, such as physical closeness, having a laugh and talking, reinforce friendships between adolescent girls, allowing them to continue and develop, and making them close and special. Mutual support, the sharing of experiences, trust and caring are all central to relationships between young women. Although 'reciprocity' (Allan 1979) or 'mutuality' (Kutnick 1988) are mentioned as features of all friendships by sociologists and psychologists, they are particularly prevalent in girls' friendships, often accompanied by a certain vulnerability (Thorne 1993). This can be seen as both caused by, and as one way of coming to terms with, social and cultural pressures on girls during adolescence (Duck 1983). These aspects are captured by an image from my fieldwork, which was provided by Jackie, describing two girls in her class who were close friends:

> Now to show 'ow close they are, Susan were, er, in Needlework, and a needle went through 'er finger, and Lorraine started to cry for, um, Susan. That's how close they were.

This vivid anecdote epitomises to me the intensity of feelings which existed between close friends. There may be a pragmatic element in giving help to other girls, but this does not undermine the sympathy and thoughtfulness shown to friends, particularly those who are vulnerable in some way.

Another particularly interesting finding is the centrality of talk in the friendships, ranging from the 'ordinary' everyday exchange of news, planning of outings or sharing of experiences, to close confiding talk, where secrets are exchanged and confidences shared. The importance of these different kinds of talking not only help friends to 'have a laugh' together, but also enhance their sense of self worth and help them sort out problems and feelings.

The keeping of confidences can on occasion lead to a fierce protectiveness towards friends, shown to other girls or teachers, and a sense of exclusiveness too which can shut out other girls. Thus the positive emotions involved in the friendships themselves can be turned outwards into a negative expression of feeling to others. The next chapter analyses what happens when those negative feelings are turned inwards to the friendships themselves.

A final point to note is that the very characteristics which are important in making the girls' friendships strong, for example, having a laugh and talking, are those which many teachers find most unlikeable in girls, and for which the girls receive most negative attention in class. I have argued that this is part of a wider denigration of women's relationships, particularly talking. In the light of this, it is not surprising that girls themselves tend to undermine their own interaction at times.

5 Falling out

On my first morning of fieldwork at Barnsdale School, Lesley Green, G2's form teacher, showed me a note about Dawn, who had been upset the previous day by some of the other girls in the tutor group, and I noted:' She was still upset today - crying, so Mrs Green took her out.' By the third week I had observed a major change in friendships among some other girls, which also caused considerable upset to the girl who was rejected: 'Lizzy was in tears this morning because she'd found a note calling her 'Stupid cow' and 'Silly bitch'. This had come from Suzanne.

During the following year I observed, and became involved in, frequent 'fallings out' of this kind between the girls, some of them minor and temporary in nature, others more serious and long lasting. They were characterised by the considerable emotional upset they caused the girls, as shown by the two examples above, and by features such as name calling and abusive notes which were not so much causes of the arguments but a part of the way in which the disputes were played out.

Reasons for friends falling out are numerous, and will be discussed in detail in the rest of this chapter. The major causes that I found, amongst both the younger and older girls, were jealousy over other girls and power struggles within or between groups.

Shallow friendships?

As with talking, there are many negative implications associated with girls falling out. Several researchers report the frequent making and breaking of children's or young people's friendships as a matter causing concern or surprise. For example, the Opies (1959) report:

> Children's friendships are far from placid. Perhaps because of the gregariousness of school life they make and break friends with a rapidity disconcerting to the adult spectator. (Opie & Opie 1959 p.324)

Robert Meyenn found the same among the 12-13 year-old girls in his study:

> There was...considerable internal fighting...with the girls 'breaking friends' with surprising (to me) frequency and usually within a very short time making friends again. (Meyenn 1980 p.118)

In the case of adolescent girls, this view is often expressed more extremely in terms of the popular stereotype of girls being bitchy and catty towards each other, and falling out because of jealousy over boys. The stereotype is reinforced by the media, for instance girls' magazines (McRobbie 1978b), where teenage girls are portrayed in constant competition over boys, with friendships between girls as shallow and mistrustful. This popular view is often taken up and expressed by girls themselves (Griffin 1985a, Lees 1986) and by teachers.

When I started my research at Barnsdale, I was struck by the frequency with which friendships between girls were seen as synonymous with falling out. For instance, the Deputy Headmistress told me that in the class of 12-13 year-olds she had taken, there had been different 'cliques' every week because the girls had so many arguments. Another woman teacher told me that the girls in her tutor group often fell out, she thought over boys. The implication was that the girls' friendships were shallow. Indeed, the second teacher said directly that she thought that boys formed stronger and more lasting friendships than girls. However, this was in contrast to the view expressed by Lesley Green, who saw the first example of girls falling out which I was aware of as 'unusual - basically this was a nice group and pretty friendly towards each other'.

Some girls themselves saw falling out as central to the interaction between girlfriends. For example, early on in the fieldwork Carly from N2 asked me why I was coming into lessons. When I explained I was looking at friendships, I noted that 'she immediately asked, 'Have there been lots of fallings out?' I asked if there were a lot then and she said yes'. I noticed that girls started to tell me about any instances of falling out between girlfriends. For example, I was told that Suzanne,

Annette and Pat were 'always falling out, that group. Suzanne with Pat or with Annette. Falling out and then making up again'.

Certainly the friendships between the second and third year girls at Barnsdale (Years 8 and 9) seemed characterised by frequent fallings out. However, what I want to argue in this chapter is that, far from being an indication of the shallow or shortlived nature of friendships between girls, making and breaking friends are essential means of reinforcing friendships between the girls, a central and as Meyenn says 'ongoing feature of each of the girls' groups' (Meyenn 1980 p.118). I very much agree with Bronwyn Davies when she questions the Opies' view (quoted earlier) of arguments and fights between children as problematic:

> Children may 'make and break friends with a rapidity disconcerting to the adult spectator', but that is perhaps because the adult spectator does not actually understand what is going on. The friendships are in fact surprisingly stable...What appear to be breakages are rather *manoeuvres within the friendship* so that the functions friendship serves can be fulfilled. (Davies 1982 p.113, my emphasis)

I am aware that Davies was referring to children of 10 and 11, rather than the early teenage years. Among the G2 girls at Barnsdale, there were some instances of changing friends, which were often related to the stage in adolescence a girl had reached in comparison to her friends (for example, Lizzy in the loose-knit foursome). These changes were sometimes connected, as in Lizzy's case, with other sources of discontent too. However, I must stress that in some instances which appeared to be changes in friendship, girls went back to their original friends, sometimes after quite a long period. This was true, for instance of Elaine, who fell out with Lorraine and the 'CB' group but made friends with them again after I had finished the fieldwork. In this and other cases, the importance of a long-term perspective was crucial.

Following on from Ward's distinction between 'ordinary' and 'confiding' talk which I used in the last chapter, in this chapter I shall make a distinction between 'ordinary' or minor, temporary fallings out between the girls and 'serious' or more major, long-lasting fallings out. Unlike many studies which report the breakdown of friendships between girls because of boyfriends or jealousy over boys, often called the 'deffing out' process (Griffin 1985a), I found this rarely between groups of friends. What I did find and what is discussed here is girls falling out because of jealousy over other girls.

'Tiff taff'

As well as the positive side of the girls' friendships, characterised by having fun and talking, a regular part of the daily interaction between many of the girls was taken up by small arguments which could lead to temporary fallings out. For example, these girls in the fifth year (Year 11) told me:

> Sarah We might just have a bit of an argument.
> Jenny Tiff taff (laughs).

Other terms used to describe this kind of small dispute were being 'narky' (Suzanne) and 'just manging' (Samara). The girls in the big group in G2 made a distinction between this kind of interaction and falling out:

> Penny We a'n't fallen out though really.
> Carol - with Janette.
> Penny We've argued but we haven't fallen out.

Anne, one of the fifth year girls, made a similar distinction when she told me that she and her friends 'complain about each other - in a joking way, but don't really fall out'. Even the girls in the self-styled 'nasty' group, who were constantly arguing or calling each other names, asserted that this was not serious but something they just did:

> Annette We can't help it really can we?
> Suzanne (funny voice) Don't know.
> Annette It just happens.
> Lizzy   We don't mean it really, we just play.

It was actually quite hard to know when these girls were being serious or not (Suzanne's funny voice interjection was typical). In their case, the daily abuse did sometimes seem to go too far and develop into more long lasting disputes, as I shall describe.

However, the phrase used by Lizzy, 'we just play', did typify much of the interaction between groups of friends. Playing the fool, or playing games and tricks, were apparent among even the fifth year girls, and were usually part of friends having a laugh together. At times the jokes rebounded, and then the situation turned sour. The girls' interaction was like two sides of a coin, with one side 'having a laugh' and the other side 'tiff taff': one could very quickly turn into another. The following is a classic example of what I mean:

77

> Janette The other week, me and two other girls had a bit of fun with Samara. We tripped her over a fence and she went off in a muff.
>
> Marie You did that other week as well.
>
> Janette Yeah, to you.
>
> Marie Yeah, we walked off and she hid behind a wall and me and Samara just walked past and she made us both jump. (Janette and Samara laugh)
>
> Samara (laughing) I tripped over, she wasn't (untrans.) I were stiff. (laughs)

The girls are actually describing two separate but similar incidents, the implication being that such situations were quite frequent as part of the girls' interaction. Such incidents were quickly forgotten and friendships made up again:

> Janette That time she (Samara) went home and she weren't me friend when she went home, and then about, about half past seven she came round and said, 'I weren't your friend this afternoon', and she were there boasting about not being me friend (laughs).
>
> Marie And then we just stood there wondering what you were on about.
>
> (Janette laughs)

In the above case it seemed as though Janette and Marie had forgotten all about the incident which had given rise to Samara's 'muff' by the end of the day, or perhaps they had never realised that she had taken offence so strongly. Another interesting aspect is the way that Samara was keeping up the argument to the very end, by 'boasting about not being me friend' at the same time as she had come to make it up. It was as if, because she saw herself as the injured party, (literally in this case), she was not going to lose face by being the one to make friends first. This was something which was more strongly evident in serious cases of girls falling out.

Making Up

There were many occasions when a small argument was made up speedily, for instance 'Half a day' in the case of one quarrel. It was also noticeable how often the original cause of a quarrel was forgotten once the girls made friends again. For instance, June told me how she and her friend Jackie fell out 'loads of times': 'But say we go, we break up and we're not talking, about an hour or so we're back to being friends again aren't we?'

I have already described in the last chapter how the talking through and sharing of experience was important to the girls. This seemed to be true even if the experiences shared or recalled were negative ones. The girls seemed to derive considerable pleasure from recounting past fallings out, particularly the making up at the end, as in the example of Janette, Marie and Samara. I was always amazed at the amount of detail that the girls remembered, although I speculated, as with other incidents recounted to me, that there was a certain amount of embroidering and elaborating of the truth in the retelling. These stories were worked up to become part of the shared history of the friendship groups. Here June and her friends Sally and Joanne whom she played with at home are recalling past events when they 'broke friends' and made up again.

June   I fell out with Sally when we were in Juniors and Sally were left on her own with Gillian. Don't you remember that, when Caroline and Jane went around with me?

Joanne Do you remember that time when we weren't her friend and then Claire were arguing with us -

June   Oh yeah.

Joanne - and then when Claire went home she wanted to make friends with us. (Laughter) I think it were that.

June   No it weren't. Tricia came down and she goes, 'Our Sally wants to make friends with you' and then Sally came down and she goes, 'Anyway, by the way I don't want to make friends with you' because Claire were there. Then she went to the shop and when she comes back she goes, 'I do want to make friends with you' and we just started talking.

VG   So did that last very long then?

Sally   We were arguing and we were laughing.

June   We were going , 'You fell out with me'. 'No I didn't, it were you an'all'.

As with Samara, it seems as though Sally was trying to 'save face' until the last possible minute, in this case until other onlookers (Claire) were not present. Sally's comment, 'We were arguing and we were laughing' also suggests that the argument was pursued to the end, even though the girls had by this time made things up again. Once again, the duality of 'having fun' and 'tiff taff' is apparent. There is also the interesting factor of Sally's sister Tricia acting as intermediary, an element which was noticeable in one of the major fallings out, as I shall describe.

Several other things strike me about the above extract. First of all the number of different incidents which were being recalled and at times confused (as in the extract between Janette, Marie and Samara above). I remember feeling totally confused myself about who was being talked about and about what was supposed to have happened. This happened frequently in conversations with other girls too, because although they could apparently recall the exact detail of the things they said to each other, they could often not remember what had caused the falling out in the first place. In a way the particular cause was no longer important. What mattered was the shared memory of the incident(s) and the reinforcement of closeness in the retelling.

Another reason for my finding it hard to follow the conversation was a feeling that it was carrying on without me or in spite of my presence. Even though I had facilitated the conversation - and in fact on this occasion had brought about a making up between June and Sally by arranging the interview - my presence was virtually ignored once the girls were in full flow, as my attempt to interject a question towards the end shows. This was an indication to me of the close-knit, private nature of the friendship group - the exclusivity which has already been discussed in relation to closeness between friends - to which I was allowed access but of which I could not be fully part.

Seeing friends too much

Just as the second and third years enjoyed looking back over shared experiences in the past, so the fifth years (Year 11) and young women who had left school laughed at recalling their younger selves. For instance, Jenny, Sarah and Jacky who had been part of a larger group of white girls at school, talked to me at their sixth form college six months after leaving school.

Sarah   We all, we used to fall out over silly things really....But now, we get on a lot better now.
VG   The three of you used to fall out sometimes did you? (Indistinct reminiscing)
Jenny   We did do that in t'first year didn't we, me and you?
Jacky   Oh that was silly.
        (All laugh)

The young women associated falling out with being younger and regarded the causes of disagreements they had had then as 'silly'.

80

Sarah suggested another reason for the greater harmony between them now:

> We all get on better don't we now that we don't see each other as often (laughs)...You don't see 'em as often, so when you do see 'em, you're a lot sort of nicer towards them aren't you?

The 'we' and 'them' referred to here were not just the three young women taking part in the conversation, but the others who had formed part of the group of seven friends at school and who had moved on to art college and different jobs. The link which Sarah suggested between the amount of time friends saw each other and the amount they fell out was echoed quite independently by other young women looking back on their days at school. For example, Anne and Michelle told me:

> Michelle Before we used to get sulky and everything with each other at school, you know we'd soon fall out and that.
> Anne   Yeah, get on each others' nerves.
> Michelle We used to see each other every day at school - used to get a bit argumentative and that.

The same point was also made by many of the younger girls. For instance, Jill thought that 'if she (Lizzy) were in t'same class we'd fall out too much'. June suggested that friends who had known each other a long time 'just fall out more, more then don't they, because they're sick of each other'. She elaborated further on another occasion:

> June You can get on with your friends at home more than you can at school, because at school they're bossing you around and saying, 'Let's copy off you' and things like that.
> Sally And they see you most of t'time any way.
> June That's why it causes you to fall out I think cos you're seeing them too much. That's what my Mum says when I went around with Joanne, cos me and Joanne have fallen out about 50 times in one year, something like that!
> (All laugh)
> Me Mum said, me Mum always used to call me home because she knew we'd fall out cos we see each other too much...she'd say, 'You've had enough of Joanne now today else you'll be falling out.

There was a certain contradiction in what June said, because she started by asserting that 'you can get on with your friends at home more than you can at school' but proceeded to describe in some detail the frequent 'tiif taff' between her and Joanne, a friend at home. She changed tack when Sally introduced the notion of time; the important factor then became not so much home or school but the frequency with which one saw friends - 'cos you're seeing them too much' - and the length of time that friends interacted - 'You've had enough of Joanne today'.

Looking back over all the other examples, the time factor stands out as dominant over whether the interaction took place at home or school. For many girls, their greatest interaction with friends took place at school rather than at home. For them school did provide more frequent occasions when friends could fall out. Paradoxically, friends who saw each other less frequently might fall out less but they might also be less close. For most of the girls, 'tiff taff' did seem to be an almost inevitable part of being close to friends and seeing a lot of them.

Serious falling out

Several previous studies (Griffin 1985a, Nilan 1991, Aapola 1992, Thorne 1993) have indicated that falling out between girlfriends can be 'emotionally traumatic' (Griffin 1985a p.6O). In my own research, 'tiff taff' sometimes overlapped into more serious, longer lasting disputes between friends. These could last anything between a few weeks to several months. In most cases which I observed, the falling out could be seen as 'manoeuvres within the friendship' (Davies 1982 p.113), and the girls made friends again, but the level of upset which the conflict could cause while it was taking place was often intense.

By far the most common reason behind this kind of falling out was jealousy, because a girl feared she was losing her friend to another girl, or conversely, because a girl acted too possessively towards her friend. Often overlapping this, the other main underlying cause was bossiness, when a girl resented being told what to do all the time by her friend. Other important factors were name calling and the breaking of trust, although these were usually associated with a falling out rather than the prime cause. There were many other ritual elements in these fallings out, such as the use of intermediaries and the question of whether other friends in the group took sides in the quarrel.

Jealousy is mentioned as an important element in friendships between girls by many researchers (Meyenn 1980, Aapola 1992, Measor & Sikes 1992, Thorne 1993), although usually in connection with girls losing their friends to boys (Griffin 1981 & 1985a), or because girls infringed moral codes on acceptable sexual behaviour (Nilan 1991). Many of the girls that I was working with were not going out with boys or even interested in them; others had boyfriends but the stereotype of girls competing over boys was not evident (Lees 1986, Griffiths 1986). In some earlier research. I argued that 'jealousy represented one aspect of friendship between girls which co-existed with strong feelings of closeness' (Griffiths 1986 p.51), and this was certainly confirmed in the study at Barnsdale.

I was usually told about fallings out over jealousy, not by the girls who had been rejected but by the girls who had, often temporarily, made other friends. For example, Pauline told me:

> One time I stopped calling for Diane altogether and just kept going to Deborah's. And she fell out with me over that.

The girl who saw herself as the injured party often reacted, understandably, with hurt and anger. For example, when Janette started going round with Vicky, her former friend Marie reacted angrily, as Janette told me:

> Me and you (Vicky) sort of got together didn't we? And I went down to her house one dinner time and Marie just said, 'Ah, get lost then, go off with her.'

Although Janette offered Marie the chance to go round with her and Vicky - 'we said that she could come if she wanted to' - Marie turned it down. It seemed as though, if she could not be exclusively friends with Janette, she did not want to be at all.

This particular incident reminded me strongly of my own adolescence, when I felt extremely jealous because my best friend of long standing started to become close friends with another girl. We had always gone round in a big group with other girls but had remained loyal to each other within the group. Although my friend was happy to keep on seeing me as well, I remember feeling extremely hurt and bitter about it, because I did not want to 'share' her with anyone else.

Bronwyn Davies, in her study of 10-11 year-olds, argues that being left alone or rejected by a friend is one of the worst things a friend can do because of 'the vulnerability experienced by children if they do find themselves alone at school' (Davies 1982 p.69). I would suggest that this vulnerability is experienced by adolescents too. Davies mentions the reciprocal behaviour engaged in by friends if they have been upset; for instance, if your friend leaves you on your own, then you leave them on their own. Davies sees this as one of the 'strategies for maintaining appropriate behaviour' within a friendship:

> What are inappropriate behaviours for a friend are appropriate behaviours for friends who have behaved inappropriately. (Davies 1982 p.69)

This can start a complicated cycle of rejection and counter-rejection, as I found on several occasions in my research.

An example of this cycle of reciprocal behaviour occurred among the girls in a large group of white girls interested in CB radio. Here hurt and anger were evident in the girl who had done the rejecting, when the girl she had fallen out with in turn fell out with her, as Elaine explained:

> Mandy's not me friend. You see they all fell out right, and then they all made friends with me and Mandy didn't... I think the reason Mandy fell out with me cos me and Lorraine were best mates, none of the rest were...I don't really care cos I hate her (laughs)...I never really liked her in t'first place. She's always been mangy.

It became quite hard to disentangle the order of events or who had fallen out with whom first. Elaine was reacting very much as the injured party, even though she admitted that it was her close friendship with Lorraine which had given rise to the falling out in the first place. There seemed to be a tension within the group over who was closest to Lorraine, and perhaps also an element of threat posed to the group as a whole by two of the girls within it becoming too close. This could explain why the whole group fell out with Elaine for a while.

Falling out because of a threat posed to a group from outside was more frequent. For example, June's friendship out of school with Sally (G1) was causing trouble with Sally's friends at school, as June explained

> If they see Sally with me they fall out with her...I'd asked her to go to t'pictures with us so we went, and her friends said I was going off with her...They just came up for her yesterday when we were

playing records upstairs, you know, she tells me, 'Keep still so they don't see you'...It's just cos I play with Sally more than she plays with them.

Sally corroborated this on another occasion:

These in my class go round together...so when I started going round with June they didn't like that so they fell out with June because they don't like me going round with her.

Sally wanted to be friends with June and her other friends, but it seemed as if they were demanding exclusive rights over her, like Marie with Janette as mentioned earlier. Sally felt that her friends were being unreasonable because she did not place the same demands on them:

There's this person in my class who's supposed to be my best friend. She goes round with someone else after school, I don't say anything about that, but if I go round with June after school she always says something about that.

This was a case of tension between parallel friends, usually kept separate because of a home-school divide, but here overlapping because Sally's school friends were extending their demands on her friendship into out of school time too. There was an imbalance too in the demands they were making on Sally which she did not reciprocate. Possessiveness on the part of friends is mentioned as one reason girls fall out by other researchers too (Griffin 1985a, Aapola 1992).

Bossing

Quite frequently girls fell put because one member of the group was perceived as being too bossy. These disputes represented another means of resisting an internal threat to the group. I noticed that such situations were more likely to arise within small groups or pairs of friends, rather than within the larger groups which less obviously had leaders.

June commented that bossing could occur over school work, 'because at school they're bossing you around and saying, 'Let's copy off you' and things like that'.This was certainly evident among the close-knit foursome, with Marilyn in particular telling the others what to do all the time. For example, Marilyn always fetched the equipment in Science lessons, even if one of the others had been asked to go. She also liked to take charge of experiments, and this sometimes caused squabbles within the group.

Bossing was most evident among the loose-knit foursome, with Suzanne wanting to take charge all the time. In terms of school work, this was again most obvious in Science lessons, because there was more practical interaction. Bossing occurred among this group out of lesson time too. Suzanne even bossed the others around during interviews, and tried to include me in her instructions too! For example, she told me: 'Ask each of us a question and nobody else is to answer it, right?' Sometimes the others would just take this kind of bossing without comment, but at other times they protested. In the second year (Year 8) Lizzy was already rebelling against Suzanne's constant bossiness and was starting to go round more with Jill and Helen from another class. By the third year (Year 9), Annette herself was beginning to tire of being told what to do and kept falling out with Suzanne because of it, as she told me:

> She wanted to go somewhere and I wanted to go somewhere else you see, so she went one way and I went the other...so she weren't me friend.

Jill summed up the situation extremely well, I thought, when she said of Suzanne, 'She thinks she's a leader - she isn't.' Suzanne certainly saw herself as the group leader; she said to Pat on one occasion, 'If I told you to jump in a lake you'd do it.'

The dynamics of the relationships within the 'nasty' group were very close to those described in Margaret Atwood's novel *Cat's Eye* (1988) where the narrator Elaine is persecuted as a girl by her friend Cordelia. Cordelia seems to exert a charismatic force on Elaine and the other two girls in the group. Each in turn becomes victim of her bossiness and cruelty, and they seem unable to break out of this pattern. The final straw is when Cordelia tells Elaine to go into a deep ravine where 'bad men' are said to lurk. Elaine nearly drowns when she falls into melting ice, but the extremity of the event opens her eyes and she realises that she does not have to do everything that Cordelia tells her.

> Cordelia says, 'I think Elaine should be punished for telling on us don't you?' 'I didn't tell,' I say. I no longer feel the sinking in my gut, the held-back tearfulness that such a false accusation would once have produced. My voice is flat, calm, reasonable.
> 'Don't contradict me,' Cordelia says. 'Then how come your mother phoned our mothers?'
> 'Yeah, how come?' says Carol.

'I don't know and I don't care,' I say. I'm amazed at myself.

'You're being insolent,' says Cordelia. 'Wipe that smirk off your face.'

I am still a coward, still fearful; none of that has changed. But I turn and walk away from her. It's like stepping off a cliff, believing the air will hold you up. And it does. I see that I don't have to do what she says, and, worse and better, I've never had to. (Atwood 1988 p.193)

Margaret Atwood vividly captures the force of feeling in this kind of situation, the conflicting emotions Elaine experiences towards Cordelia whom in other respects she idolises, and her feeling of being trapped (literally in the above example) in an inescapable situation. When she finally has the confidence to stand up to Cordelia, the cycle is broken and the friendship reestablished on different terms.

It seemed to me that this is what was happening with the so-called 'nasty' group. As Lizzy and Annette got more mature and confident, they refused to go along with Suzanne's bossing. Pat never seemed to reach that point during the time I was at the school. I was also interested in Suzanne's admission to me that she was 'less narky' with friends at home. She could not really explain why this was the case, so I can only speculate that Suzanne too felt caught in a role that she no longer enjoyed.

Another similar case of a girl refusing to be pushed around any more was Pauline. When I talked to her in the 5th year (Year 11), she had fallen out with her friend Diane because of Diane's bossiness:

Well she's been right funny with me, ordering me about and everything and she just gets me mad at times, so I've stopped you know, we still go out together a bit - went with her last night that were it.

When I met Pauline again nine months later (now on a Youth Training Scheme), she had fallen out more permanently with Diane. This was for a mixture of reasons which included Pauline's refusal to go out with Diane's brother, and Diane's jealousy of Pauline's new friend Deborah. The reason which came through most strongly, however, was Pauline's determination not to be pushed around any longer:

I told her what I thought, I says, 'I'm not going to be used by you cos you're using me'. When every time she used to babysit she used to ask me to go with her right. And when I got there she was saying, 'Do t'washing up for me, do this, do that'. I said, 'No I won't'. I said, 'It were you using me not me using you'.

Pauline threw some interesting light on the reasons she had gone along with Diane's bossing in the past: 'I used to take it from her because I was scared of her, but now I mean I'm not scared of her, I tell her exactly what I think and she doesn't like it.' Pauline also suggested that people did what their friends told them 'just to mek them pleased with you', but now she was older she would tell them to 'do it yourself'.

Looking back over my own adolescence, I would suggest that there may be another, more positive aspect to bossing which did not emerge in my research, but which may help explain why girls sometimes stick with friends who, to outsiders at least, are pushing them around. One of my own friends as a teenager was a girl who was decidedly bossy. However, unlike Pauline with Diane, I was certainly not scared of her. I can remember feeling irritated with her, and frequently ignoring what she told me and simply going my own way anyway. Looking back, I think that her bossiness had a motherly, protective aspect which was right for me at the time. My friend may have bossed me, but she also looked after me and was very supportive during stressful times.

I include this personal example in order to suggest that the dynamics of 'bossiness' may be quite complex and based on more than simply fear. In the case of Suzanne's group, the strong supportive element in their relationships described earlier may have outweighed or at least counterbalanced the negative aspects. Tension between the need for emotional closeness and independence is mentioned as a cause of quarrels in Aapola's research too (1992). For some girls, the need to be mothered may be important at some stages of adolescence, in order for them to find their own feet. Thus, at times an apparently unbalanced power dynamic in a relationship may actually suit the friends in question, as Sonia Avgitidou (1994) found in her study of younger children in Italy and England. 'Lopsided' friendships are also mentioned in other crosscultural studies (Brain 1977), and these can sometimes be remarkably successful and sustained over long periods.

Breaking Trust

In the last chapter I described how important it was for girls to be able to confide secrets to their friends and know they could be trusted to keep them. The breaking of such a trust is mentioned in several studies as a reason for girls falling out (Ward 1976, Aapola 1992, Thorne 1993). In my own research, the breaking of this trust did not usually cause girls to fall out, but if friends had already fallen out, telling other people their secrets was an effective way of making things worse, 'getting back at' one's friend and causing hurt. Many examples of this kind, where stories are spread behind a friend's back, are described by Sue Lees (1986), and it was certainly a feature of my research too. For instance, Pauline told me about her former friends Diane and Deborah:

> They're two faced. You could tell 'em owt, then if you fell out with them or had a slight argument they'd go blocking it all up the street what you told 'em. I have nowt to do with them now.

Pauline was bitter about what she saw as a betrayal, and was wary of becoming close to anyone again. John Ward (1976) mentions this kind of response to a breaking of trust in his research too.

Marilyn and Charleen fell out once when a secret was spread, as they described:

Marilyn   Another time we broke friends were when -
Surinder   When she (Charl.) went and told that, that you wanted to go out with, er, Dean Clark.
Marilyn   Oh yeah, she went and -
Charleen   Yeah, cos then she (Mar.) just says, 'Oh I want to go out with Dean Clark'. So she goes, 'No it isn't'
Marilyn   No, weren't that one. When you told me he wanted to go out with me, and then you told, um, you told Mary that time.
Charleen   I didn't tell Mary.
Marilyn   You did. That's why I weren't your friend.
Surinder   She did. Mary told him.
Marilyn   And Mary told us you told her.

As with many of these incidents, the chain of events was hard to follow, and the friends nearly started an argument over what was the 'true' version. I was interested that Marilyn insisted that the boy in question had told Charleen 'he wanted to go out with me', and Charleen had spread that secret, rather than Surinder's version, that Marilyn had confided in Charleen that she wanted to go out with Dean. It was as if Marilyn saw it as a sign of weakness to admit that she had confided a secret, whereas her version put her in the stronger position of being the one who was sought after. The secret seems to have been spread from Charleen to Mary to Dean. Because Mary did not owe any particular loyalty to the group, she also 'told us you told her' and so the story came back full circle.

The above example did not seem to have caused too many repercussions and was quickly sorted out. However, when Marilyn and June fell out, Marilyn in her turn spread June's secrets around. A particularly hurtful element of this to June was the one-sided nature of this betrayal of trust:

> Marilyn's told me as well, she's got loads of secrets she's told me and I've never told anybody. But all my secrets I've told her she tells everybody now we're not friends.

Name calling

As with breaking trust, name calling was not usually the start of a dispute, but one of the means by which that dispute was enacted. Sue Lees (1986) puts both features under the category of 'bitching', and makes the distinction between simply being nasty about a friend behind their back and casting slurs on a friend's sexual reputation, for instance calling them a 'slag'. Finding examples of this kind of behaviour may simply reinforce the stereotype which I discussed earlier and suggest that girls' friendships are shallow. It does seem to me that Sue Lees' account (1986 p.65-8) runs into this problem. Christine Griffin makes the important point:

> It is important to differentiate between 'bitching' as it is applied to young women's cultures in derogatory ways according to dominant 'common sense', and these young women's actual cultural practices and their associated meanings. (Griffin 1981 p.10)

Christine Griffin sees 'bitching' as a means by which young women try to resist the break up of their friendship groups, rather than because of the stereotype of girls vying with each other for boys. In my research this certainly seemed to be the case.

The only example of name calling which actually seems to have started an argument between friends sounded relatively mild. This took place between Penny and Dawn from the 'big' group. However, in Penny's account, there was the suggestion that the name calling may actually have been a good deal worse than she was prepared to tell me:

> She called me a name, you know she kept calling me names all night. Then she called me a spotty, er I won't say what she called me...Well there was this picture on the wall, this man had his tongue stuck out on t'wall, and he had spots all over his tongue.

> She goes, 'Look Penny, he's caught your disease'... and she was
> calling me names all night.

It may also have been that girls were more prepared to use abusive terms about their friends behind their backs rather than to their faces, or in the notes which often formed part of the falling out process. Other researchers (Goodwin 1991, Aapola 1992, Thorne 1993) report that girls are more likely to use name calling and abuse behind each others' backs, and that indirect forms of conflict between friends are more characteristic generally of girls than boys. Sinikka Aapola (1992) suggests that this is because girls are learning such 'delicate social skills' (1992 p.9) as 'empathy, sensitivity to others' feelings, care' (ibid. p.10). This may be true, but I would argue that it does not diminish the real hurt engendered by such indirect means of communication.

Being aware that someone is calling you names or spreading stories behind your back, even if you never hear what it is, can perhaps be as hurtful as hearing it directly. For example, when June heard that stories were being spread about her, she said, 'If people are saying things about me, I want to know what it is'. June made an interesting distinction between types of name calling and their effects:

> It upsets you when they call you bad names...If it's just silly it
> doesn't really bother you cos you know that you're both being
> stupid.

June also made another distinction in terms of gender:

> I'm not bothered if boys call me names, it's just girls cos I'd think
> they'd understand more, but all they do now is call me names.

The implication was that one expected boys to be abusive, but it was somehow worse if girls did it. It was particularly hurtful in June's case because Marilyn and the friends she had fallen out with were calling her 'cripple' because of her slight disability.

This gender difference may have been involved in another case. During the second year (Year 8) Elaine was very unhappy because some boys kept calling her 'dog' and 'slag'. The other girls in the big group in G2, who went around with these boys sometimes at break, apparently colluded in this name calling by laughing along with it, although I never heard them calling Elaine names themselves. As with June, this may have made things more hurtful to Elaine.

There were many aspects of behaviour associated with falling out which amounted to an unwritten code of practice among the girls. I have already mentioned name calling, spreading stories and sending notes. The other main factors I observed were the use of contingency friends and intermediaries, and the question of whether to take sides or not.

Contingency friends   This phrase is used by Bronwyn Davies (1982) to describe the strategic withdrawal to other children for support when friends fall out. This occurred a lot in my research. Contingency friends were often former close friends, as Bronwyn Davies also found. For example, when June fell out with Marilyn, she turned to Karen who had been a close friend in Junior school. As June said, 'she (Karen) knows all about me and everything, and she's happy to let me go about with them...just sit with 'em.' Karen let June go round with her and her friends for a while so she would not be on her own.

Certainly having such friends to fall back on in an emergency made life more bearable during that time. June seemed to cope quite well because she not only had Karen but also Jackie, another former close friend, in another class. In contrast, when Dawn fell out with the big group she had no one, which may explain why she stayed away from school during this time. Bronwyn Davies argues that children who do not have contingency friends have a much harder time than those who do, because they are in that extremely vulnerable position of being on their own. Bronwyn Davies also suggests that having contingency friends gives children strong bargaining power because they can negotiate from a position of strength. This may be one reason why June was able to hold out so long before making it up with Marilyn.

Intermediaries   The use of intermediaries in a dispute was frequent, and could be related to contingency friends as Bronwyn Davies found:

> Withdrawal to contingency friends does not spell the end of friendships. Negotiations...where messages are sent via others to find out if the friendship is still on, take place fairly soon after the withdrawal. (Davies 1982 p.26O)

In my research, this was particularly noticeable when June fell out with Marilyn and Jackie talked to Marilyn and Charleen on her behalf, as I noted:

At one point June wanted to say something so she beckoned Jackie down. Marilyn said, 'Let her come up to us, don't go down to her.' Jackie acted as go-between, reporting what Marilyn had said. June came and whispered in Jackie's ear.

On this occasion, I felt that Jackie was being over-friendly towards Marilyn and Charleen, and wondered on whose behalf she was really negotiating. This also seemed to be connected to the question of whose side other friends were on.

Intermediaries were not only used by the girl who had withdrawn to a contingency friend. For example, Annette acted as a go-between for Suzanne when Lizzy fell out with her, delivering messages with her own added insults. It was perhaps in Annette's interest to keep this dispute going as long as possible, because Suzanne was less likely to start an argument with her when she had already fallen out with Lizzy.

Taking sides   When two friends fell out, the question of other girls taking sides in the dispute was quite complicated and seemed to depend on a number of factors, such as which class the girls were in or how big the group was. For example, according to the seven girls in the 'CB' group, they were able to contain disputes between two members without the rest of the group being disrupted:

Elaine   If one falls out you still go round together until you've made friends don't you?

Mandy   Yeah, cos Kathy, she's (Elaine) fallen out with 'er for about three weeks, but she still comes round with us. You just fall out, you're still friends in a way.

Lorraine You've still got to get on together.

The assumption was that falling out was a temporary affair and that the girls in question would make it up after a while. However, this did not stop the whole group falling out with Elaine a few months later. Parallel friends from other classes of the girls in the close-knit foursome in G2, who formed an extended friendship group, also kept out of individual members' disputes up to a point. Marilyn was still friendly with Manjeet when she fell out with Surinder; similarly Martine was still friendly with June when she fell out with Marilyn. Marilyn suggested that this was because they were in different classes or forms:

Martine's my best friend, but we broke up with June and seeing tho' she's not in t'same form as us, June a'n't done owt to her so she still speaks to June.

The crucial point seemed to be that 'June a'n't done owt to her'. Because Martine was in a different class she had not been directly involved in the dispute, whereas Surinder and Charleen were, so they also fell out with June. Hence Marilyn talked about 'we' and 'us' rather than just 'I'. However, June suggested that Charleen's and Surinder's taking sides with Marilyn was more to do with Marilyn being leader of the group:

> Charleen and Surinder aren't involved in it, they're just going along with Marilyn....because Charleen and Surinder, they do everything what Marilyn does....When Marilyn fell out wi'me they fell out with me for no reason at all. They just fell out wi'me because Marilyn fell out with me.

Jackie suggested that Surinder and Charleen were scared of losing Marilyn's friendship if they did not go along with her:

> If they say, sort of talk to June, Marilyn'll fall out with them...I think that's what they're all scared of, making one -if one falls out, then they'd all fall out wi'er.

Jackie felt that Marilyn had the power to make, for example, Manjeet fall out with Surinder if she wanted, and 'then she'd (Surinder) have no one to go round with'. In the same way she and June felt that Marilyn was trying to get Jackie on her side so that June would be left on her own:

June   Marilyn came up to me and told me that Jackie hated me. And she's been telling all these lies what other people have said.

Jackie Just so I'll fall out with June and June'll fall out with me.

June   So that she - they can have Jackie on their side. But Jackie's on nobody's side and I don't want her to be on anybody's side.

That 'Jackie's on nobody's side' certainly seemed confirmed by my earlier observation that she was acting in a friendly way towards Marilyn and the others whilst supposedly acting as June's intermediary. I wondered if June really meant 'I don't want her to be on anybody's side' or whether she meant 'I don't want her to be on anybody's side but mine'. In this particular case, the protracted quarrel

94

between Marilyn and June had many repercussions, and involved a mixture of factors already discussed, as well as issues such as class, race, disability and academic ability (see Griffiths 1989 for details).

This complex interweaving of different factors which seemed to determine whether friends took sides or not may have diminished as girls got older, as some of the young women at sixth form college suggested:

> Sarah   Sometimes it would be - this were when we were a lot younger - it would be, 'Oh so and so's fallen out with so and so, so I'm not teking their side.
> Jacky   So I'm not their friend (laughs).
> Sarah   But then, to t'fifth year, if somebody had an agreement (sic) between them two, nobody took sides did they?

Closeness or independence?

In this chapter I have argued that falling out between friends was a normal part of interaction and a mark of closeness rather than a sign of the shallow or temporary nature of the friendships. I have noted 'strategies for maintaining appropriate behaviour' (Davies 1982 p.69) within a friendship, as well as resistance to threats posed from outside.

Two points emerge as particularly important in reviewing the considerable amount of data on falling out which I accumulated during fieldwork. Firstly, looking at the main reasons why girls quarrelled, there seems to be a tension between a fear of being rejected or left alone (jealousy and possessiveness), and a need to retain a certain degree of independence and control within a relationship (resistance to bossing). Sinikka Aapola (1992) sees the balancing of closeness and independence as the central tension in adolescent girls' friendships:

> Girls look for mutual understanding, closeness, trust and emotional support in their friendships, but at the same time they want an independent position in the social world. (Aapola 1992 p.6)

In an earlier study, John Ward (1976) describes a similar tension between adolescent girls' need for closeness, in particular to a best friend, and the pull towards what he calls 'individuation' (Ward 1976 p.28). Ward sees the individuation process in girls primarily directed at becoming attractive and desirable to boys and ultimately leading to a distancing between a girl and her friends. This is very much a reiteration of the stereotype described at the beginning of the chapter; although he describes the 'strong bond' (ibid. p.54) between girlfriends, Ward goes on to assert that 'pairs of boys may very well be deeper and truer friends' (ibid. p.54). In my research, the need for independence expressed by girls was not associated with a desire to be seen as attractive, but with a growth in confidence and maturity. The determination not to be pushed around by another girl (see examples in bossing section) could be seen as part of a transition to young womanhood, but not in the sense that Ward describes it.

The second point which struck me forcibly in reading through the interviews and fieldnotes is the intensity of emotion which falling out, be it 'tiff taff' or more serious, could occasion. This was particularly apparent in Lizzy and June, both of whom were extremely upset by their respective quarrels with friends. In June's case, the protracted dispute with Marilyn and the other black girls left its mark even when the girls had made friends again. June was very subdued, and unwilling to talk about it further, which was most unusual for her. At the time I wrote that the sense of betrayal of trust which some of the girls felt was 'a crucial indication of the depth of positive feeling between the girls, and the emotional security they derive from these relationships''. The nearest analogy I can find is to describe the emotions generated as akin to lovers quarrelling (heterosexual or homosexual). Because I was drawn into the quarrels as a sounding board, counsellor and occasionally intermediary myself, I could experience the intensity of emotion in a very real and direct way.

Coincidentally, at the same time as I was carrying out my fieldwork, I was going through a similarly intense 'falling out' with two close women friends, similar to those described by Orbach and Eichenbaum (1987), which arose out of a misunderstanding and revealed different attitudes. My personal experience also made me unable to dismiss falling out between girls as either simply an adolescent phenomenon, or as a 'practice run' for future relationships with boys. These explanations seem to undermine the importance of the girls' relationships themselves, as (perhaps unwittingly) in this quote from Angela McRobbie:

> The female twosome...anticipates future boyfriends, but for the moment its members are thoroughly involved in each other. In fact there is a huge emotional investment put into these relationships by the girls; it is as though they transfer all their emotional energies later to be focused on a boy, on to the 'best friend'. (McRobbie 1978a p.106)

96

Although McRobbie does stress the strength of emotional involvement between girlfriends, there is the implicit suggestion that once boyfriends appear on the scene, the best friend will simply be ditched. The image of the fickle and transient nature of girls' loyalties is once again reinforced. A similar view was expressed by the Art teacher, Mrs Jebson, who commented on Lizzy being upset about Suzanne, 'This year it's over girls. Next year it'll be boys. I think it's lovely'. Although Mrs Jebson recognised the degree of emotion generated by girls falling out and, unlike some of the other teachers, was always positive about girls and their friendships, (her 'I think it's lovely' was a typical comment), there is the same implication as in McRobbie's quote that these emotions will simply be transferred from girls to boys. In chapter 8, I argue that this is a misrepresentation. Just as the girls resisted both internal and external threats to their friendships posed by other girls, so they resisted the break up of their friendship groups because of boyfriends.

6 School: interaction and attitudes

In previous chapters school has provided the backdrop against which girls' friendships have been described. In this chapter the focus shifts so that school, particularly lesson time, comes to the fore. The question of perspective provides one strand running through the chapter. Ian Birksted (1976), in his study of six comprehensive school boys, wrote:

> I was interested less in seeing how they fitted into the structure of the school than in how the school fitted into the structure of their lives. (Birksted 1976 p.65)

In my own research, I was similarly interested in seeing to what extent the girls were able to carry on their interaction during lessons, and how their attitudes to school affected their classroom behaviour.

The chapter starts with a discussion of interaction sets: to what extent and under what circumstances these are evident in girls' classroom behaviour. The effects of classroom organisation, teaching styles, and the attitudes of boys and teachers, are all important interlocking factors here. This is followed by an analysis of girls' friendship groups and their orientations to school. I shall also highlight patterns of resistance, and identify how girls find their own space, either in or out of lessons, within a positive alternative to the traditional 'misery model' (Wernersson 1992).

Gender divisions in school

The context within which girls' interaction takes place is crucial and, until recently, has often been detrimental to girls' achievement, particularly in mixed-sex schools (Measor & Sikes 1992). Previous research has shown that gender divisions in school, in both organisation and the hidden curriculum, can at worst render girls invisible in the classroom (Stanworth 1981, Spender & Sarah 1980); teachers have often given less attention to girls in class than boys, and held lower expectations of their academic achievement (Spender 1982, Whyld 1983). Moreover, girls have often been subject to verbal and physical abuse from boys (Jones 1985, Mahony 1985, Lees 1986).

At Barnsdale, this kind of situation was very evident. For example, there were many gender divisions in the everyday organisation of the school, such as sex-divided registers and girls and boys lining up separately. Girls were not allowed to wear make-up, jewellery or high-heeled shoes, restrictions which caused a great deal of resentment and were often ignored or directly flouted.

Barnsdale High was unusual in having both a woman Head and a female Deputy Head. In other respects staffing was more traditionally male-dominated: men headed most departments except Home Economics. In the classroom, gender divisions in seating occurred more often by pupils' choice than by teachers' organisation. Teaching was largely traditional, and materials often gender-stereotyped. The most blatant sexism occurred in Careers lessons, where the (male) careers teacher actively discouraged non-traditional choices for girls and boys, and hardly encouraged the girls in any careers.

In interaction with teachers, gender-stereotyped attitudes were often revealed. In general, boys got away with more misbehaviour than girls. On the other hand, girls were not often encouraged to take an active part in lessons. Boys dominated lesson time and received more teacher attention, firstly by being more active participants in the lessons, and secondly by disruptive behaviour. Girls and boys engaged in much negative interaction both in and out of lessons, as I shall describe, although for much of the time they simply ignored each other and led very separate school lives.

Within this kind of school context, many classroom interaction studies have looked at how girls relate to each other at school, and highlighted patterns of girls' accommodation or resistance (Griffin 1985a, Stanley 1993, Wolpe 1988, Wernersson 1992). Although some of the studies of gender and schooling mentioned earlier present girls as victims of an oppressive system, the detailed findings particularly of more recent studies show clearly that this is an over-simplification, and that girls are active in constructing their own distinctive and different responses to structural and cultural pressures (Anyon 1983, Wolpe 1988, Thorne 1993). As AnnMarie Wolpe writes, girls as well as boys 'are not passive actors in the classroom or in school in general' (Wolpe 1988 p.101):

> They act as already constituted gender subjects which has direct consequences on overt forms of behaviour which are far more complex than straightforward situations of domination and submission. (ibid. p.101)

In general, the research shows a less polarised picture of girls' attitudes to school than comparable studies of boys (Birksted 1976, Willis 1977); orientation is more complex than a clear pro- or anti-school position, and there is no necessary correlation between ability, attitude to school and involvement in teenage culture (Lambart 1976, Pollard 1984, Lees 1986).

Common definitions: interaction sets

There is some disagreement in classroom-based studies as to whether girls interact in close-knit peer groups (Lambart 1976, Meyenn 1980) or looser interaction sets (Furlong 1976, Llewellyn 1980). Furlong's article (1976) has been particularly influential in challenging the peer group model. Furlong argues that interaction is fluid not static, and constantly changing as participants define and redefine the situation. Thus, pupil interaction does not always include friends, and can vary frequently according to circumstances. Furlong also stresses that behaviour between friends can change with different teachers and that there is 'no consistent culture for a group of friends' (Furlong 1976 p.26).

Furlong's article is certainly important as a caveat to an over-rigid conception of friendships and interaction between peers. However, on the basis of my previous teaching experience and my own research, I cannot reject the peer group model so absolutely as he does. I shall argue that girls in the classroom do not operate exclusively either in friendship groups or interaction sets, but exhibit a clear hierarchy of preference, starting with their own friends where possible.

At Barnsdale, the girls in G2 were, as already explained, divided into three main friendship groups, which were evident in form time and in lessons which they had all together (Fig. 3.1). These groups provided the main unit of interaction for most of the girls. However, if friendship groups were split up, the girls formed (usually small) interaction sets with other girls; girls with parallel friends in other classes also enjoyed the opportunity to get together at times. Other

100

(sometimes larger) interaction sets were also apparent in lessons when pupils demonstrated that they were defining the situation in the same way, although the two kinds of sets often overlapped. Often a whole class would behave similarly, usually responding to a particular teacher. This kind of reaction was evident whether G2 were together or separated into different sets.

Four main factors affected the extent and frequency of these two kinds of interaction sets: school organisation, classroom organisation, teachers and boys, and these will be looked at in turn. A certain amount of overlap occurred between these factors and should be taken into account.

School organisation: sets and options

Interaction sets may well be a more common feature of forms of school organisation where there is constant change in the composition of class groups for different subjects. (Meyenn 1980 p.111)

For G2, setting already existed for many subjects (see Table 6.1), which sometimes divided the main friendship groups and brought about some degree of temporary interaction with pupils from other classes. This was particularly true for Maths and English, which had five sets each. The most frequent contact was with pupils from N2, who shared all lessons for subjects with two sets (History, Geography, German) and PE, which was sex-divided.

Such variations became more marked as pupils moved up the school, when setting was introduced for Science, and options were chosen. However, within the divisions which school organisation created, friendship groupings still remained the primary unit of interaction where possible, taking precedence over other possible interaction sets. I identified a hierarchy of preference which operated among the girls as to whom they would sit with in lessons.

Looking at the fifth year (Year 11) girls first, friends were able to keep together for quite a lot of the time, although there was some variation between the groups. For example, Michelle and Anne were together for English, Maths, Geography and German, whilst Debbie and Joanne only had English together, being in different ability groups for the other subjects they both took. The fifth year girls told me that it was easier for large groups of friends to keep together in lessons, because it was more likely that at least some of the group would coincide for each subject. This was certainly true for the group of seven white girls, whose various combinations of set and option

Table 6.1
2G2 Subject Sets

Name	Engl.(5)	Maths (5)	Geog.(2)	Hist.(2)	German(2)	Tech.St.	Home Ec.
Suzanne	3	4	2	2	2	Y	-
Pat	4	5	2	2	2	-	Y
Lizzy	4	2	2	2	2	-	Y
Annette	3	2	2	2	1	-	Y
Marilyn	2	2	2	1	1	-	Y
Charleen	5	5	2	2	2	-	Y
Surinder	3	2	2	1	1	-	Y
June	4	4	2	2	2	Y	-
Carol	1	2	1	1	1	-	Y
Vicky	1	1	1	1	1	-	Y
Penny	2	3	1	1	1	-	Y
Karen	3	3	2	2	1	Y	-
Pam	3	2	1	1	1	-	Y
Janette	1	1	1	1	1	Y	-
Elaine	2	2	1	1	1	Y	-
Dawn	3	2	1	1	1	-	Y

Figures in brackets = total number of sets for that subject.

group look similar to those for Lambart's 'sisterhood' (1976, p.156). As Jacky said, 'we've always got you know two friends in each group when there's lessons'.

The girls in this group were very clear about the permutations of friends for each subject, as three of them explained:

Sarah Got English with Sue.
Jenny Yeah. We've got Maths with Marje.
Jacky And I've got English with Kath...
Jenny And I've got Geography with Tricia.

Jenny and Sarah, who were best friends within this group, had all their lessons but two with each other. They told me whom they would interact with in other lessons:

Sarah I've got all my lessons with her (Jenny) except for one, when I've got Computer Studies with Jacky.
Jenny And I've got all my lessons with Sarah, except when I've got one with Marje...Except I haven't got anyone in Chemistry, so I talk to Michelle an'all, and then you (Sarah) haven't got anyone in Chemistry have you?
VG So who do you sit with in Chemistry?
Sarah I sit with all t'lads (laughs)

It was from these girls that I got the idea about a hierarchy of preference. In their case, it would be:
(i) best friend;
(ii) other girls within their friendship group (eg. Jacky or Marje);
(iii) other girls not in their friendship group (eg. Michelle);
(iv) boys.

A similar hierarchy was evident among the girls in G2 as well, which I was able to observe in action. As with the fifth year girls, it was easier for at least some of the big group to keep together than for girls in the two smaller groups. Only Karen from the big group was ever on her own (Geography and History), whereas girls from the two smaller groups were frequently separated from their friends, especially in English and Maths. On these occasions, the girls sat with other girls. From my observations, I drew up a provisional hierarchy of interaction for girls in G2:
(i) girls in their friendship group at the same table (usually from G2);
(ii) girls in their friendship group at different tables;
(iii) other girls in G2;
(iv) girls from N2 (or other classes);
(v) boys.

An example will make the order of preference clearer. Fig. 6.1 shows the seating for German Set 1. The teacher, Mrs Jackson, allowed friends to sit together so long as there were not more than three friends from the same group on one table. This meant that the big group were spread across three tables, sometimes four if Elaine was also there; (she usually played truant from German). Surinder and Marilyn from the close-knit group were joined by Annette, the sole member of the loose-knit foursome in this set. What is immediately obvious looking at the diagram is the almost total separation of (a) G2 girls from N2 girls, and (b) girls from boys.

Most interaction took place between friends at the same tables, but in the case of the big group there was also a considerable amount of interaction across the tables, as the following notes indicate:

> Most interaction between Carol and Vicky laughing and chatting in whispers. Also Vicky and Janette across to Karen at next table...Penny and Pam looking round...Vicky pushing Dawn in friendly way...Pam taking lead in finger cracking game, trying to attract attention of Carol and Vicky. Karen and Pam laughing a lot together, Dawn joining in.

All this was conducted quietly behind Mrs Jackson's back, so she would not notice. Marilyn and Surinder spent a lot of time laughing and joking together, whilst Annette generally worked separately. However, when Janette was moved to their table because of bad behaviour (an occasion when Mrs Jackson did notice), they acted as an interaction set, murmuring and complaining about Janette having to join them, and then making critical comments about her work when she was sitting with them.

Dislike of Janette (because she was bright and commonly regarded as 'teacher's pet' in this and other subjects) was a general uniting force among otherwise separate groups in German lessons, and even girls in the big group shared in this response. For instance, when Janette was told off and was near to tears, Fi, Abby and Sharon (2N2) were very obviously 'looking across at Janette and laughing'. On this occasion, Karen 'looked round and laughed with them'. In the next German lesson, when Janette took her book up to Mrs Jackson to show she had finished the work, Darren 'mouthed "Janette" to Penny – Penny grinned back' at this example of Janette 'sucking up to teacher'. The temporary interaction sets which these incidents concerning Janette occasioned are marked in dotted lines on the diagram. The marginalisation of Janette by her friends because of her perceived ability will be discussed later.

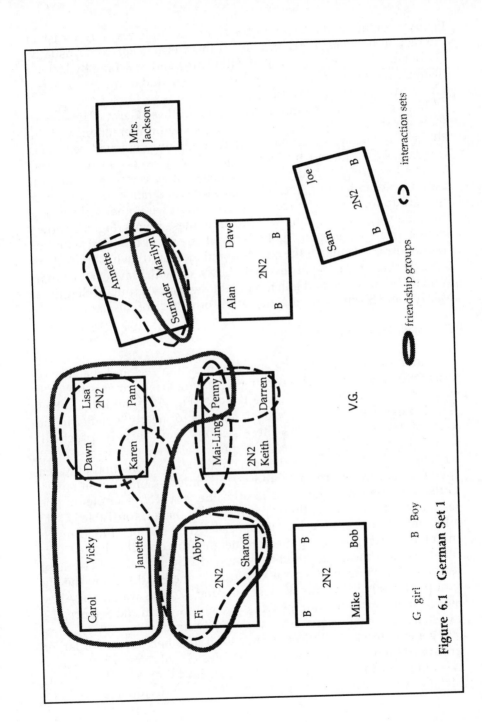

Figure 6.1 German Set 1

Penny's contact with Darren in the above example was a rare case of interaction between a girl and boy in this German set. More usually, Darren and Keith communicated with Penny and Mai-Ling by kicking them under the table. This was the more usual kind of contact between girls and boys in other lessons too.

I have described the kind of interaction in these German lessons in some detail in order to convey the complexity of interaction, and the kinds of occasions which gave rise to different interaction sets. This was largely borne out by looking at other subjects too. Variations occurred where girls had parallel friends in other classes and sat with them in certain lessons, and when girls who had fallen out with their own group for a while moved their place to sit with other girls during this time. Another example will illustrate these points. Fig. 6.2 shows seating arrangements for Maths Set 2. Elaine sat at the front with her friend Lorraine from F2 (the only lesson they shared), whilst the others from the big group sat at the back. Lizzy sat with Dawn rather than Annette because she had fallen out with the 'nasty' group at that time. Marilyn and Surinder sat together at the other side of the class.

Classroom organisation: seating

Considerable variation in the size of interaction sets and the ease of interaction also occurred according to seating arrangements for each subject. For example, in Science lessons (Fig. 6.3), the large tables enabled the friendship groups to sit together, or nearly together in the case of the big group. As these lessons were largely practical, interaction on each table was positively encouraged whilst experiments were being carried out. Apart from interaction between members of the big group, there was little interaction between tables. Girls and boys only interacted in a hostile way, for example, in one lesson boys from Table B threw paper darts at the girls on Table D.

In contrast, the seating for History Set 1 (Fig. 6.4) precluded much interaction except with immediate neighbours or with the teacher; otherwise work was supposed to be individually carried out. For these lessons, Marilyn from the close-knit group joined with girls in the big group. The only interaction between G2 and N2 girls was when Abby asked Janette for help with the work. As with German and Science, the division between girls and boys was visually striking.

In general, teachers allowed friends to sit together, in pairs or larger groups depending on the size of tables. I only observed a few exceptions to this; for example, in English Set 4 (Fig. 6.5), the teacher, Mrs Grey, allocated seating, mainly on an individual basis, and

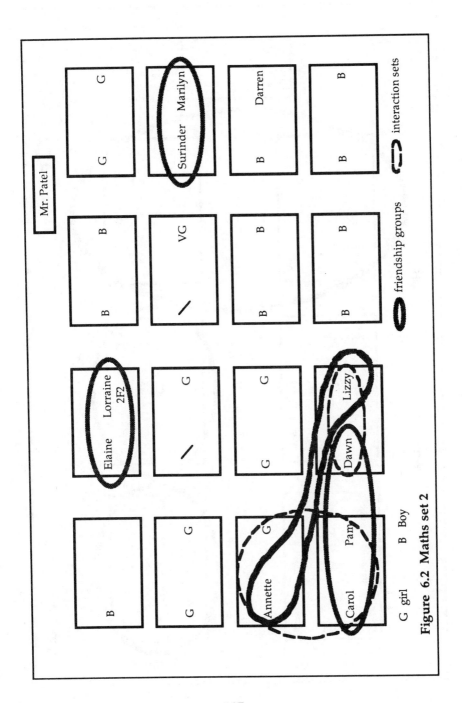

Figure 6.2 Maths set 2

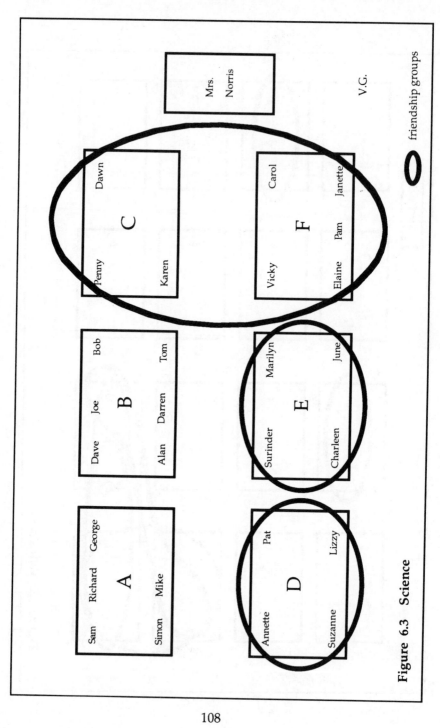

Figure 6.3 Science

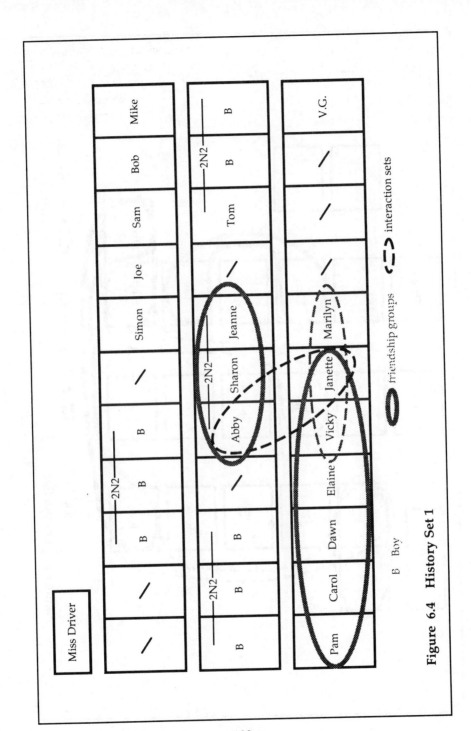

Figure 6.4 History Set 1

109

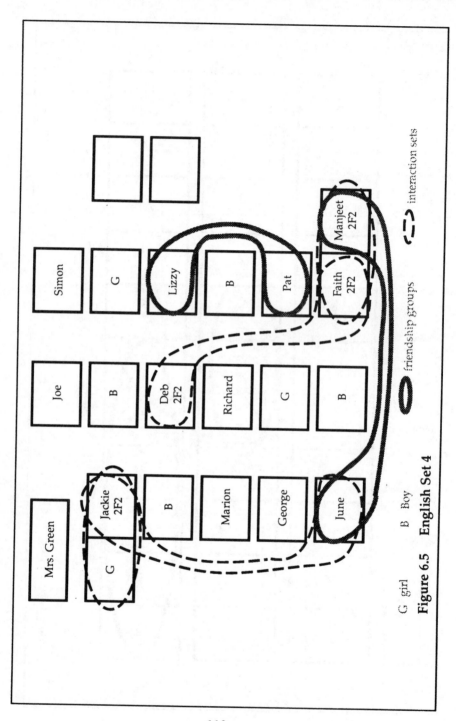

Figure 6.5   English Set 4

G girl   B Boy

○ friendship groups   ⌒⌒ interaction sets

alternated girls with boys. This meant that it was difficult for friends to communicate, as June and Jackie explained:

June   We can't sit next to each other in English can we?
Jackie She sits right at the back, I sit right at the front (laughs)...Can't mess about, just everyone sits like that, don't they?
June   Mrs Grey won't let us sit together, she don't like it. She just separates us all t'time.

In Mrs Grey's lessons, there was little interaction except at a distance, involving much turning round, smiling and mouthing words; for example, Deb 'laughing, put out her tongue' at Faith (both 2F2). In spite of the difficulties, most communication was within friendship groups, with little interacton between classes, except for June and Manjeet who were parallel friends, and no interaction between girls and boys, even though they were sitting next to each other. Mrs Grey apologised for there being 'no interaction' in her lessons: 'I don't know what you'll be able to see'. In fact, the type of interaction which was possible in her lessons told me a lot about her teaching style and the way pupils responded to this.

Similarly in Art, the teacher, Mrs Jebson, divided the largest friendship group and alternated girls with boys (Fig. 6.6). Because Mrs Jebson insisted on quiet, virtually silent working conditions, it was difficult for girls in the big group to interact across the tables. However, if Mrs Jebson went to fetch materials from the stock room, there would be a frenzy of movement between the tables, as in the following extract:

Whilst Mrs J. there, movement between the tables only for purpose of borrowing felt tips, eg. Elaine over to Karen...Simon managed to get round all boys' tables and chat. Girls only seem to move when Mrs J. goes out...Vicky to Karen, Penny to Carol. then Penny, Vicky and Elaine to Dawn and Janette...Karen gave muttered warning, 'You'd better get back', to Vicky as Mrs J. returning - Vicky rushed back to her place. Boys (Tom, Simon) still wandering around.

There were some interesting gender differences in the above example: boys did not seem to mind being seen to infringe classroom rules, whereas girls did. There was a certain amount of differential treatment of boys and girls from the teacher to which they were responding here: any infringement of classroom behaviour seemed to be tolerated more from the boys than the girls, and this was common in other lessons too.

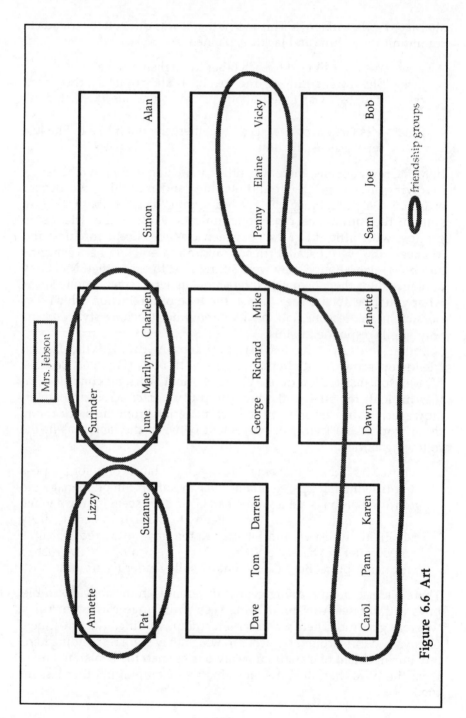

Figure 6.6 Art

From the examples already given, it is clear that the teachers had a strong influence on the kind of interaction which took place between pupils. At Barnsdale, teaching was largely of the traditional 'chalk and talk' variety, with strict discipline imposed in most lessons; or to use Bernstein's terms (1975), there was strong classification and framing. As Bernstein observed:

> The stronger the classification and framing, the more the educational relationship tends to be hierarchical and ritualised, the educand seen as ignorant, with little status and few rights. (Bernstein 1975)

The degree of power and control exerted by the strictest teachers was considerable. The 'hierarchical and ritualised' elements were noticeable from the start of lessons onwards: pupils were frequently made to leave a classroom and line up again, or to stand in silence behind their desks, if they entered the room too noisily. Likewise, at the end of lessons, if any pupils started clearing away too soon, they were made to unpack their things, take their coats off, and sit down again until the bell rang.

However, within this general framework, there was considerable variety, as my initial impressions of teachers show: for example, Mr Wilson (History Set 2) was 'very strict', and shouted a lot to keep order, in contrast to Mr Bartlett (Geography Set 2) who was 'firm but kindly' and used a 'half joking/abusive' manner to discipline pupils, or Mrs Jebson (Art) who always insisted on quiet or silent work but 'uses very quiet manner, never shouts'. There were also a few teachers who stood outside the strict norm and allowed a more relaxed atmosphere in the classroom.

As I went from lesson to lesson, it was immediately obvious how the same pupils changed their behaviour according to which teacher they were with and what standards were expected. Through their actions, the pupils demonstrated that they were absolutely clear about the personality and teaching style of each teacher, and consequently what would or would not be allowed in each lesson. In Furlong's terms, the class as a whole shared:

> a common definition of the situation, by drawing on similar commonsense knowledge, and making common assessments of appropriate action. That is, they 'see' what is happening in the same way and agree on what are appropriate ways to behave in the circumstances. (Furlong 1976 p.26)

Drawing on this shared knowledge and understanding, a class would often act as a large interaction set, demonstrating similar reactions and behaviour, which could vary dramatically from subject to subject. For instance, in History I noted, 'Hardly any interaction except furtively when Mr Wilson writing on board'; whereas on the same day in Music, I observed 'Highish noise level and some silliness from all class'. The pupils were so restricted by most teachers that they could not cope with any degree of freedom, such as that given in Music lessons, and so responded with misbehaviour.

A particularly interesting example of shared expectations occurred when Mr Harris, who had a reputation as a bully, was covering for Mrs Johnson's absence. The pupils were expecting Mrs Johnson, who tried to treat them 'like adults' (her words), and behaving in a way which she would have found acceptable: for example, talking whilst lining up outside the room; some arriving late because they had been to the toilet first. Mr Harris took everyone by surprise when he arrived, 'bellowed that this wasn't how they should behave and ... proceeded to give the class a lecture on how they should line up'. He also gave a 'rollicking' to the latecomers.

The effect of Mr Harris's outburst was dramatic; everyone seemed to be in shock, and there was total silence. Then, when Mr Harris left the room to fetch some books:

> Janette put her hands to her face, still red, breathed deeply and looked at Karen and Carol. Carol smiled and raised her eyebrows, commiserating. Alan (next to Carol across gangway) and Carol passed comments. Tom also looked round and made some comment to Janette. Everyone whispering, but quietly now.

Mr Harris had been particularly angry with Janette, who had been kicking a boy from another class when Mr Harris arrived (because the boy in question had made rude comments about her clothes). The general feeling of (albeit muted) support towards Janette on this occasion provided a contrast to German lessons, where interaction sets formed out of pleasure at her being told off. Although the main interaction here was between friends from the same groups, there was also (unusually) quite friendly communication between girls and boys, arising out of the situation and their shared response to it.

A shared reaction to trouble, or potential trouble, was often evident. For example, greater interaction, in the form of increased noise level and movement around the class, was possible if a teacher had to leave the room for a while. One pupil would often act as look out and warn the rest of the class when the teacher was on the way back. On other occasions, large interaction sets were formed in common response to small acts of defiance; for example, in Maths Set 3 the class was united in laughter against a strict teacher when Fi from N2 fell off her chair on purpose just as he was about to start a test.

The teachers, therefore, exerted considerable influence on the type of interaction possible within a lesson, by setting the boundaries of acceptable behaviour. The size of interaction sets arising from a shared definition of the situation varied from small groups of two to four girls (often including members of different friendship groups), to the whole class. However, there were also many differences observable between girls' friendship groups in the way they responded to teachers, which will be explored later in the chapter.

Boys

Other studies mention negative interaction between girls and boys in school (Spender 1982, Thorne 1993), including physical and verbal abuse (Jones 1985, Mahony 1985, Lees 1986), and my own findings were very similar. In the previous sections, I have included a few examples of interaction between girls and boys, either on an individual or group basis. However, these were not frequent; in general, interaction between girls and boys was marked more by its absence than its presence. I have scoured my notebooks for examples, but found more cases of negative or aggressive interaction than any resembling friendly contact, particularly in the classroom. Some of these have already been noted above. Physical aggression between girls and boys was quite common, and most frequently involved girls from the big group in G2, as in the following example from an Art lesson (when the teacher had gone out):

> Penny thumped Dave twice ...Carol and Dave thumping each other ... Carol, Penny and Dave all got compasses out pointed at each other.

There was often a thin borderline between jokey and hostile interaction, and Penny in particular often engaged in mock fights with the boys, involving kicking and hitting, which characterised the boys' physical interaction with each other. Usually this was done with a certain amount of good humour, and I got the feeling that to some extent Penny was treated like an honorary boy. However, this could also easily turn to real hostility.

The most serious incidents between the sexes that I was aware of occurred between Elaine and boys in G2 and N2 who started calling her 'slag' and 'dog', as I mentioned in chapter 5. Two brief examples will give an idea of how Elaine reacted and the effect this sexual abuse had on her:

> Darren and Tom over with Elaine's table. Shouting then Elaine head down on table, crying and Tom's rubbing his chest, 'She thumped me'.

> Before she went into Maths, Elaine had been greeted by a chorus of barks (ie. 'dog' again) from the boys - she thumped one as she walked past.

The first incident followed on from a note the boys had passed Elaine in the previous lesson. She was obviously upset, but retaliated by hitting the boy (Tom in this case), as she did in the second incident too. An aggressive physical response by a girl to a boy's verbal abuse was also the pattern in the example involving Janette, mentioned earlier. Sue Lees (1976) discusses how important it is for girls to protect their sexual reputation, and the Barnsdale girls were certainly not slow to hit back (literally). Perhaps one reason why girls tended to retaliate physically rather than verbally was because 'there aren't rude names for boys', as a girl in my previous research put it (Griffiths 1982 p.88).

Most of the time in lessons, I got the impression that girls and boys inhabited separate territories which were guarded carefully, with the occasional skirmish across the battle lines. Barrie Thorne (1993) describes similar gender separation, 'opposite sides' and 'borderwork' (Thorne 1993 p.64) in vivid detail in her study of elementary school children in the USA. At Barnsdale, this territorial divide was demonstrated visually by the seating division which existed in form time (Fig. 3.1) and most lessons where there was a choice of seating (Figs. 6.1, 6.2 & 6.4). Penny thought this preference for separate seating was more on the boys' side: 'Boys don't like it cos they think, "Sitting next to girls - eer!"'. Perhaps it was a basic antagonism towards girls (suggested by Penny's comment), or simply a wish to annoy them, which made it the boys who most frequently started hostile interaction, either by shouting or literally throwing things across into the girls' space. For example, in Science:

> Boys at far table chucking paper at Lizzy, Suzanne and Annette when Mrs. Norris out of room. They threw it back.....Boys all playing with water, Darren flicking it to next table (close-knit group).

Apart from the big group, the so-called 'nasty' group were particularly liable to be shouted at or otherwise receive negative attention from boys in G2; I noted many incidents, particularly in Music and form time, so it was newsworthy to record in an Art lesson:

Darren talking to Suzanne and Pat, joking. First sign of contact I've seen with them that's not totally abusive.

The close-knit group were less liable to have hostilities directed at them, perhaps because one of the main protagonists of abuse was Tom, a Black-Caribbean boy with whom the black girls generally maintained friendly relations. Marilyn told me:

I get on with them (boys) all right, cos sometimes we mess about with boys at breaks and dinnertimes...one of them's me cousin.

I was surprised at how positively girls talked about boys with whom they shared lessons, given the kind of interaction which took place. For example, Jackie (2F2) said, 'We get on with the boys very good in our class' . Even Elaine said, 'I can talk to 'em (boys) right easy an' that. I just get on with 'em'. June, who had also been at the receiving end of hurtful comments from boys (about her disability), was less generous, saying they 'got on my wick'.

The fifth year girls were less positive. For example, Pauline tried to avoid any contact with boys: 'Never spoke to 'em', but she was inclined to blame herself for not getting on with them: 'Suppose it's me really'. Some of the others were more directly critical, regarding boys as immature and silly:

Diane   Always fooling about like in school.

Anne   Just gets on your nerves, they don't know when to shut up.

Margaret If they're not with their mates we get on with them OK, with their mates they act stupid.

In general, I felt that boys were regarded as a fact of life, sometimes tolerable, sometimes a nuisance. As Carol said, 'Doesn't really bother me...we're mixed cos it's normal'. As noted earlier, the boys were bottom of the girls' preferred choices of pupils they would interact with in lessons. Although on some occasions girls and boys appeared to share a definition of the classroom situation, it seemed that more often they came to lessons with very different starting points, as indicated in other research (Wernersson 1992), hence the lack of frequent interaction sets formed with boys.

This section will end with some important qualifying points. Firstly, as other researchers have found (Wolpe 1988, Thorne 1993), only some boys expressed the aggressive behaviour described above; others remained quietly separate. Secondly, such total separation may be school, region or time-specific: at Barnsdale, and Millbrook generally in the 1980s, the sexes were markedly polarised (the long-running TV programme *Last of the Summer Wine* was made in the region and demonstrates just such a strong division, albeit highly stereotyped). In contrast, Barrie Thorne (1993) found many examples of children crossing the gender divide in her own research, and questions the usefulness of an oppositional model.

Finally, it seems hard to equate the boys of these lessons with the boys about whom girls talked as potential or actual boyfriends. In fact, they were rarely the same boys, because boyfriends were usually older or from different classes. The difference also seems to stem from the gap between the boys of romantic fantasy, and the reality of the boys with whom girls had daily contact.

Different attitudes: friendship groups

Interaction sets based on common definitions of the situation did not preclude the existence of different types of behaviour. Within the general boundaries of behaviour possible within a particular lesson, the main friendship groups in G2 carried on their own interaction. Whilst acknowledging individual differences within each group, distinct attitudes, behaviour and orientations to school were observable for each group, as other researchers have also found (Delamont 1976, Meyenn 1980, Pollard 1984), ranging from quiet conformity to open resistance. Although Furlong questions the existence of 'pressure on group members to conform to the group's demands' (Furlong 1976 p.26), this was clearly evident at Barnsdale, and was part of the process of defining and negotiating 'sameness' within groups.

The loose-knit foursome

The four girls in the self-styled 'nasty' group were the most conformist in terms of classroom behaviour, and the most pro-school in orientation, even though they had low aspirations. In terms of attainment, the girls in this group were perceived by the school to be of moderate to low ability (Table 6.1), Annette being the strongest academically, and Pat the weakest (perhaps because of her frequent absences rather than because of a lack of ability). Suzanne summed up their attitude to school work:

> We have to try. And if we can't try they help yer out. They don't exactly tell you what the answer is but - they help you out.

There was a clear hierarchy in terms of who helped whom with work. The others always asked Annette first 'cos they think I'm t'brainiest of us lot' (Annette) ; then they asked Suzanne in subjects such as German where Annette was in a different set. Annette herself turned to Suzanne for help if she needed it:

The girls' assertions about effort were certainly confirmed by my own observations: they worked hard and were generally well behaved, rather like the younger working class girls in Bjerrum Nielsen and Rudberg's Scandinavian study (1992). The girls' generally pro-school attitude was exemplified by the fact that they always stayed behind at the end of Art lessons to see if they could do any tidying jobs. One reason for choosing Mrs Jebson to help was because the 'nasty' girls liked her. Their attitudes to different teachers were clear: basically, they disliked any teacher whom they considered too strict, who shouted too much or was unfair. For example, they disliked Mrs Norris because:

Annette   She picks on me for nowt. She tells me to shut up and everything.

Suzanne   She doesn't say, 'Can you be quiet?' She says 'Shut up!'

Pat   And she goes, she goes, 'Who gave you permission to talk?'

The girls made a direct association between the teachers and the subjects they taught; in general, they disliked subjects taught by teachers they disliked. As Suzanne put it, 'Well it's them (teachers) that puts yer off it'.

In terms of behaviour and attitudes, the loose-knit foursome exhibited the kind of behaviour described in Stanley's study of the 'quiet schoolgirl' (1992), and were similar to Meyenn's 'nice' girls (1980) or Pollard's 'good' girls (1984). However, whilst both the latter groups were regarded as 'goody-goodies' by other girls, the so-called 'nasty' group never were, as the name implies. This was mainly because of the level of abusive interaction they carried on amongst themselves in lessons, alongside their generally high level of effort and application. The group also presented a hostile front to other girls, most often through Annette, but the group as a whole were thought of as unfriendly. Other aspects of the girls' interaction - the playful, imaginative side which I saw at break or lunchtime, or the supportive element which emerged during the field trip - were hardly ever visible in lessons, and may never have been observed by other girls.

The big group

Also pro-school, but very different in their classroom behaviour, were the big group. Of the three girls' friendship groups in G2, this group was the closest together in ability. All eight girls were of average to high ability; most were above average. Janette and Vicky were in the top sets for every subject; none of the eight was below Set 3 for English or Maths (see Table 6.1). In organisational terms, this meant that most of the group were together in most lessons; even in English and Maths, there were always at least two of them together. The general attitude of the group was summed up by Penny:

> We do us work, we don't mess around when we're doing us work, we do us work, then if we've got time left we mess around then, but we don't mess around in lessons.

Penny's remarks about the group's attitude to work and behaviour in lessons sum up the fine balance and near-contradictory stance they exhibited in practice. From my observations, I would make a rather different distinction from Penny's about the big group's behaviour, between covert misbehaviour, usually in lessons with 'strict' teachers, and overt misbehaviour, in lessons with 'soft' teachers, the categorisations used by the girls themselves.

Unlike the loose-knit group, who hated the strict teachers, the big group considered 'you could learn better with strict teachers' (Carol). Whereas the loose-knit group believed in trying hard, even though they often found lessons difficult, the motivation for the brighter big group's behaviour seemed to come from the teachers rather than themselves. Penny's final comment 'but we don't mess around in lessons' was important in showing how the girls wanted to be seen to behave by the strict teachers.

The most striking examples of covert misbehaviour occurred in German lessons (Set 1, Fig. 6.1). A large part of each lesson was taken up by written exercises, which the pupils were expected to complete in virtual silence. The following extract is typical of what the big group were doing whilst they were working:

> Vicky calling in whispers across to Penny...whilst Mrs J. checking work at Sam and Joe's table...Carol fiddling with Elaine's hair and fingers....Then Karen calling to Penny, Pam whispering to Karen,

> Karen making funny faces to Pam, Dawn laughing. Carol pushing Elaine right over to Dawn, almost on to floor. Not noticed by Mrs J.

Another similar example from a German lesson is included earlier. When I re-read these lesson notes, I have to remind myself that this abundance of interaction occurred within a silent classroom. Mrs Jackson, the teacher, expected high standards of work and behaviour. It was therefore essential that the funny faces, laughing and pushing took place when Mrs Jackson was the other side of the room or had her back turned. To teachers like Mrs Jackson, the big group tried hard to keep up an image of hardworking, well behaved pupils. The girls had got the art of covert misbehaviour down to a fine art, and were rarely caught out.

These examples of covert misbehaviour, largely undiscovered, contrasted greatly with the overt misbehaviour of the big group in lessons where they considered the teacher 'soft', such as Music:

> Broadcast with percussion instruments. Recipe for chaos! Girls particularly: Vicky banging Janette on head with tambourine. Penny, Karen and others singing song (unrelated to broadcast).

Far from attempting to conceal their misbehaviour, the big group openly and obviously messed about in Music lessons, and were at times completely unrestrainable, as when Vicky and Carol were 'almost hysterical with giggling'. It was as if all the appearances of good behaviour which they sought to maintain in other lessons were abandoned, because they knew they could get away with it.

The big group, then, were basically an academically able, pro-school group who enjoyed having a laugh and were not averse to misbehaving. In these respects, they were very similar to Pollard's 'netball' group (1984), or Meyenn's 'PE' group (1980), who preserved a tension between school and peer group norms and found a way round the rules, whilst largely maintaining a good reputation among teachers. They were not so openly non-conforming as Lambart's 'sisterhood' (1976) or Fuller's black girls (1980), but they shared with the former group a love of mischief and a desire not to be seen as too 'brainy'.

I was particularly interested in the way that this sometimes precarious mid-path was preserved by the big group amongst themselves, as well as with teachers. There was considerable pressure put on the three more marginal members of the group, Janette, Dawn and Elaine, to adhere to the group's norms on behaviour in lessons. For example, Dawn was ostracised in the second year (Year 8) because she was not prepared to misbehave as much as the others, as Penny explained: 'She wanted to behave, but she's all right now'. Similarly, Janette was marginalised in the second year because she was too concerned about being top of the class and being seen to be good at school work. However, by the third year (Year 9), she was trying to play down her ability, as Penny said: 'She doesn't brag about it as much. She doesn't go, 'Oh I got ten out of ten', stuff like that'. Whereas Dawn and Janette were left out by the 'big' group for being too obviously pro-school, Elaine was marginalised for a time for being too anti-school (see below). In this way, the 'sameness' (Bjerrum Nielsen & Rudberg 1992) of the group's norms were preserved by the majority exerting pressure on the minority.

The school itself was providing little active encouragement of their academic abilities, and the girls were reluctant to consider themselves 'brainies' (Penny). Lesley Green, the class teacher, saw a potential conflict between the girls' school work and growing interest in boys and teenage culture, stemming from a concern expressed by the girls' parents. However, from my observations, this was not in practice an area of conflict for the girls themselves, who seemed to balance the two sets of interests well. Given that the school appeared to offer these girls so little to aim for, it was perhaps surprising that they remained so pro-school, and were so concerned to maintain a good reputation among the stricter members of staff.

The close-knit foursome

Although the close-knit group gave the impression of being pro-school, on closer observation they spent far more time in lessons getting on with each other than getting on with work. Many of the activities which they engaged in during lessons were a form of quiet (or not so quiet) resistance to school. Surinder told me that lessons were 'so boring' that they had to do something to pass the time. As well as 'grooming' and other forms of physical closeness, they also spent a good deal of lesson time talking and laughing amongst themselves, often quite openly and loudly. Unlike other girls whom I saw kept behind or moved for similar behaviour, the close-knit foursome seemed to get away without more than a telling off. This may have been to avoid possible accusations of racism towards the black girls in the group.

At this stage, their behaviour was not out and out resistance, like that exhibited by working class girls in some studies (Llewellyn 1980, Davies 1984), but more an ignoring of the school perspective (Birksted 1976), like the older working class girls in Bjerrum Nielsen and

Rudberg's research (1992), or the Black-Caribbean girls in Fuller's study (1980).

The activities I observed were more noticeable in lessons which the four girls had together, such as Art, Science or Music, than in subjects where they were separated into sets. For example, in German (Set 1), Marilyn and Surinder generally worked quietly together, as they also did in Maths (Set 2). There was a certain amount of competition between these two, which was expressed when I asked them if they helped each other with school work at all:

Marilyn   I help 'er (Surinder) in lessons, in German.
Surinder   And I help you as well in Maths.
Marilyn   In German, I help you in German.
VG   Why, are you good at German, Marilyn?
Marilyn   I'm better than Surinder.
Surinder   And I'm better than you at Maths.

Marilyn, who was the brightest academically of the four, did seem to want to do well; this was most obvious in History (Set 1), where she was on her own with girls from the big group. In contrast Charleen, who was the weakest academically, did not seem interested in lessons. Charleen's favourite lesson was Home Economics. Like other pupils, she often took meals cooked in these lessons home for family tea later. Charleen had considerable domestic responsibilities; in her case, the school curriculum was not just preparing her for future commitments, but assisting her with present ones.

At break, lunchtime and even after school, the four girls spent a lot of time with each other and with their joint parallel friends talking about what had happened in lessons. Apart from simply 'having a laugh', anecdotes about lessons also seemed to represent a form of resistance in retrospect, as the following example indicates:

Charleen recounts, full of giggles, how Mrs Sharp told her to stop laughing in Needlework earlier. Surinder tells tale of how she prodded Mrs Winter's buns in Cookery. Martine joins in this anecdote. Much laughter.

In reporting these incidents afterwards, the girls were not only catching up on news about lessons and sharing experiences which they might have missed through separation, but also transforming misdemeanours into triumphs. This was true whether the particular action or behaviour had been detected, as in Charleen's case, or had gone unnoticed. Experiences of this kind could be worked up afterwards into part of a group mythology, what Lynn Davies (1984) calls 'shared reality transformers' (Davies 1984 p.4O).

Although the four girls had many friends in other classes, particularly among other black girls, there was a generally hostile dynamic between them and the other small group in G2, who regarded them as 'enemies': as Suzanne explained, 'If you look at them they'll fight you'. To the close-knit group, however, the aggressive behaviour which I observed between these two groups on many occasions confirmed their opinion of the 'nasty' group's unfriendliness.

The close-knit foursome liked to go out of school altogether at lunchtimes, 'cos there's nowt to do 'ere' (Marilyn). The main appeal of school for these girls seemed to be in the social interaction with friends which it afforded, but if this could be carried on out of school, so much the better. School itself seemed to have little to offer them, and all but Surinder had low academic aspirations for the future. This may have been at least in part because of the teachers' low expectations of working class and black girls, found in other studies (Grant 1992, Mickelson 1992, Measor & Sikes 1992). There were underlying dissatisfactions with school, and by the fourth year (Year 10) they had become much more openly anti-school in their behaviour.

The 'CB' group

The most clearly anti-school group that I observed consisted of seven white girls from three different classes, including Elaine from G2 during the second year (Year 8). To distinguish them from the big group in G2, I shall refer to them as the 'CB' group because of their out of school involvement in Citizens Band (CB) radio. Their interests were generally subcultural, a mixture of punk, skinhead and heavy metal, epitomised by their hairstyles (spikey and dyed blond), and their eclectic tastes in music: Toyah, Madness, Siouxsie and the Banshees. This made them very different from other 'mature' girls whose interests in fashion and music were much more mainstream. In terms of attitudes to school, the 'CB' group were also very different. Although quite academically able, the group had a general anti-school orientation, exemplified by Mandy's comment: 'Hate it!'

The girls saw each other in lessons where possible; some of them were in the same English and Maths sets. In the classroom, their resistance to school took the form of keeping a low profile, trying not to be noticed. Although not overtly disruptive, their behaviour was sometimes regarded by teachers as 'sullen'. At break time, they would congregate 'round t'back of Sports Hall wi't'smokers' (Lorraine), but for much of the time, they were simply absent, 'legging it', or 'bunking off', that is, deliberately missing school:

Mandy We used to go to my house cos me Mum went to work you see.
Elaine Every dinner time we'd leg afternoon.

In particular, they would try to miss lessons taken by teachers they regarded as 'bullies' (Lorraine). When this was discovered, the girls were put 'on report', which meant getting a signature every lesson to prove they had attended. However, although they insisted on the girls attending lessons, any interest or encouragement on the part of the school stopped there. Elaine became more involved with school again through the pressure of her other friends in G2's big group, rather than by anything the teachers did, and by the third year (Year 9) was saying how the 'CB' group had been a bad influence on her. Although anti-school in orientation, the CBs were very different from anti-school groups portrayed in other studies (Llewellyn 1980, Ball 1981, Davies 1984), both because of their quiet classroom behaviour, and their unusual variety of outside school interests, which included Air Cadets as well as 'CB' and music (see ch.7).

Forms of resistance: an alternative model

I shall conclude this chapter by bringing together the girls' forms of resistance to school, and ways in which they made space for themselves in and out of lesson time, against the backdrop of gender divisions in school. This will parallel the discussion in the next chapter of ways in which the girls found their own space within the constraints imposed on their leisure time.

Many forms of resistance engaged in by adolescent girls at school are mentioned in other research. For ease of comparison with my own findings, I have summarised these in Table 6.2. Some of these activities, such as doing hair or making school uniform look more fashionable, could be seen as an accommodation to traditional female interests or behaviour rather than a form of resistance. Angela McRobbie (1978a) expresses this paradox when she writes:

Marriage, family, fashion and beauty all contribute massively to this feminine anti-school culture and, in doing so, nicely illustrate the contradictions inherent in so-called oppositional activities. Are

125

Table 6.2
Adolescent girls: resistance to school

Form of resistance	Reference
(a) Individualised:	
day dreaming	Llewellyn 1980, Griffin 1985a
writing on desks or on books	Wolpe 1988
combing or sucking hair	McRobbie 1978a, Wolpe 1988
reading magazines in class	Fuller 1980
(b) Collective:	
passing notes	Griffin 1985a
sticking up for each other	Davies 1984
being slow or late	Furlong 1976, Fuller 1980
sullen resentment	Davies 1984
cheeking teacher	Furlong 1976
'exploits' (eg. firebell)	Davies 1984
talking in class	Fuller 1980, Davies 1984, Wolpe 1988
alteringuniform	McRobbie 1978a, Griffin 1985a
physical contact	Wolpe 1988, Thorne 1993
teasing, humour	Wolpe 1988, B. Nielsen & Rudberg 1992
(c) Making space:	
Science lab	Meyenn 1980
girls' toilets	McRobbie 1978a, Thorne 1993
smokers' corner	Davies 1984, Wolpe 1988
talking about school:	
'reality transformers'	Meyenn 1980, Davies 1984
missing lessons	Davies 1984, Griffin 1985a
truanting	Davies 1984, Griffin 1985a

the girls in the end not simply doing exactly what is required of them - and if this is the case, then could it not be convincingly argued that it is their own culture which itself is the most effective agent of social control for girls? (McRobbie 1978a p.104)

Paul Willis explores just this process of cultural reproduction in *Learning to Labour* (1977) in relation to working class boys.

The contradiction must not be ignored. However, I do not think it undermines the importance of girls claiming some measure of control in their lives, albeit within limited confines. I would also argue that much depends on the context and girls concerned: the same activity may have different meanings and serve different purposes depending on who is carrying them out. Anyon makes just this point when she writes:

Accommodation or resistance, even when it takes the form of turning away or withdrawal, is an active process. The analysis above suggests that girls are not passive victims of sex-role stereotypes and expectations, but are active participants in their own development. (Anyon 1983)

The findings of my own and other studies confirm the point that young women actively shape and construct their own responses, often to severe restrictions, in a variety of personal and often unique ways.

In relation to the young working class women in my own research, this was certainly the case. Table 6.4 summarises some of the main forms of resistance to school which I observed among the girls. In comparing the two tables, it strikes me that there was no evidence of individualised resistance among the Barnsdale High girls. This was true even when seating was arranged on an individual basis; as I have described, in these circumstances, the girls would communicate by signalling, whispering or note passing, or by finding ways of getting physically closer such as coming up to the front of the class together.

As I have already described, none of the groups was anti-school in the traditionally feminine way that the girls in Angela McRobbie's research (1978) seem to have been. In the case of the big group, interest in teenage culture went hand in hand with high ability and a generally pro-school attitude. In an earlier chapter, I argued that important features of the girls' friendships, such as 'grooming', served several different purposes at once, and did not necessarily represent an adherence to fashionable appearance. The most anti-school group, the CBs, were certainly not traditionally feminine in many of their interests.

Table 6.3
Barnsdale High girls: resistance to school

Form of resistance	Girls involved
(a) Collective: signalling, smiling chewing gum in class sticking up for each other	all groups
talking in lessons having a laugh hand games	all, partic. big & close-knit groups
mutual grooming writing on books, bags hugging, holding	close-knit & big groups
altering uniform hairstyles	big, 'CB', other 'mature' groups close-knit
(b) Making space: *In school* girls' toilets classroom (form time) Art room smokers' corner 'reality transformers'	all groups big group loose-knit group 'CB' group partic. close-knit group
Out of school churchyard anywhere missing lessons truanting	loose-knit group close-knit group 'CB', other 'mature' groups 'CB' group

There was no simple correlation, then, among the Barnsdale girls between attitude to school, ability and involvement in teenage culture or 'feminine' interests. To paraphrase Birksted (1976 p.65), all the girls fitted school into the structure of their lives to a greater or lesser extent, rather than the other way round. To do this within the considerable strictures imposed by most teachers at Barnsdale High was no mean achievement. Although there were many instances of small groups or whole classes sharing a common definition of the classroom situation, there was clear evidence of girls interacting within their friendship groups, and operating within group norms.

The view of young women using friends as their main reference group in school, and as a positive way of coping with constraints, rather than as a 'negative of boys' (Wernersson 1992 p.6), provides a positive alternative to what Wernersson calls the 'misery model' (ibid. p.4) of girls at school. Rather than seeing girls as low in self esteem because they receive less attention than boys, Wernersson argues that girls maintain high self esteem through building competence in social relations; thus they achieve highly in their own terms. Added to this the most recent findings of girls' higher attainment in academic terms (Mickelson 1992, Grant 1995), and a very different picture starts to emerge of girls, to reword Anyon (1983), as active participants in their own achievement.

7 From playing out to dossing out

In this chapter, I shall discuss the effects of some of the changes which take place during adolescence on young women's leisure patterns; examining, for example, the transition from 'playing out' to 'dossing out', the relative importance of the 'culture of the bedroom' for girls of different ages and their friends, and the transition from school to work or unemployment. Whilst acknowledging that young women's leisure activities are located within and shaped by restrictions, such as where and when they can go out, the positive strategies which young women use to overcome constraints on their leisure time and negotiate their own space will be stressed.

Young women and leisure: an unproblematic picture?

Whatever their age, the Barnsdale girls enjoyed themselves a great deal together out of school: 'having a laugh' and 'messing about' were frequently mentioned. Most went out every evening, at least in the summer months, as John Ward also found in his research (1976). Whether mature or younger-seeming, the second and third year girls (Years 8 & 9) followed a wide range of leisure activities. Some went to youth clubs and other organisations, such as dancing classes; many went to local discos. Others filled their time without going to any formally arranged events; for example, June and her friends: 'play records, go for a walk, go out, go to t'swimming baths, go to town, go to t'pictures - when I get money'. Leisure patterns for the fifth years (Year 11) and school leavers were rather different. As well as some of the activities mentioned already, they went to pubs and clubs in town, and to parties at each others' houses.

Looking at the young women's patterns of leisure in isolation, suggests a largely unproblematic picture of unrestricted leisure, based on individual choice and interest. However, to leave it at that would be totally misleading and obscure important factors which actually shaped the young women's leisure. Feminist researchers (Griffin et al 1982, Deem 1986, Wimbush & Talbot 1988) have argued that leisure has usually been defined by sociologists implicitly, if not explicitly, with reference to men. They stress that leisure is a problematic concept for women, not least because of the unclear division between paid work and unpaid domestic responsibilities which can take up so much of women's supposedly 'free' time. Liz Stanley stresses the importance of 'putting context back in' (Stanley 1988 p.18) to leisure studies and explains:

> 'Leisure' certainly does not make sense on its own; it has to be understood as part of a conjunction of interests, needs, skills, commitments and obligations in women's lives, most importantly including those of 'work'. (ibid.)

Similarly, what adolescent girls and their friends do in the evenings and at weekends cannot be fully understood without knowing what restrictions they have on their leisure time, and it is to these which I now turn.

Restrictions on young women's leisure time

Girls' leisure activities are both constructed and restricted by their class, race and gender (McRobbie 1978a, Griffin 1985a, Aapola 1992). In the industrial towns of West Yorkshire in the 1980s, young working class men and women had very little money, and there were few places to go locally. Although bus fares were subsidised (30p maximum fare outside peak times), the girls' spending money was limited (£1.50 a week average) and few of them had bikes. This restricted the young women to their immediate area, as other studies have found (McRobbie 1978a, Griffin 1985a). For the many young people who faced unemployment after leaving school, this situation was unlikely to change. Those lucky enough to find employment might experience a slightly higher degree of financial independence, but leisure provision was still restricted. However, young women face further constraints on their leisure not experienced, and indeed in some cases caused, by men.

These gender and class-specific restrictions affect most girls to a greater or lesser extent, regardless of ethnic background. However, in my own research, compared to white and Black-Caribbean girls in general, the Indian girls were virtually invisible in any out-of-school activities. Laxmi Jamdagni (1980) explains that, for Asian (Indian and Pakistani) girls, leisure centres on the home and family, and suggests that activities such as youth clubs would be considered unsuitable because they take place in public and clash with an emphasis on modesty and traditional roles in the home. However, Pratibha Parmar and Nadira Mirza (1981) question explanations premised on Asian girls' 'supposedly innumerable problems at home' (1981, p.9), and argue that institutional racism lies behind their relative invisibility in youth culture.

As a white researcher, I am wary of making generalisations based on insufficient knowledge and thus perpetuating stereotypes. There are considerable cultural and religious variations within what is often unproblematically called 'Asian culture' which must not be overlooked (Amos and Parmar 1981), as I certainly found in my previous research between Moslem and Sikh communities (Griffiths 1986). The passage of time is also bringing important changes; for instance, more recently in West Yorkshire traditional Indian dancing has become very popular among Indian and non-Indian girls, both at school and in the community. I must also stress that there were many white and Black-Caribbean girls whose leisure patterns were similar to the Indian girls', spending a lot of time at home either through choice or because of restrictions. In both this and my previous research I was struck by the degree to which young women's common experiences overrode divisions of either class or race.

My own and other studies indicate that three main gender-specific factors give rise to restrictions on the young women's leisure time, and these will be discussed in turn.

Domestic responsibilities

Home responsibilities are commonplace among girls, particularly working class young women (McRobbie 1978a, Griffiths 1986). At Barnsdale, most of the girls had to help with everyday domestic chores such as washing up, cooking and cleaning. Childcare also formed a common part of the girls' home commitments. The actual amount of time spent on these jobs varied considerably, from lending an occasional hand to running the household. In almost every case these domestic commitments impinged on the girls' leisure time, and were

132

regarded as a taken-for-granted aspect of their lives. As June put it, explaining why a friend sometimes had to stay at home in the evening, 'Shirley has to wash up, things like that, everybody does'.

Domestic duties seemed to increase as the girls got older and were regarded as more responsible; they impinged on the girls' leisure activities at the very stage the young women wanted to go out more often. For example, Karen went to a local youth club quite frequently in the second year (Year 8), but by the third year (Year 9) she had stopped going 'cos I have to go baby-sitting'. Karen looked after her cousin's one-year old baby three times a week 'till about half past eleven' plus weekends, which was quite a sizeable commitment. Charleen, one of the Black-Caribbean girls, was virtually running her large household single-handed at the age of 13: she had to 'do t'baking, make tea and do dishes' as well as shopping and cleaning. She rarely went out, and could only see friends 'after I've done me work'.

For girls like Karen and Charleen, their experience was preparation for unpaid domestic work as well as maternal duties. They were already learning to sacrifice their own time and interests to others' needs. The sense of familial obligation was strong, and in only one case (unlike McRobbie 1978a) did a girl receive regular payment for these domestic duties. This was Pat who was paid £5 a week by her sister-in-law 'our Sue' for looking after Sue's daughter Tracey whilst Sue was at work:

> I look after her every night, go straight down for her after, after I've finished school I go straight down to t'nursery for her, then she pays me at end o't'week.

It was noticeable that Pat described the arrangement as being between her sister-in-law and herself rather than her brother; childcare was obviously seen as a female responsibility. Pat tried to combine seeing her friends after school with looking after Tracey: 'I tek her to my house an' we've got a den what we made out of the bonfire and we tek her in there'. She also managed to see her friend Tina, who lived next door, by helping her make the tea for her three younger siblings while her mother was at work in the evenings. In this way the two friends were still able to see each other, and provide reciprocal help for each others' domestic duties.

However, this represented a major change in the leisure pattern for these two girls, who had divided their weekday evenings the previous year between Pendleton and Redfern youth clubs, including at least two discos a week. Now the girls were virtually restricted to each others' houses; Tina could not leave the house until relieved of her domestic responsibilities: 'When Tina's Dad's home she can come out'. Otherwise the girls relied on friends calling round, or occasionally they managed to go out and meet friends in the park.

Parental fears about safety

Many studies (Griffin 1985a, Griffiths 1986, Lees 1986) have found that young women experience restrictions on where and when they go out at night, and this was further corroborated by the Barnsdale study. For example, Lizzy was typical of the girls in G2 in telling me 'I can't stay out late'. This was also the case for many of the fifth years (Year 11), such as Sarah who told me her parents 'won't let me out if I'm on me own'. Such restrictions are generally imposed by girls' parents because of worries for their daughters' safety at night. There are very real dangers to women from male violence and sexual harassment, which the Barnsdale girls recognised. They talked about the threat from gangs, and violent incidents which had happened locally (including one of the so-called 'Yorkshire Ripper' murders). For example, Charleen who had to be in by half past seven in winter told me, 'Me Mum don't like me staying out too long in t'dark cos all these people get kidnapped and killed.'

Ironically, one of the actual incidents which affected some of the older girls going out was the murder of a young boy which had happened in the area the year before I started my research. Jenny explained:

> You see we used - we used to go down (the youth club) ages ago, but then you know when there were that little boy who were killed (Sarah: Murdered), murdered, and so we stopped going cos us Mums wouldn't let us go then ... and so we just didn't bother going did we?

This example highlights some of the contradictions and confusions involved in interpreting sexual violence. Although the victim in the above case was a boy, and there was every indication from media reports at the time, that it was a homosexual murder, girls' leisure activities were directly curtailed as a result. This is in sharp contrast to a more recent murder in Brighton of two girls in their early teens, which resulted in girls only in the area being sent home from school early for a while afterwards. Even though young children of either sex are vulnerable to sexual violence, parents appear to 'read' such incidents differently for sons or daughters. So whilst boys' leisure activities may be temporarily curtailed after a particular incident such as the above where a boy is the victim, such restrictions rarely touch boys' lives and are not introduced when a girl is the victim, whereas girls experience restrictions all the time and these seem to be reinforced more strongly after an attack or murder of a girl or boy.

In Millbrook, many places were considered too 'rough' for girls to go, for example, certain youth clubs or parts of town. Few girls were allowed out alone, but most were allowed to go out with a girlfriend or group of girls. As Jacky, one of the fifth years said, 'Safer i'n't it when you're with all your friends'. However, safety in numbers was not usually considered sufficient safeguard by the girls' parents when the evenings grew darker earlier. Far more restrictions were imposed in winter, and this brought about a radical seasonal difference in many of the young women's leisure patterns. For example, Carol told me: 'I can't see them (girlfriends) much after school now, cos me Mum won't let me out cos it's getting too dark'. The girls had to come in earlier in winter (anything from 6.30 onwards), and some places such as the park which had been considered safe in summer became no-go areas. As Janette explained:

> We used to be able to go out on a night as well into the park ... but now we can't because it's got dark and there's gangs around the park where you don't know what they're doing and what they're going to do to you, so we don't bother.

Some of the girls were not allowed out in winter at all unless there were going to be boys in the group too. This struck me as somewhat ironic since it was dangers from male 'gangs' which gave rise to the restriction in the first place. Interestingly, both Janette and Jenny in the ealier quote used the phrase 'we don't bother', making what was a parental restriction in both cases into a seemingly personal choice.

Lack of transport was a further problem. Apart from the financial constraints on using public transport, buses late at night were not considered safe. Most girls had to walk to and from local activities, but this in itself was often forbidden in winter. Having parents who were able to drive their daughters to and from clubs or discos was rare and is more likely to be a middle class phenomenon (Griffin 1985a).

Such constraints were perceived as most severe by the 'mature' 12-14 year-olds who wanted to go out a lot, in contrast to older girls who tended to be allowed more freedom, especially after they had left school. For instance, Sarah (now at 6th form college) told me: 'cos with us being older we can stay out later now can't we? It's a lot better'.

135

As Angela McRobbie described in her study of working class girls (1978a), one of the few places for young people to go locally may be the youth club. Near Barnsdale was Redfern youth club, but very few girls went there because it was considered 'rough' and 'mainly for t'lads' (Jacky and Jenny). Facilities provided were football, pool, space invaders and table tennis, all of which were dominated by the boys. Girls needed to be particularly confident and persistent to face out the lack of facilities within the club and the predominance of boys. As Jenny explained, 'there's no other lasses who go, so we don't bother going'.

Two girls who did carry on going to the youth club in spite of these drawbacks were Lizzy and Jill who went twice a week. Lizzy was not a particularly assertive girl and would probably not have gone without Jill, who could hold her own in any situation and told me once that she'd 'flatten' any boy who gave her trouble. Lizzy told me, 'Stick with Jill mainly' at the youth club. She and Jill did sometimes mix with the boys, usually by playing table tennis with them (always girls against boys), but otherwise they tended to watch television or stand around talking and watching the boys.

The problem of youth clubs being geared to boys' interests is now widely recognised (Youth Work Unit 1981, Nava 1984), but Redfern youth club provided very little which interested the girls, except for trampolining once a week, and girls' nights were non-existent. Some other youth clubs in the area held discos and encouraged disco-dancing (Griffiths 1988), and this was one way in which young women could find their own space within the otherwise male-dominated atmosphere. Just before I moved away from the area, a youth worker for girls was appointed in Millbrook. She was hoping to organise girls' nights in some youth clubs, more facilities for girls on 'mixed' nights, and in-service training for youth workers. Hopefully her appointment will have brought about some recognition of the problem and improved conditions for young women.

Finding their own space

In the light of the restrictions described above, which in some cases limit young women's leisure activities considerably, I want now to look at ways in which girls negotiate their own space, either on their own or within mixed-sex situations.

Angela McRobbie and Jenny Garber (1976) coined this term to describe what they regarded as one way in which girls resisted boys' domination of the streets, that is using their own homes as the base from which to explore aspects of teenage culture. Activities like reading magazines, dancing or listening to records could all be easily accommodated in the girls' bedrooms, along with talking about boys, fashion and music. In my research, the extent to which the culture of the bedroom was evident varied considerably among different groups of friends. I found no girls who stayed at home to the exclusion of going out, but staying in had different meanings and took different forms depending on what age they were and at what stage of adolescence. Ethnicity was another important factor.

Bedroom culture depends on having your own private space, but many of the girls I worked with did not have their own bedrooms. Even when a girl had her own room, privacy was not guaranteed. For example, Janette's sister and parents often came into her room, so she and her best friend did not feel free to discuss boys or family relationships, and had to go out if they wanted to talk without interruption.

Staying at home was seen as least satisfactory to the 'mature' 12-14 year-olds who wanted to go out as much as they could. This preference for going out has been reported in other studies of adolescent girls (Ward 1976, Griffiths 1986). Time at home was often seen as the prelude to going out rather than an end in itself. The girls would call for each other and go out after doing school work or jobs in the house. For example, Vicky told me: 'We'd probably do our homework or something, then we'd go out with Pam and everyone else you know'. Those girls who were not allowed out during winter evenings described what they did at home rather negatively, like Pam: 'Not much really. Just watch telly or play some games, just do owt'. It was as if staying in forced these girls to resort to more childlike activities.

One activity mentioned by the 'mature' girls as a positive reason for staying in was playing records. For example, Mandy and her friends: 'all stay in to tape Top Twenty ... all go to us own houses, and then we meet when it's finished'. Even in this case, listening to the records was a prelude to going out, meeting their friends and comparing notes about which groups they liked. Some of the girls also stayed in to do CB radio. Elaine and Lorraine ('CB' group) had their own CB radios for which they paid £10 a year in licence fees - a lot of money for these girls - on top of buying the 'rig' itself. Talking over the radio was an activity which fitted into the 'culture of the bedroom' rather like talking to friends over the phone. Lorraine and Elaine used it in this way to talk to each other. With CB, there was the added interest that you could make new friends, including boys, as the girls explained:

> Lorraine You just talk to loads of people and get to know them.
> Elaine Cos we wouldn't know none of them lads if we didn't do CBs would we? You shout 'Breaker'
> Lorraine Yeah (laughs).
> Elaine and then you get talking to 'em and if you ask them for an eyeball and you go and meet 'em somewhere and then you've got a new friend.
> Lorraine You don't use your proper name though ... I'm Queen Bee (laughs) -
> Elaine And I'm Prawn Cocktail.
> (All laugh)

I thought this was particularly interesting because it gave the girls a legitimate means of taking the initiative in starting relationships with boys, which might have given the girls a bad name in other circumstances (Lees 1986). They were also able to size up boys over the radio without necessarily having to meet them. The girls obviously enjoyed the excitement involved, the fun of adopting a radio persona, and using the CB language. Apart from playing records and CB, going to each others' houses was something these girls were more likely to do in mixed-sex groups.

A more positive attitude to staying in was shown by the younger-seeming girls, particularly those who were friends with younger girls in their neighbourhood. They enjoyed the ritual of going to each others' houses to play games. For example Suzanne described what she and her younger friend Dot did:

> Sometimes we can go in each others' houses. We take turns at that. One night she comes in mine and another night I go in hers ... We play twist or monopoly, stuff like that.

Other activities mentioned were knitting and reading, very different from the interests of the mature girls. The Indian girls also spent much of their time at home, usually in extended family groups rather than with friends, although they did see Indian girlfriends at weekends at the gurdwara (Sikh temple). Their interests were similar to the younger-seeming girls' and they talked about what they did positively. These girls were certainly not involved in adolescent culture.

At the other end of the age range I found that some of the older girls also enjoyed spending evenings in with girlfriends, perhaps because they experienced fewer restrictions on their leisure time and had plenty of nights out. Those who lived close by would 'pop round' to each others' houses for a chat very frequently and informally. Friends who lived further away had to make more definite arrangements. For example, Michelle told me: 'Anne'll come down here on Tuesday and I'll go by on a Thursday or other way round. We usually just stay in, watch a bit of telly and talk'. As with the younger girls, the reciprocal nature of the arrangement was obviously important. For young women like Michelle and Anne who had left school, these evenings together were a way of keeping in touch, catching up with news and sharing problems.

The Black-Caribbean girls in some ways came closest to McRobbie and Garber's description of bedroom culture. Like the Indian girls, these girls did much more in extended family groups, so finding privacy at home was not such a priority. They did not seem to experience such pressures as the white girls to go out or have boyfriends (Fuller 1980, Griffin 1985a) so although they were generally free to go out, they were often happy to spend evenings at home. One activity which occupied a lot of the black girls' time at home was doing each others' hair. They often came to school with beaded braids, which could take a whole evening to complete. Although doing each others' hair was a favourite activity among all the girls, in the case of the Black-Caribbean girls it was an important part of their black identity, as I have already described. The black girls also spent time at home playing records, reading, helping each other with homework and talking.

Sue Lees has argued that bedroom culture is not a form of resistance for girls as Angela McRobbie and Jenny Garber suggested, but 'if anything, an adjustment to their expected feminine role which, by and large, is anticipated to centre on the home' (Lees 1986, p.60). I regard this as an over-simplification. In my research, for example, activities such as CB radio enabled girls to go against an 'expected feminine role' by taking more initiative and control in starting relationships with boys. For the older girls in particular, bedroom culture was a way of resisting pressures to spend all their time with boyfriends. It is important to distinguish between time spent at home on domestic chores, which did represent an 'adjustment' to traditional female roles, although even here the girls sometimes managed to negotiate their own space, and time spent at home engaged in other activities. Apart from those girls with extensive home responsibilities, most of the girls spent time going out as well as time at home, as I shall now describe.

Playing out, 'dossing' and going out

As feminist researchers have pointed out, from Angela McRobbie and Jenny Garber's critique (1976) onwards, much previous research on young people and subcultures (usually done by men) suggests that girls are invisible on the streets except as 'appendages' to boys (e.g. as girlfriends to gang members), and do not hang around in groups of girls. However, other studies (Smith 1978, Wilson 1978, Campbell 1984) show that girls can be full members of gangs or mixed-sex groups, and can also associate in groups of girls, suggesting that the differences in findings can be attributed to the perspective and gender of the researchers. Other more recent research (Griffin 1985a, Lees 1986) shows that girls in general, not just deviant girls, are often highly visible on the streets in groups together, and I certainly found this in my research.

What the girls did depended on their age and stage of adolescence. There was a gradual transition from 'playing out' at the younger end, to 'dossing' or hanging around as the girls got older. Dossing was gradually replaced by 'going out', which depended on having more money and consequent access to places to go, and was therefore most evident among those young women who had left school and were at college or in work. However, there was not always a clear demarcation between these stages. In particular, the self-styled 'mature' 12-14 year olds often combined playing with more adolescent activities. Most of the girls 'went out' in the more formal sense at least occasionally, to the cinema or local disco, but opportunities were more limited for the younger girls still at school.

The younger-seeming girls still spent a lot of their time 'playing out' after school. For example, Annette told me: 'We just mess about and come up to school and play in t'sandpits'. However, even some girls who regarded themselves as mature referred occasionally to playing out, usually when talking to me on their own. For example, Karen told me that she and her friends 'just sit down and talk and play stuff - hide and seek and that'. This combination of playing and talking was typical of many of the girls, and is acknowledged in other studies too (Connell 1987, Thorne 1993).

At weekends the younger-seeming girls tended to stay at home playing out with friends, although they sometimes went swimming at the Sports Centre in town. During the holidays they might go to the river or nearby countryside with their friends. I was told about activities such as pear-picking and fishing expeditions, which the girls described with great enthusiasm. For example, Marilyn, Martine and Shona described their attempts at butterfly catching:

Shona	We just get somethings that's fallen off a tree or a branch.
Martine	And you just go like that (gesturing) and you can catch them.
Shona	Put them in a jar and then when we get home we just let'em go.
VG	Oh, how many did you catch?
Martine	We didn't catch none!
Marilyn	We only caught one but ...
Shona	We caught one and it were red.
Martine	Yeah, we kept catching them and they kept escaping.
Marilyn	If you put them in a jar they won't be able to fly no more so we just let them go.

The three girls told me this very excitedly, all speaking at once. As with the games they played at home, these activities were similar to those pursued by younger children. The adventurous nature of some of these trips, an aspect which the girls obviously enjoyed, also provided a contrast to some of their home-based pursuits.

For the 'mature' 13-14 year-olds upwards, the most common activity after school was hanging about together or 'dossing', as other studies have also found (Griffin 1985a, Lees 1986). As Pam said, the girls would 'go for each other and doss out'. Although apparently casual, dossing was quite a ritualised procedure. The girls woud call for each other, as they did on their way to school; for example, Mandy (CB group) told me:

We meet at one person's house, say if Lorraine says, 'Come for me at half six', then we'd all t'lot of us'll go to her house and then we'll go somewhere else so that we can meet.

Once gathered together, the girls would 'just stay on the street' or 'just wander round'. The word 'just' which often prefaced comments about dossing sounded slightly self-denigrating, as though the girls felt they should have been doing more. It also seemed to indicate a certain dissatisfaction at the lack of things to do locally. There was a constant tension between this and the girls' determination to make the best out of limited circumstances, as the following comments from two fifth year girls indicated:

> Sarah   There's nothing much to do any time really is there?
> Jenny   (interrupting) But we always find summat good to do, cos we go down t'chippy and have a laugh don't we?

The chip shop was one of the popular places to gather, especially on Saturday nights: 'eight o'clock everybody's round chip shop aren't they?' (Sarah). Other good places to doss locally were the Co-op, and the grounds of Barnsdale or other schools. For the 'CB' group, the off-licence was a popular place to go, as Lorraine told me:

> Sometimes we go up Pendleton or we just sit around Heyton ... or we go to off-licence, we sit outside off-licence cos a lot of breakers, CB breakers go up there.

The local park was perhaps the favourite 'dossing' ground. Janette described what the girls did: 'Sometimes we just walk around and sit on the swings and talk', another example of the combination of playing and talking which characterised these girls' behaviour. In spite of its limitations, dossing was generally seen by the girls as a positive occupation, equated with 'having a laugh'. 'Just a right good doss' was the highest accolade.

However, dossing came to an abrupt end in winter. It was very noticeable how, during the dark winter evenings, groups of boys still hung around the street corners but the groups of girls had virtually disappeared. Nevertheless, this does not undermine the fact that for part of the year at least, the streets were girls' space as much as boys'. Many of the girls preferred hanging around the streets to going to youth clubs, because they could enjoy themselves with their friends without boys taking over. They might join together with a group of boys on occasions, but they could choose not to do so. Dossing gave them this kind of freedom and control, and a strong sense of independence.

Largely because of lack of money and because it was considered unsafe at night, the girls rarely went into Millbrook on weekday evenings unless they belonged to a club such as St. John's Ambulance Cadets which met in town. Dossing around the streets in town would have had a very different connotation from hanging about the estates where they lived (Lees 1986). However, Saturdays were usually spent in town. Many of the older girls had Saturday jobs such as shop work or waitressing, which restricted when they could meet their girlfriends. For those who did not have jobs, and more particularly for the 'mature' 13-14 year-olds, most of the time in town on Saturdays was spent dossing, hanging around the shops, where I sometimes saw them 'running round the shopping precinct laughing and playing hide and seek, as well as looking in the shop windows' (another example of girls combining childlike and adolescent activities).

What little spending money the girls had, which averaged £1.50 a week, they would use to buy records or magazines. Fashionable clothes were extremely important to the 'mature' girls. As Pam said, 'I wouldn't want owt that was out of fashion'. However, clothes were generally too expensive for the girls, and were usually bought by or with their mothers, which was often a cause of conflict as other studies have found (Griffin 1985a, Griffiths 1986). Whilst with their friends, the girls were therefore restricted to window shopping. For some of the girls, going to town was also an opportunity to meet groups of boys, as Carol explained: 'We meet them in town every Saturday and go round in a big gang. About ten of us'. By and large, however, Saturdays and Sundays durng the day were times to see girlfriends.

In contrast to these girls, young women who had left school were less likely to spend time dossing either in the evenings or at weekends. Those who had gone to college (sixth form, art or Technical college) had access to far more social activities such as discos organised by the college or parties held by other students. Although they were all still living at home - 'keeping close and spoiling' (Leonard 1980) was very much the norm here - these young women had greater freedom than when they had been at school. They were allowed to stay out later, and sometimes stayed overnight with girlfriends. Those in work had greater financial independence and could go into town to pubs and clubs, or shopping for clothes at the weekends. Going out became the norm rather than the exception.

However, for unemployed young women the picture was very diferent. With no spending power, they were cut off from the goods and services to which their money-earning peers now had access. The wider social activities of the students were not available to them either, so they remained trapped as it were in the previous stage. Some could be seen dossing around the streets or gathered outside the Job Centre. Others became isolated in their homes, depressed and filling their time with domestic duties, as I learnt from Pauline about some of her former school friends.

Very little has been written about young women's involvement in clubs, apart from youth clubs (McRobbie 1978a) and some sports activities (Talbot 1988, Farran 1990). At Barnsdale, the girls went to various different clubs and societies and I visited many of these in the evenings. These included Girl Guides, which had been popular but by the age of 14 was considered babyish; and orchestra, which only Janette went to, and which gave her entry into a middle class world very unlike school. Although many of the girls enjoyed sporting activities at school, few engaged in them outside, apart from Janette who did athletics, and one of the older girls, Jacky, who was in the county under 18s hockey team. I shall give three contrasting examples of clubs to which several of the girls went: the all-female Girls' Friendly Society, the predominantly male Air Cadets, and the mixed-sex St. John's Ambulance Cadets.

(i) Girls' Friendly Society   Some girls got over the problem of boys dominating youth clubs by going to all-girl groups. For example, three of the big group in G2, Penny, Pam and Dawn and a friend Becky, went to the Girls' Friendly Society (GFS), a Church of England organisation for girls between the ages of 7 and 16. They had a somewhat ambivalent attitude towards the group. Sometimes they talked about it in lukewarm terms: 'it's just a bit boring at times'; 'it's summat to do'. However, at other times they described what they did enthusiastically. For instance, Penny told me, 'We do games and have parties and things like that and we go on trips and camping'.

A clue to the girls' ambivalence was provided by Penny who called GFS 'a bit babyish'. As part of the big group, these girls were keen to appear grown up. Going to a club which included 7 year-olds, where you played games and did model making, could easily have been regarded as childish. Because the girls were at a transitional stage in adolescence, they did still enjoy these younger-type activities, but they could only bring themselves to admit it when talking to me on their own.

What tipped the balance in favour of GFS was that these girls were encouraged by the women running the group to create a dance for the local disco-dancing competition (Griffiths 1988). This was an acceptable activity in the eyes of the other 'mature' girls so they could talk about it more openly. For a while at least it put GFS in the spotlight and made it seem like an exciting place to go.

There was a pleasant, caring atmosphere at GFS, rather like a big family, and it did create space for girls to meet together and take part in activities without interference from boys. In spite of the wide age range, there was scope for the older girls to pursue their adolescent interests, such as the disco-dancing, as well as joining in with the younger girls. The two women in charge obviously tried to give the girls opportunities to develop their own particular talents and interests. I found it interesting that these women had very similar aims to many feminist youth workers, although they approached their work with girls from a different, that is, a religious angle.

(ii) Air Cadets In contrast to this supportive all-female environment, two of the 'CB' group, Elaine and Lorraine, followed later by Carol (big group) were pioneers because they were among the first girl members of the local Air Cadets. This was certainly a non-traditional interest, and (to me) a somewhat surprising choice for these girls who were among the most fashionable of the 'mature' girls. However, they were extremely enthusiastic about the activities, as Elaine described, 'You can go at rifle range, you can do engines, radar and radio.... You do all sorts of stuff. It's a good laugh really'.

There were 12 girls in the group and about 60 boys. The group was affiliated to the Royal Air Force (RAF) although it met in the local Territorial Army centre. Members paid 10p a week subs, and took part in a variety of courses which led to exams (rather like the St. John's Cadets) as Elaine explained:

It's just like RAF you see. You start from t'bottom and work up. When you go down there you're in initial training flight. That's what Carol were in but she's passed her first exam so she's a First Class Cadet now ... and then there's a Second Class Cadet and then there's Leading. I'm a Leading Cadet. Then there's Staff Cadet and then you just get into higher ranks.

Although Elaine talked about the group at great length and with obvious enthusiasm, I wondered at first if she and the other girls' main interest in going was to meet boys, especially as I knew that she and Carol both went out with boys from the Cadets. Elaine's description of how they joined the group did suggest that the social side might have been the initial reason for their interest:

Well we went to RAF Finingley you see, and I took me cousin Jane camping there and we had a right good time an' that talking to all these RAF blokes, so we went down to, um, recruitment office in town and they told us about t'cadets.

Even if there was an element of wanting to meet boys involved, it seemed to be an added bonus rather than the major reason why the girls kept on going. The girls never talked about the boys in the group unless I asked, but they did talk unprompted about the activities:

Carol We do all sorts. We're going to Creighton next week on like an adventure trip sort of thing wi'em.

Elaine ....Airmanship, things you're supposed to fly, er, First Aid, and skiing when you get some snow.

From the way the girls talked about the group I felt that they took the activities seriously. Both girls wanted to join the RAF after they left school, Elaine as an air-traffic controller, and Carol in the WRAF or as a secretary. The girls needed to be genuinely dedicated in order to continue with what sounded like arduous training exercises on the weekend 'adventure trip', as Elaine described:

We'll probably have to walk to Fuller Rocks which is about nine miles, then go out to the airway ... and you have to go jogging on a night, about a three mile run but we all walk it (laughs) ... You do all sorts of stuff. It's a good laugh really.

The girls also had to overcome the initial opposition they faced from the men who ran the Cadets. They were fighting a battle to become 'official': girls were not yet able nationally to be full members of the Air Cadets. Until that rule was changed they would not be allowed to fly or wear a uniform. So although the girls were allowed unofficially to go to Air Cadets, take part in the classes and move up the ranks - a big step in itself as they had at first been classified as canteen ladies - their membership was still only partial, was on different terms from the boys and barred them from one of the main purposes of joining, learning to fly. Their situation was unsatisfactory, but it nevertheless represented a considerable achievement and the girls were determined to continue.

(iii) St. John's Ambulance Cadets Many girls from Barnsdale High were members of the St. John's Cadets which met in Millbrook one evening a week, including Marilyn and Martine, Lizzy and Jill. I felt that part of the appeal of the Cadets was that the girls could legitimately go into town at night, which many of them would not normally have been allowed to do, especially in winter. As Marilyn explained, 'It starts at 7 o'clock but we usually go down and mess about in town first'.

146

Although the Cadets admitted girls and boys, and classes were mixed, evenings started in single-sex groups. The groups then split up according to how advanced they were; for example, beginners went to a basic First Aid course, and after passing an exam in this could go on to a more specialised course, rather like the Air Cadets. On the evening I went, girls were going to Home Nursing or Motorcycling if they had already passed the basic First Aid course. Those who had passed the first exam could wear a uniform, but this seemed to be a mixed blessing: most of the girls wore jeans, and Lizzy told me that she would rather wear her own clothes than the uniform. This was a contrast to the girls in the Air Cadets, who saw the acquisition of a uniform as a major goal which would mark their full membership status.

Martine and Marilyn were still beginnners and I went with them to the First Aid class, where there were six girls and five boys. In contrast to lessons at school, the girls were generally more forthcoming than the boys, and the woman instructor addressed more statements and questions to the girls. This may partly have been because she saw first aid as a female activity, akin to nursing. Certainly, that was the main reason Marilyn gave for belonging to the group: she wanted to be a nurse, like her mother, and saw the classes as useful preparation.

However, it seemed to me that the St. John's Cadets provided a social activity, like a youth club, as much as a place where young people went because they were seriously interested in first aid. There was a pleasant, friendly atmosphere, with a curious mixture of formality and informality. Girls seemed to have a far better chance of taking an equal part than they did at an ordinary youth club. The popularity of St John's Cadets among 'mature' girls such as Lizzy and Jill as well as 'younger seeming' girls like Marilyn and Martine suggested that the club had a wide appeal.

Dancing

Dancing was a favourite activity among the young women in my research. Many of them had been to dancing classes - ballroom, tap or ballet - when younger, but by the age of 13 most had transferred their interest to dancing at discos or at youth clubs. This was just one of the ways in which childhood interests were being transformed into aspects of female youth culture (Griffiths 1988).

Discos were one of the most popular leisure activities among the young women. Given the lack of other places to go locally, it was hardly surprising that they were always 'packed out'. Angela

McRobbie (1984) draws a contrast between the 'respectable' city discos and subcultural or punk discos. In my research, a similar contrast existed between the school discos and those held at the local working men's club. Discos were also held at some of the local youth clubs.

Because school discos were organised and supervised by teachers, they were regarded as 'safe' places for girls; even girls who hardly ever went out were allowed to go. However, because of their respectable image they were considered 'boring' by most young people, and were eventually cancelled because of poor attendance. In contrast, 'thousands' went to the discos at Barnsdale Club every other Friday night for young people between 13 and 18 years old. The popularity of these discos actually made dancing difficult; this was both a cause of some complaint from the girls and the reason for the good atmosphere which attracted them in the first place.

One of the main attractions of the Barnsdale Club disco was that it provided young women with a 'real night out', as one of them described it, rather than another evening hanging around the streets with nowhere to go. The girls could get dressed up in their most fashionable clothes, which they normally had few opportunities of wearing. A mixture of styles was accommodated, from mainstream to subcultural, and the discos were popular with both Black-Caribbean and white girls. Some girls were into punk; whilst their appearance had to be toned down at school, they could appear at their most outrageous at the disco. Others adopted styles of dress linked to popular film and television series about dance, ranging from *Saturday Night Fever* to *Fame* and *Flashdance.* What links these diverse styles, as Angela McRobbie argues (1984), is that they provide non-traditional images for girls as active and independent rather than passively feminine, whilst at the same time maintaining elements of romance and fantasy. The girls were given a sense of confidence by their appearance which carried over into their behaviour.

Groups of girls went together to the disco rather than with their boyfriends. For example, Marilyn and five other Black-Caribbean girls aged 13-14 all went to the disco in a big group. Unlike many of the white girls of the same age, Marilyn and her friends were not interested in boys; they went to the discos because they enjoyed dancing. Although some girls did meet boyfriends at the Barnsdale Club it was primarily a place where young women went to dance with their friends. In fact, a fundamental reason for the popularity of these discos among the girls was that, unlike the formal dances of my early adolescence, which were 'a conventon of courtship, dating, and sexual bargaining' (Mungham 1976, p.85), girls did not have to go with a boy or depend on a boy asking them to dance to enjoy themselves. This meant that, like the punk girls in Angela McRobbie's study (1984), the girls went out with the active intention of enjoying themselves, rather than with the more passive aim of being 'picked up' that Simon Frith describes (1978 p.67).

Interaction between the sexes did take place, but in a way that gave the girls far more freedom and control than in their everyday relationships with boys at school. I would argue that this was due to the present day conventions of dance culture, evident both in the attitude of independence with which young women went to the discos and in the styles of dancing themselves. Although I never visited the Barnsdale Club disco myself - I would have felt out of place in terms of age alone and regarded it as an intrusion into the girls' private lives - I did hear about what happened in some detail from the girls themselves. I also got an indication of the kind of interaction which took place when a disco was organised during the field trip to the Yorkshire Dales which I went on with some of the second years from Barnsdale High. This was rather too much like the respectable school discos for the girls' liking. Apart from the fact that adults were present, there were complaints that the room was too big and no-one would start dancing until the lights were turned down. Once under way, however, the girls started dancing with obvious enjoyment either on their own or in groups, while the boys stood at the other end of the room and watched. My fieldnotes record:

> Lesley leaping about ... Penny, Karen and Pam started doing steps (like 'Shadows' routine) ... Some boys started moving down to girls' end. It was only when a slow number was played later that a few of the girls and boys paired off.

The dance routines which some of the girls followed reminded me vividly of my own adolescence when the Twist, Madison, Mashed Potato and Shake were popuar dances. In contrast to the ballroom dances which I went to in my early teens, where I suffered agonies sitting around the edge of the wall waiting to be asked to dance (very similar to the mass-dances described by Geoff Mungham, 1976), I remember the tremendous sense of freedom I experienced when pop music started to be played at dances in the mid-6Os. My girlfriends and I could get into a circle or a long line and dance freely without worrying about having partners, as Mary Ingham also remembers (1981). We used to practise the dance routines in the lunch-hour at school (a girls' direct grant) and had great fun in this girls-only environment. When at mixed-sex dances this enjoyment of being all girls together was still strong. At the same time there was an element of showing ourselves off to the boys who would gather round to watch - as happened with the Barnsdale young people - and perhaps part of our enjoyment was in the unusual freedom this afforded us.

I felt that this double edge was present at the field trip disco. As they danced, the Barnsdale girls were obviously having fun together and seemed to some extent oblivious of the boys' presence; but when the boys moved closer the girls' dancing took on a 'courtship display' element, indicated by slightly self-conscious movements and quick glances at the boys. I would suggest both from my own experience and what the girls told me, that part of young women's enjoyment of dance is in the active yet acceptable sexual expressiveness involved, very different fom the passive wallflower syndrome of my early teens. This provides at least a temporary escape from girls' daily subordination, where any form of open sexual display, through dress or behaviour, is regarded as provocative and liable to give girls a bad reputation (Lees 1986).

Relative freedom

The picture which emerges of young working class women and leisure is a complex one. I have outlined some of the different ways that the young women in my research negotiated their own space within the context of restrictions, and according to what stage in the transition to womanhood they had reached. There was no single pattern of leisure, even among girls of the same age. Many preferred places where they could meet together and enjoy themselves without interference from boys, whether at home, 'dossing' or at groups like the Girls' Friendly Society. Others preferred the challenge of creating space in mixed-sex or predominantly male environments, such as the local youth club or Air Cadets.

In spite of cultural and ideological pressures, there was by no means a simple transition from childlike to adolescent interests or from girlfriends to boyfriends. The girls often combined home-based and outside interests, or traditionally feminine with non-traditional activities. Girls with extensive home responsibilities and unemployed young women experienced most pressure to conform to traditional female roles. This was true regardless of ethnic background. These young women suffered from isolation and a contracting rather than widening of opportunities as they got older.

However, the young women generally retained a positive approach in spite of often considerable restrictions on their leisure time. Most held traditional views about the future: marriage and motherhood were taken for granted. They saw adolescence as a period of relative freedom, a time to enjoy themselves and 'have fun' before they settled down. As Vicky said, 'I don't want to get tied down at 16. I fully intend to enjoy my life to the limit before that happens'.

8 Transition from girlfriends to boyfriends?

As girls move into adolescence, they not only experience bodily changes, they become sexual beings. Girls are also heavily sexualised and eroticised (Walkerdine 1990, Thorne 1993), particularly in the media, although at the same time there is often a 'moral panic' around the expression of girls' sexuality, and it is often denied in some arenas such as schools (Holly 1989, Wolpe 1988). Such cultural contradictions make this a difficult time for young women, especially as double standards still often prevail for boys.

Finding boyfriends, dropping girlfriends

The cultural and ideological pressures on girls to get a boyfriend are enormous and have been well documented (McRobbie 1978a & 1978b, Griffin 1981 & 1985). For instance Christine Griffin writes,

> Getting a boyfriend was seen as proof of young women's 'normal' heterosexuality and more 'grown-up' femininity. (Griffin 1985a p.59)

Within this context of 'compulsory heterosexuality' (Rich, 1980), to continue close relationships with girls without a corresponding interest in boys might be regarded as abnormal or deviant. As mentioned earlier in the book, positive role models for young gay women are still lacking (Jones & Mahony 1989), although some important changes are taking place in this area (Cooper 1989, Gardner et al 1992). As well as a way of avoiding the negative designation 'lez', often used as a term of abuse (Mahony 1985), finding a steady boyfriend may also be a way of protecting a girl's reputation from the label 'slag' (Lees 1986).

152

One way in which heterosexuality may be presented as the norm is through the media. Angela McRobbie's analysis of *Jackie* (1978b), a magazine for young women, shows that:

> the stories consist of isolated individuals, distrusting even their best friends and in search of fulfilment only through a partner ... *Jackie* stories ... elevate to dizzy heights the supremacy of the heterosexual romantic partnership. (McRobbie 1978b pp. 17 & 20)

Here the friendships between girls are undermined; young women are divided in competition with each other to get a man.

Although there are a growing number of accounts, particularly from feminist researchers, demonstrating the importance of friendships between girls (Ward 1976, McRobbie 1978a, Griffin 1985a, Aapola 1992, Naber 1992), much of the literature states that girlfriends take second place or are dropped altogether as girls start going out with boys. For example, Diana Leonard writes:

> As they grow up girls go out less with groups of girls or one girlfriend ... they go out with a boyfriend, or they stay at home ... the girls' peer groups frequently dissolve once they leave school ... At this point (mid teens) they seem often to transfer their affection to one boy ... and they may regard other girls as rivals. (Leonard 1980 pp. 80 & 81)

The model which emerges is a polarised one: girlfriends or boyfriends. The two are seen as incompatible, and inevitably the boyfriends win in the end - just like the *Jackie* stories. However, there are some important differences in emphasis between these studies. Some accounts, usually those written in the 1970s, state that girls drop their girlfriends unquestioningly. For example, Trisha McCabe writes:

> Once the steady appears girls ... accept that girlfriends must be abandoned. As *Jackie* says, 'Your best friend will just have to accept that she has to take a back seat - invite her round on the night you wash your hair.' The girls' 'voluntary' abandonment of their own interests is always lived through the ideology of femininity and it is always over-determined by romance. (McCabe 1980, p.127)

and in a similar vein, Dorothy Hobson writes:

> When they began 'courting', they (the women) abandoned their spare time activities and their girlfriends. There is an acceptance that women 'give up' their freedom, there was no sign of assertion

of their right to continue their own leisure activities. (Hobson 1980, p.137)

The picture which comes across is that girls are passive victims of ideological pressures. The suggestion is that, even when young women plan to keep their girlfriends, they will eventually succumb to pressures to drop them, or at worst accept this unquestioningly, through a total endorsement of the cultures of femininity and romance.

In contrast other studies, some more recent (Griffin 1985a, Naber 1992), present the process as more complex. Whilst the final outcome may be the same - that is, boyfriends eventually take over from girlfriends - girls do not drop their girlfriends without some resistance. For example, Christine Griffin stresses:

Most young women are well aware of the threat posed by 'deffing out' to supportive female friendships and feminine cultures in 'leisure' and the school. They take steps to avoid the loss of these collective female networks. (Griffin 1981 p.8)

Diana Leonard notes a strategy by which girls resist the breakup of their friendship groups:

Should one girl start seeing too much of one boy she was drawn back into the group by her friends ridiculing her choice, by their ignoring her (e.g. by not calling for her), or by their whispering about her in front of her. (Leonard 1980 p.80)

This process of inclusion or exclusion has already been noted in terms of other behaviour, particularly at school, and can be seen as part of the larger process of defining 'sameness' (Nilan 1991, Bjerrum Nielsen & Rudberg 1992). Pauline Naber (1992), in her study of young women's friendships in the Netherlands, stresses that the transition from girlfriends to boyfriends is not inevitable or irreversible. At the end of *Typical Girls?* Christine Griffin lists a number of positive strategies, such as two-timing or taking 'blokes for a ride' (Griffin 1985a p.192), which girls adopt to resist the pressures to 'get a man' and abandon their girlfriends. Young women here are presented as taking a direct and active role in their own lives.

In my research, I expected to find a relatively unproblematic transition from girlfriends to boyfriends. I was surprised to find considerable evidence of the kind of resistance illustrated above and, unlike most previous studies, friendships between girls being largely maintained alongside relationships with boys. In the rest of this chapter I shall describe and elaborate on the strategies the girls I worked with used to keep their girlfriends. The pressures on young women to 'break friends' are undoubtedly strong - all the studies are agreed on this - so I shall also highlight what causes those pressures and at what stages they are strongest.

Ages and stages

Girls' relationships with boys can be seen as divided into clear stages, according to their age and how well they know them. From 'going round with' a boy, usually in a mixed-sex group at the age of about 12 onwards (or earlier in American studies, Best 1983, Thorne 1993) girls 'progress' to the more clearly delineated 'going out with' a boy from about 14 years old, and from there to more regular boyfriends. In West Yorkshire more serious relationships with boys which might lead to engagement were known as 'courting'; 'going steady' is often used as an alternative term. I use the term 'progress', because as Diana Leonard explains,

> there is a sense that the stages and types of relationship passed through are 'achieved abilities', with each subsequent relationship more 'advanced' than the last, (Leonard 1980 p.72)

the final goal being marriage. In practice, as Leonard points out, the progression is often not so straightforwardly linear, but that is the 'model' within which the girls may operating. In my own research the young women were very clear about the boundaries which existed between one stage and the next. Angela McRobbie describes how these stages are exploited by magazines like *Jackie* and by advertising in general:

> The whole range of consumer goods directed at female youth is intricately sub-divided into 'phases' and 'stages'. Not surprisingly then the girls who are the subjects of this ideological commodity-based offensive do operate within these categories. (McRobbie 1978b p.99)

The implication here is that girls are passive recipients of cultural pressures, inexorably pushed along the road to marriage. McRobbie actually goes on to demonstrate how the girls, whilst largely taking for granted that they would end up getting married, actually used the stages to keep control in relationships with boys and to maintain their friendships with their girlfriends.

Studies of younger girls show the strength and closeness of friendships between girls persisting alongside boyfriends (McRobbie 1978a, Lees 1986), and I found this to be the case in my own research. At this stage, boyfriends posed little threat to the friendships between girls.

Most of the 12-14 year-old girls either went out with groups of girlfriends in the evenings or in mixed-sex groups. The mixed groups were usually two single-sex peer groups who started to hang around together, a pattern reported in other studies of early adolescence (Ward 1976, Leonard 1980). The mixed group was at first just an extension of the all-girl group. The ritual of the girls calling for each other was still maintained, and the boys were something of an afterthought:

> Mandy   There's about, normally about ten of us, about five girls and a few boys ... and they (the boys) say meet them at a certain place and you'd go in at a certain time.
>
> Elaine   You don't consider them as boyfriends really. They're just good mates.
>
> Carol   Have a good laugh with 'em ... We meet them in town every Saturday and go round in a big gang. About ten of us ... Usually go and sit in Pilkington's and have a coffee. (laughs)

What made the girls mentioned above slightly untypical was that they followed non-traditional interests (CB radio and Air Cadets), and they met the groups of boys through these. It was from these mixed-sex groups that the first boyfriends came, rather than an individual girl meeting an individual boy, as I had assumed. For example, when I asked Karen, 'How did you meet him?' she replied, 'Just went round with him' and this was typical of other girls too.

I also assumed that when the girls started talking about having a boyfriend, that this meant going out with a boy on an individual basis. The girls soon made it clear that I was jumping a stage. As Pam said, 'I didn't go out with him, I just sort of went with him'. Having a boyfriend to these girls usually meant being nominally attached to a boy within the group, but still hanging around with the rest of the group, as Janette explained:

> It happens that if someone's got a boyfriend from one class and then all her friends have got people who they could go with even if they're not going out with them, they all gather together and go out

somewhere on a night, to a disco or to the park or something and meet there.

Relationships with boys formed through these mixed-sex groups were very brief, lasting from one night to two or three weeks at most. I found it hard to keep up with the girls' boyfriends, they changed so quickly. Speedy turnover of boyfriends is something that I remember vividly from that stage too. These temporary attachments to boys were a great contrast to the intense, long-lasting friendships between the girls themselves. The girlfriends formed what John Ward calls a 'social anchor' (1976 p.53), a stable point in the ever-shifting configuration of boyfriends.

There was a sense in which the girls were keeping a deliberate distance in relationships with boys, 'trying out' several before they felt prepared to get more involved with one, as Janette explained, 'before you do (go out with a boy), got to decide whether they're right for you first'. A strategy which helped the girls do this was boyfriend swopping which I experienced myself during early adolescence. Going round in mixed-sex groups meant that the girls could actually rotate boyfriends until they had all gone round wth all the boys in the group. One group of girls all liked a particular boy, and virtually passed him round from one to the other, as Vicky explained:

> I think it were Karen she used to like him and that, and she asked him to come to Bankside, and then everyone got to like him you know Elaine and Carol and that we got to like him, and they all got to like him, and then Carol and Elaine had got their own sort of boyfriends and then Karen sort of like went off with him a bit, and then I were left on my own - going out with each other now.

Boyfriend swopping enabled the girls to keep control over their relationships with boys. They could compare notes amongst themselves about the boys, and this was important in some cases: for example, to warn each other about which boys 'tried it on' and about which boys were 'boasters' (Wilson 1978 p.69) as in the following case:

> Carol Well, I didn't really like him anyway cos he used to lie a lot. He used to say he was going into RAF and he hasn't got in yet. He used to say loads of things didn't he?
> Both He lied to everyone.
> Elaine He said he'd got 200 quid from the Motorcross. And nearly every lass from Cadets gone out with him. (laughs)
> VG And did he tell the same stories to everybody?

Carol   Yeah ... he said he had a 36O bike and he only had a 1OO, and he says his Dad won't let him ride it, but we goes, 'Come down to Cadets on it,' but he never did, did he?

It obviously took some time for the girls to work out that the boy was spinning yarns, but once he started repeating the same stories to each girl, they sussed it out by comparing notes, and then his bluff was called.

The picture which emerged from this stage was very different from the usual stereotype, perpetrated by girls' magazines and popular belief, that girls compete with each other for boys, and fall out with their friends because they both like the same boy. I found that this might happen between different girls who were not friends, but between girlfriends there was a cooperative supportive approach, as exemplified at this stage by the boyfriend swopping, and later in a very different way, by a strict code of practice not to poach each other's boyfriends, as I shall describe.

Boyfriend swoppping not only enables girls to keep control in relationships with boys, it also means that girls can keep control of each others' behaviour as well. Several studies (Measor & Woods 1984, Lees 1986, Nilan 1991) describe the way that girls reinforce sameness in terms of appropriate sexual behaviour too, expressing disapproval of over-sexual appearance and behaviour by warnings, name-calling ('slag' or 'tart') and at worst exclusion from the group. This 'policing of the boundaries' as Llewellyn (1980) calls it, can occur between girls who are not friends as part of other aggressive behaviour, but it is only likely to have an effect if it takes place between friends.

'Going out with' : foursomes and chaperoning

By the age of 14, many girls are still hanging around with boys in mixed-sex groups rather than going out with a particular boy, and some girls are not mixing with boys at all, but only seeing their girlfriends, so there is considerable variation, or what Barrie Thorne calls 'uneven transition' (Thorne 1993 p.147). At Barnsdale, there were differences between the younger-seeming and 'mature' girls, and also some ethnic differences as mentioned earlier. For example, the Black-Caribbean girls were most scathing about the white girls' preoccupation with boys.

For those girls who did have boyfriends, relationshps with boys were sometimes longer lasting than they had been the previous year. For instance, Elaine had had the same boyfriend for three months. Some of the girls were beginning to go out individually with a boy on occasions, though still meeting in the mixed group too, as Vicky described:

> We usually go round together, but now and again if there's something good on at t'pictures, we usually go there or something like that.

Elaine painted a similar picture of where she might go with her boyfriend, 'Well, sometimes we went up to his house, and sometimes we just went out for a walk, went to t'pictures, swimming, stuff like that'. Outings were not particularly exotic, because these young people had very little money, and there were few activities for their age group.

I had to be careful not to assume that seeing a boy meant the same as going out with him on an individual basis. For example, Carol said that she saw her boyfriend four times a week. However, on closer questioning, it emerged that she rarely went out with him alone. She either saw him in a large group, or more usually in a foursome:

> cos Elaine knows him as well, cos she's been out with him, and she's going out with a lad now as well, who is his friend sort of, so we can go round together ... and Karen, her boyfriend Wayne, if we see her, we sometimes go round with her, so we still see schoolmates.

There is still the sense in Carol's description of the close-knit mixed group, where girls and boys swopped partners. Foursomes of this kind were a frequent pattern, and usually a way in which the girls were able to maintain their close girlfriendships too.

However, in one or two cases, the foursome was founded more on the boys' friendships than the girls'. For example, Janette told me:

> And now I go round with him and his friend Alan ... we go to each other's houses and to the park and up to this girl called Christine up Heyton ... and to town sometimes.

Christine was not one of Janette's usual friends, and she did not see her outside the foursome. Some studies report that going out with a boy and his friends seriously undermines girls' own friendships and interests (Griffin 1985a, Lees 1986). In my research, I did not find this happening to any great degree: Janette still saw her close girlfriends at other times, whilst one of the older girls, Jenny, enjoyed extending her friendship group in this way:

We see a lot of other lasses, girls, through going out with these boys ... you kind of chum up with some others because they happen to be around at that time.

Nevertheless, I recognise that there may be a real danger for some girls of dropping, or being forced to drop, their own friends. It is certainly mentioned as a feature of married women's lives (Naber 1992, O'Connor 1992) when a couple's friends may be based round the man's rather than the women's friendships. However, Naber stresses that this does not undermine the importance of friendships to women, although it may change the composition of their friendship networks.

At Barnsdale, some of the girls did their best to resist this possible breakdown of their friendship groups by adopting a strategy I shall call 'chaperoning'. For example, even when girls went out with a boy alone, they sometimes started the evening with their girlfriends and met them again later, as Lizzy told me, 'We set off together ... (after) half an hour we'd leave 'em to go off to us boys, then we'd come back ... to go home'. This was true of the fifth year girls (Year 11) too, even when they had regular boyfriends; for example, Jenny and her friend Sarah:

Jenny   When I'm going to meet him she walks me, don't you?
Sarah   I walk around until he comes and then we might chat a bit -
Jenny   Then she goes.
Sarah   - and then I go missing.

Like boyfriend swopping, 'chaperoning' enabled the girls to maintain their close girlfriendships, and to assert solidarity and control in relationships with boys. The girls were able to keep their pattern of calling for each other, and to compare notes about what had happened with their boyfriends afterwards. The fact that whatever happened when the girls were alone with their boyfriends would be reported back to their girlfriends immediately afterwards may have acted as something of a check on the boys, as well as the girls' behaviour.

It is important to stress that even the girls who were beginning to pair off with boys or go out in foursomes still saw their girlfriends separately. Any reduction in time spent with girlfriends was largely due to the onset of winter, and the fact that many of the girls' parents would not let them go out at night with just girls once the evenings were darker. Without necessarily wanting to, the girls therefore found themselves in mixed company more often in winter than in summer.

By the age of 15 or 16, some girls have regular boyfriends and these relationships may start to last longer. In my research, for instance, Sarah (Year 11) had gone out with a boy for five months. Two of the girls had been going out with their boyfriends all year and were deemed to be 'courting'. There seems to be general agreement in the literature that a steady boyfriend or courtship constitutes the greatest threat to girls' friendships (McCabe 1980, Hobson 1980, Leonard 1980, Griffin 1985a). I found that while courtship did pose a serious threat, regular boyfriends did not, and the girls clearly differentiated between the two stages.

Even when the girls were going out regularly with a boy, most of them saw their girlfriends frequently, not just in school, but in the evenings too. This happened particularly when the girls lived close to each other; for example, Sarah and Jenny saw each other every night, as Sarah said, 'I'm always popping round to her (Jenny's) house ... I see her more than I used to see me boyfriend didn't I?' As these two girls were part of a larger group of seven white girls who went round with each other all the time at school, there was no question of fitting their girlfriends into hair-wash night (as *Jackie* suggests) for most of these girls; boys were fitted into a busy social life with their girlfriends rather than the other way round. Their leisure activities seemed much closer to the male pattern described by Annie Whitehead, who writes about men in rural Herefordshire:

> Boys and men do not give up the old pattern of going out with their mates when they are courting, but often reserve special nights - Friday and Saturday - for their girlfriends. They spend the other evenings drinking with their peers. (Whitehead 1976 p.195)

The girls too had clearly allocated girls' times and boys' times. School and most of the weekends were for girlfriends. On Saturdays, those who did not have Saturday jobs would go round the shops together; Saturday nights were spent with their boyfriends (if they had one), and Sunday nights they would all meet at the local chippy. The Sunday night meeting anticipated the more institutionalised 'Friday night girls' night' which developed after they had left school.

Holidays were particularly good for seeing their friends, as Jenny explained:

> When it's holidays you see we - in an afternoon we don't see none of us boyfriends, and so through all t'holidays we've got all t'daytime with, you know, all us mates, and so we see a lot of each

161

other, more in holidays don't we, and at weekends, during Sunday, Sa'day.

Boyfriends were definitely restricted to evenings, but some evenings were for girlfriends too, as I have said. Even when the girls were going out with their boyfriends in the evening, they often chaperoned each other (see previous section), so girls' times could spill over into boys' times.

Talking about what had happened with their boyfriends was something the girls looked forward to, as Sarah described:

> (laughing) As soon as we come up to school in t'morning we're all walking up going, 'Oh! This happened and this happened' aren't we? ... Especially after that party on Saturday, all t'gossip were flying round! (claps hands)

Sarah made it clear that the pattern of calling for each other on the way to school was still being maintained, and introduced the point that the girls sometimes saw each other on a 'boyfriends' evening', for example at parties. Talking through what had happened actually seemed to add to the excitement, as though experiences with boys were incomplete until they had been relived with their girlfriends. Talking about their relationships with boys was just one part of a general sharing of experiences, which provided the girls with emotional feedback and mutual support, as I have already described.

Confiding and comparing notes may have helped build up trust and loyalty, and prevent the rivalry between friends over boys which *Jackie* and other magazines present as commonplace. Like Sue Lees (1986), I did not find girlfriends competing for men to any great extent. Indeed, an informal code of practice had evolved among some of the girls to prevent this occurring:

> Sarah That's never happened!
> Jacky Not yet!
>   (All laugh)
> Jenny Yeah, we've all got different tastes ... if we knew that someone liked him (the same boy) tho', we wouldn't go flirting or owt would we?
> Sarah Oh no, no we wouldn't would we?
>   (All laugh)

The girls' laughter and self-mocking suggests that they were well aware of the possibility of rivalry, and they went on to describe how this did sometimes occur between them and girls outside their friendship groups:

> Sarah There are some people that flirt with your boyfriend and it gets you very mad.
> Jenny Yeah, it makes you mad.
> Sarah But we won't go into details (laughs).
> Jenny No!

Courtship presented a far stronger threat to the girls' friendships, and the girls were aware of this:

> Jacky If you've been going out with a boy for a long time, and you don't see them (your friends) quite often, they just reject you.
> Jenny We don't tho'. No.
> Jacky No, but you know, other people do, other groups.

As with the rivalry issue, there were vehement denials that this might apply to them. There was a recognition that 'deffing out' occurred, but only among other girls. Nevertheless, there were severe tensions in this group because Marje and Tricia were courting and beginning to see less of the others. This was not fully admitted until I spoke to the girls six months after they had left school. Jenny explained how the 'girls' times' had been encroached upon, because Marje and Tricia had been seeing their boyfriends

> all t'time, they always have done. Like at dinner times, soon as they could be together, they would be together. And like Dale were with Tricia practically all the time cos they had the same lessons together as well, so that's how it went. And then they'd just walk home together and then we just wouldn't make any arrangements with them.

This had even impinged on the girls' day time meetings during summer holidays, as Jenny described:

> Usually over the summer, Marje and Tricia'd come down to t'park and things ... but this year it's just been me and Sue and Sarah, we were in t'park, and Julie ... with Kathy.

However, even in this case there was evidence of resistance against the breakup of the girls' friendship group. Whilst Marje had started seeing her boyfriend during the day without any qualms, thereby following the more traditional pattern, Tricia had been extremely unhappy about the situation and had eventually withstood the pressures from her boyfriend to spend all her time with him. Even six months later, Tricia talked vividly and at great length about what had happened. Her description almost takes the form of a confessional statement:

> When I went out with my boyfriend I neglected me friends a lot. In the last five months (before I left school) I used to see my boyfriend every night and then friends were just out then. I hardly ever saw them at school. I got sick of that - I used to hide under the table (at dinner time) so I didn't see him didn't I? I'd have my lunch with them, and then when he'd been for his lunch and he'd come back - cos he used to go down to the chip shop - he'd come back and then he used to stand outside the common room windows, and I used to say, 'Oh, is he there? Is he there? Oh God, he's not there! If he's coming tell me, give me a shout', didn't I? ... But just before that started happening, I did used to go out and stand there, but I felt - I don't - I wanted to but I didn't, if you know what I mean, cos I thought, well I'll be seeing him tonight anyway and I won't see me friends tonight... School was friends' time and then night was boyfriend's time.

Tricia was aware that because she was encroaching on the 'girls' times', she might lose her girlfriends and felt absolutely torn between wanting to be with her boyfriend and her girlfriends, ('I wanted to but I didn't, if you know what I mean'). Tricia's eventual solution was to restore some balance in the allocation of time, so that 'School was friends' time and then night was boyfriends' time.'

Much of the motivation to see less of her boyfriend during the day came from within Tricia herself, because she valued her girlfriends and felt bad about neglecting them. There was also some teasing from the other girls to get her back into the group; as Tricia put it, 'It'd be more of a joke but to get it over', and this obviously had its effect. As Diana Leonard found (1980, quoted earlier), the girls were not going to let their friend go without a struggle. However, in Tricia's case it was less drastic for the remaining girls than it would have been had she been in a pair of best friends. As Sue said:

> Well you realised there were one missing but - but you know it didn't - it wasn't as if you were left on your own because she was gone off with her boyfriend.

I shall describe the impact of courting on a best-friend pair in the next section. In contrast to this example, it is important to stress that some girls of the same age (15-16) did not have regular boyfriends and spent their time almost entirely with their girlfriends.

After leaving school, the young women from Barnsdale went on to college (6th form college, Technical and Art college), jobs (bank clerk, secretary, shop work), Youth Training Schemes or the dole. The pressures on young women to lose touch with their girlfriends may be particularly strong at this point, especially when the daily contact at school has gone (Griffin 1985a).

Diana Leonard (1980) found that this is when a steady boyfriend is most likely to take over from girlfriends. However, my research indicates the persistence of many previous friendships, particularly between best friends who lived close to each other. Large groups of friends were harder to maintain and were being replaced not by boyfriends, but by the formation of new friendship groups among young women at work and college. My findings accord most closely to those of Kris Beuret and Lynn Makings (1986), who describe a group of hairdressers with steady boyfriends whose friendships with other young women were still important. In my study, friendships between girls also existed alongside regular boyfriends.

Sarah, Jenny and Jacky had kept in touch most easily because they had moved together to the local sixth form college, and were therefore still seeing each other every day. Sarah and Jenny were still seeing each other most evenings too, in spite of the fact that Sarah now had a boyfriend whom she had met at college. Sarah's reason for not seeing her boyfriend that much was school work:

Sarah Me school work comes before him ... I don't bother seeing him on a night really, unless we're going out somewhere, and that's it.

VG And how often might that be?

Sarah Not very often ... I don't see him every night at all.

Jenny She sees me more than him (laughs).

Sarah Yeah, I'm round at her house more than I see him. I don't know, it suits me better cos then I haven't got an excuse to say, oh well, I'll put off me homework till tomorrow and go off and see him. I just don't do that, you see I have to do me homework now.

In spite of Sarah's protestations about homework, she did not use this as an excuse for seeing less of Jenny. The two girls were obviously still following the same pattern of seeing each other as they had done the previous year. It seemed as if Sarah did not want to become too serious about this boy. One possible reason for this was that he was

Black-Caribbean, and Sarah was having a lot of trouble at home because her mother was unhappy about the relationship.

I would suggest that another reason for Sarah's not seeing her boyfriend very often in the evening was the less sex-divided atmosphere of the sixth form college. The girls mentioned that one of the things they liked best about the college was that, unlike school, they could 'get friendly with lads without anybody making silly jokes about it'. Girls and boys mixed more naturally in the day, without necessarily being girl and boyfriend. Even at night, mixed-sex groups were informal: parties were frequent occurrences, and girls were not expected to go with a partner. All this added up to a very different atmosphere from the polarisation of school where, as Tricia had so vividly described, you were either with your girlfriends or with your boyfriends. The girls who had gone to Technical and Art college also valued the informality and felt that the pressures to courtship were much diminished.

Paradoxically, Beuret and Makings (1986) suggest that the 'freer' culture of college life may lessen the importance of all-women groups as young women mix more freely with men. This raises the important question of whether a strong female friendship group depends on, or thrives best in, a polarised situation. However, age and class background may be crucial factors. The students in Beuret and Makings's study were aged 19 to 24 and middle class; whereas the young women at college in my study were 16-17 years old and working class, and there were no signs at this stage that their friendships with each other were being undermined.

The 'developing primacy of the heterosexual couple' (Griffin 1981 p.8) posed more of an obvious threat to the friendships between girls who had gone straight from school to work. Marje, who had been courting since before she left school, was now very much following the stereotyped pattern, seeing her boyfriend 'nearly every night ... We mostly meet in each other's homes but we go out sometimes'. She only rarely saw her old schoolfriends, and only occasionally went out with girls from work. However, some of the young women who were now at work were still strenuously resisting this pattern. For example, Tricia who was also courting, said,

> I used to see my boyfriend every night ... but I just got bored with it, just arguing all the time, so I don't see him so much now. We just see each other at weekends now, and maybe one night or two nights in a week ... it leaves me time to do stuff in my spare time.

The same had been true for Sue: 'Used to see him every night'. She had now finished with her boyfriend, and both she and Tricia were going out with girlfriends again.

In another case, Anne's relationship with a boy had nearly caused the breaking up of her best friendship with Michelle, as Michelle described:

> Anne was sort of going out - she had a boyfriend right, and I didn't, so she'd be going out with her boyfriend at t'weekend and I didn't want to stay in, so I phoned another friend and we started sort of going out at weekends and sort of saw her more than I did Anne. And then - I don't know - I didn't get on right well with this other girl ... sort of fell out with her and I came back to Anne.

This was the closest I found to the example of 'deffing out' given by Christine Griffin (1981 & 1985a), where best friends take second place to boyfriends. The emotional impact on Michelle of Anne's courting was much stronger than Tricia's had been on the large group. However, Anne and Michelle had not split up for good. When they realised that they missed each other's company, they made things up, as Michelle explained:

> I see her twice a week now usually ... Anne'll come down here on Tuesday, and I'll go by on a Thursday or other way round. We usually just stay in, watch a bit of telly and talk.

Although both Anne and Michelle were going out with boys now, they were retaining time for each other, and they were determined not to split up again.

For the young women at work, there were not so many opportunities to socialise in the day as there had been at school. However, there was evidence that the girls were still maintaining time for their closest previous friends and also making new friends at work. Apart from the kind of arrangement Anne and Michelle had made, groups of friends tended to go out together on a Friday night, and see their boyfriends on Saturday evening. Michelle did this as well as seeing Anne individually during the week: 'I might go out with him on a Saturday and go out with them (the girls) on a Friday'. Tricia also reported this Friday night outing. According to Tricia:

> All the girls I know, they all have a - we go out with each other on Friday night, and then Saturday night is with your boyfriend.

This certainly seemed to be the local custom for young working class women. It was most noticeable that the streets in town on Friday night were full of goups of young women, all dressed up, arms linked, talking and laughing together and off to have a good time. They presented a strong, positive image and contradicted my expected finding that female peer groups would disappear when the girls left school. 'Lasses nights', as they were known, are mentioned in other research (Westwood 1984, Beuret and Makings 1986), which suggests that this is a widespread custom for young working-class women.

However, keeping in touch with girlfriends may not be so easy for young unemployed women, as Christine Griffin stresses (1985a). For example, Mandy had been unemployed since leaving school. In the end she moved away from the area to try and find work. Her best friend Pauline was upset that they might lose touch. Neither of these young women had boyfriends.

Affirmation of friendship

Contrary to my expectation and the findings of much previous research, the friendships between the girls in my study did not break down, but were largely maintained alongside boyfriends. As I have mentioned, I did not always ask the right questions, and sometimes made faulty assumptions about the degree to which boyfriends might be taking over from girlfriends, but the girls were always ready to put me right.

It is important not to underestimate the very real pressures the girls face to 'break' friends. I have identified strategies which the girls I worked with used to prevent the break up of their female friendship groups. For the younger girls, the mixed-sex groups and boyfriend swopping enabled them to keep control in their first superficial and temporary relationships with boys. Whilst boyfriends came and went, girlfriends provided a secure reference point with whom experiences could be shared and assessed. As they got older and went out with boys more individually, foursomes and chaperoning still enabled the girls to see their girlfriends. The main danger at this stage was the boys' friendship groups taking precedence over the girls'.

Courtship presented one of the strongest threats to the girls' friendships, especially after they had left school and did not necessarily see their friends during the day. But by means of girls' times and for those in work the more institutionalised girls' nights, many of the young women maintained close relationships with girlfriends. I was particularly heartened by the reassertion of friendship which occurred, as Pauline Naber also found (1992), when girls who had split up or nearly split up with their girlfriends realised the importance of what they were losing, and renegotiated a relationship which persisted alongside their boyfriends. This seemed to me to be a real affirmation of the strength and value of friendship between women.

The girls who stayed within the polarised culture of school or work faced greater pressures on their friendships than those young women who went to college. At college the girls gained access to a less rigid culture where, for a time at least, the sexes were not in such strong opposition, and it was easier to maintain both girl and boyfriends, and to have boys as friends without the pressures to exclusive courtship.

My emphasis throughout this chapter has been a positive one, reflecting the girls' attitudes themselves. Most of the girls I worked with held traditional views about the future: they took it for granted that they would get married and have children. Nevertheless they still hoped to have women friends. How far they would be able to achieve this in practice I can only speculate. I should like to end on a hopeful note by giving the last word to one of the young women. Jenny, of whom it was said by one of her friends, 'never loses touch with anybody', may have derived some of her sense of the importance of women friends from her mother:

> Me Mum says that it's best to (keep in touch with your friends), cos she tried to, and she lost contact with her schoolfriends, and she were you know a bit unhappy about it ... but luckily she has now (met up again) with two of them, and it's two of her best ones ... and she won't break up again, so it's all right.

9 Keeping together, keeping strong

Close friendships and positive strategies

In general, a strong positive picture of friendships between young women has emerged from the research. As other studies have found (McRobbie 1978a, Griffin 1985a, Aaopla 1992, Naber 1992, Thorne 1993), these friendships are close and supportive, characterised by trust and loyalty. Talking, especially confiding with a close friend, is central to the relationships. Enjoyment of each others' company, or 'having a laugh', is also an important component. Friends are often inseparable, and physical closeness such as hugging or 'grooming' is commonplace.

Many findings from general studies of friendship are also confirmed by this study. First and foremost, friendship can be seen as a vital means of establishing a positive self-identity and enhancing self-worth. This may be particularly important among school children who do not want to be seen to be alone (Davies 1982), and among adolescents who are going through a period of intense change and need support from friends (Ward 1976, Duck 1983). Other general characteristics of friendship, such as reciprocal obligations and mutual support (Allan 1979, Kutnick 1988) are also evident in girls' relationships. Whilst these may in part have a pragmatic basis, the intensity of feeling between girlfriends is undoubtedly strong, and the caring and sharing elements of the friendships.

Friendships between adolescent girls are made within the context of a patriarchal society where women still occupy a largely subordinate position. In relation to the young women in this research, and in other studies (Griffin 1985a, Bjerrum Nielsen & Rudberg 1992, Measor & Sikes 1992, Thorne 1993), this manifests itself in terms of gender divisions at school, constraints on girls' leisure time, and pressures towards heterosexuality. More generally, friendships between girls are often devalued, and construed in stereotypical terms, such as 'shallow' or 'bitchy' (Lees 1986). In particular, those qualities which are central to young women's relationships, such as 'having a laugh' and talking, are often denigrated as evidence of girls' silliness, and made the reason for disciplinary measures at school.

Within this negative context, friendships between young women can be seen as a major way in which they maintain some degree of power and control in their lives. I have identified many positive strategies which the girls I worked with employed in order to keep their female friendships strong in different aspects of their experience. For example, the girls exhibited various forms of resistance and provided mutual support at school, ranging from helping each other with homework to talking and having fun in class. Outside school, there were various ways in which the young women found their own space, including 'dossing out' together, dancing or 'bedroom culture' (McRobbie & Garber 1976). When girls started to go out with boys on a regular basis, they kept time for their girlfriends and resisted the breakup of their friendship groups, maintaining girlfriends alongside boyfriends, unlike the findings of many previous studies (Ward 1976, Llewellyn 1980, Griffin 1985a).

These positive strategies are summarised in Figure 9.1. I have restricted the diagram to those areas on which the research focused, but it could be used as the basis for a model of young women's friendships, incorporating other elements such as family, work or the media. As Angela McRobbie and Jenny Garber wrote:

> When the dimension of sexuality is included in the study of youth subcultures, girls can be seen to be negotiating a different space, offering a different type of resistance to what at least in part can be viewed as their sexual subordination. (McRobbie & Garber 1976 p.221)

Variation in friendships

In a recent study, Sinikka Aapola (1992) sees the culture of girls' friendships as a 'special kind of youth subculture' (Aapola 1992 p.5):

> This subculture is geographically scattered, socially and historically varying, but nevertheless, it shares some common

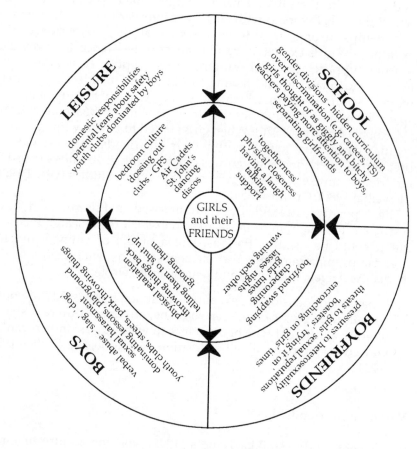

Outer circle - constraints
Inner circle - forms of resistance

Figure 9.1 Adolescent girls: positive strategies

cultural notions, such as ideals and meanings....democracy, honesty, harmony, continuity and variety. (ibid.)

I would stress variety as a crucial aspect of girls' friendships. Whilst acknowledging the other common elements mentioned here and above, I have some reservations about any model of girls' culture as identical or uniform. Like Barrie Thorne, I feel that 'terms like "culture" and "subculture" are too often used to reify contrasting images' (Thorne 1993 p. 108) in an oppositional way. What struck me particularly forcibly in my own research was the diversity of possible responses which groups of girls made to the same situation. The active role which girls play in making sense of their experience and shaping their own unique perspective has been stressed throughout the book (Anyon 1983, Connell 1987). Hence the importance of Tables 6.2 and 6.3 in identifying the wide range of possible forms of resistance to school. In Figure 9.1, the particular positive strategies employed by the young women at Barnsdale are noted, but they were mediated in different ways by the various friendship groups, and might well be different again for a different group of young women.

Although I identified common features in the young women's friendships, the variation between them was striking. At school, the girls interacted neither exclusively in close-knit peer groups (Lambart 1976, Meyenn 1980), nor in looser interaction sets (Furlong 1976, Llewellyn 1980). However, I did identify distinct groups of friends among the girls, which formed the most frequent basis for their interaction. These groups were largely but not totally bounded by school class membership. Many girls had close friends in their class and parallel friends (Aapola 1992) in other classes; these groups did not necessarily overlap.

Parallel friends were often younger and marked the division between school and out of school activities. Friends outside school were sometimes distinct and different; this largely depended on where the girls lived and what interests they pursued. Out of school friendships were particularly marked among neighbours or near neighbours, and were often of a long-standing and close nature. They also differed from school friendships in being less clearly differentiated in terms of age, race or gender, as other studies have found (Wulff 1988, Thorne 1993). Parallel friends offer young women the possibility of veering between childhood and adolescent interests, and avoiding the hurt that exclusive friendships may bring about if they break down. They also enable girls to keep more control in their relationships, and to keep a balance between closeness and independence.

Factors affecting the formation of the girls' friendships are numerous, including personality and appearance, academic ability, involvement in teenage culture and other interests, class, ethnicity and school organisation (Griffin 1985a, Wolpe 1988, Grant 1992, Thorne 1993). In my own research, no single factor accounted for a group of girls being friends, although once friendships were established, the groups defined themselves according to their sameness in certain respects (Bjerrum Nielsen & Rudberg 1992). The negotiation of sameness through inclusion and exclusion was a hallmark of the girls' interaction, as other research has indicated (Nilan 1991, Aapola 1992). Among 12-14 year-olds, the transition to adolescence was an important factor: the friendships groups could roughly be divided into 'mature' and 'younger seeming' girls, and this sometimes accounted for changes in friendships of a temporary or more permanent nature.

Size and structure of friendship groups

There is also a tendency in much of the literature to contrast girls' friendships with boys': instead of large close-knit groups, it is suggested that girls either interact in pairs of best friends and small groups of three or four (Ward 1976, McRobbie 1978a, Griffin 1985a), or large but uncohesive groups (Llewellyn 1980, Davies 1984). However, more recent studies (Lees 1986, Aapola 1992) including my own have found large cohesive groups of friends as well as smaller groups, and less interaction in best friend pairs. At Barnsdale, the size of girls' friendship groups ranged from small (three to four girls) to large (seven to eight girls). At school, the girls did not generally go round in pairs, although best friends were often part of a larger group. Best-friend interaction was more likely to occur outside school, especially when girls met in each other's houses; however, even outside school, the girls often met in larger groups.

Groups of three girls seemed the least cohesive, perhaps because of the possibility of rivalry for a dominant member's affections. Groups of four could be close or loose-knit, depending on the membership. Large groups were close and loyal in spite of their larger numbers; even though there might be a certain amount of shifting membership or changes in pairings within the group (eg. the big group in G2), the groups as a whole remained remarkably constant. The seven white girls in the fifth year (Year 11) formed the most cohesive group, perhaps because they were older and had withstood both earlier fallings out and the division into different sets as they went up the school. Age and school organisation may be crucial factors in the structure and cohesion of groups.

The structure of the groups also differed from some previous findings. Eleanor Maccoby and Carol Jacklin (1974) note:

> The fact that boys travel in larger groups (than girls) probably has considerable significance. We suspect that the size of social groups has a great deal to do with dominance patterns. Large social groups cannot so easily function without a dominance hierarchy as can small groups. (Maccoby & Jacklin 1974 p.226-7)

Maccoby and Jacklin were working on the assumption that girls interacted in smaller numbers than boys. In my research, the large groups were notable for their absence of leadership or any clear hierarchy, but this did not seem to prevent them from operating effectively as groups. This might suggest, as Robert Meyenn does, that 'equality of status is a feature of girls' peer groups' (Meyenn 1980 p.140). Sinikka Aapola (1992) also suggests that equality is an ideal that girls aspire to in their friendships, and found non-hierarchical patterns among large groups of girlfriends. However, the small groups in my study did have a hierarchical structure and clear leaders, showing that equality in girls' friendships is by no means universal, and providing a contrast to other studies which show non-hierarchical small groups (Griffin 1985a, Bjerrum Nielsen & Rudberg 1992).

Orientations to school

Unlike studies of boys (Hargreaves 1967, Lacey 1970, Willis 1977), numerous studies of girls (Griffin 1985a, Lees 1986, Wolpe 1988, and others below) have found that there is no direct correlation between academic ability, involvement in teenage culture and attitudes to school; that is, girls are not simply pro- or anti- school. Although studies which focus on low-stream or 'deviant' girls (Furlong 1976, Llewellyn 1980, Davies 1984) indicate a similar pattern to boys in some respects, even these show less cohesiveness in anti-school orientation. When looking at a spread of studies over a wider range of class, ability and race, the gender differences become more marked. In particular, high attaining nonconformists seem to be a regular feature of studies of girls at school (Lambart 1976, Delamont 1976, Meyenn 1980, Fuller 1980, Pollard 1984, Lees 1986), across a range of class and ethnic backgrounds.

This was certainly the case at Barnsdale. At 13-14 years old, some of the brightest girls academically were also the most heavily involved in teenage culture (the big and 'CB' groups). The 'CB' group were 'academic but alienated' (Lees 1986 p.123), disliking certain aspects of school life, but the big group were generally pro-school, although anxious not to be seen as too 'brainy', and not averse to misbehaving. In contrast to studies by Llewellyn (1980) and Davies (1984), many of the less academically able girls at Barnsdale (notably the loose-knit foursome) were strongly committed to school norms, a pattern also noted in some previous research (Meyenn 1980, Pollard 1984). Like Meyenn, I found the whole range of possible orientations to school among the girls, even though the majority were from a similar working class background.

The hallmark of most of the girls' interaction at school was enjoyment of each others' company, which helped to provide them with a positive reference point, and sense of achievement in their own terms (Wernersson 1992), in spite of a lack of encouragement from most teachers at the school.

Out of school activities

Considerable variation was also noted between the girls' leisure activities, even within the limited choice available. Although the girls' leisure time was constrained by domestic responsibilities or parental fears about safety, I identified many ways in which they found their own space. As with the formation of the friendships, this to some extent depended on the girls' relative maturity. For example, the younger seeming 12-14 year-olds still talked about 'playing out', whereas for the more mature girls 'dossing' was a favourite activity.

Whereas some girls favoured all-female environments such as the Girls' Friendly Society, others preferred mixed-sex groups such as the St. John's Ambulance Cadets, or the largely male Air Cadets or local youth club. This seemed to depend on a mixture of personality and interest. Dancing was enjoyed by most girls, usually at local discos.

The culture of the bedroom was not particularly evident among the girls, partly because there was a lack of privacy at home. It was most common among the Black-Caribbean girls, who experienced less pressure to go out, and older girls who had more freedom to go out on other occasions. The nearest to a subcultural interest was Citizens Band radio, which a group of girls followed. Although largely based in the girls' homes, groups of CB 'breakers' also met locally, so the girls were part of a larger network of young men and women.

Black girls

Black girls suffer from a double subordination by race and gender (Fuller 1980, Riley 1985), which may lead them to group together, particularly at school. At Barnsdale, because of the relatively small numbers of black pupils, Black-Caribbean and Indian pupils were often part of the same friendship groups, which cut across divisons of age, ability and gender. However, most black girls also had white friends, both in and out of school, as other studies have found (Wulff 1988, Phoenix 1992, Thorne 1993). Context is an important factor, and may give rise to different groupings. For example, in a school with larger numbers of black pupils (Griffiths 1982), a greater variety of mixed-ethnic groupings was evident, as well as distinct ethnic and religious groups, particularly Muslims and Sikhs.

At Barnsdale, the Rastafarian subculture was the strongest element amongst the Black-Caribbean pupils (boys and girls). Whereas the Indian girls' wearing of trousers to school seemed unproblematic, the Rastafarian headgear and hairstyles (boys' dreadlocks and large caps as well as girls' beaded styles) had caused problems vis a vis the school rules. That these were now accepted was seen as a triumph and a symbol of black identity and strength. Miss Jones, the Head, certainly saw the Black-Caribbean pupils as problematic in terms of discipline, because they were so strong in collective support. Although I rarely observed or overheard any examples of racist abuse from teachers or pupils, according to the black girls it was commonplace and something the Black-Caribbean girls countered vociferously.

Indian girls were so few in number at Barnsdale that they did not constitute a separate group, as some studies report (Amos & Parmar 1981, Brah & Minhas 1985). This might have changed since I undertook the research, with the increase in Indian families moving into the area. The two Indian girls whom I got to know best were both Sikhs; family and religious life were strong, and were kept quite separate from school life. However, this may have been because, as a white researcher, I did not find a 'way in' to their experience as Indian girls, and they may have sensed that I was bringing certain preconceptions about 'cultural conflict' to our conversations.

Another interesting factor which I did not follow up to any great extent was the contrast between those girls of mixed race who had predominantly white friends, and those who associated mainly with black girls. From what I could find out, this seemed partly dependent on which parent was white or black, and with whom the girl lived (ie. one or both parents). Ann Phoenix's research (1992) suggests that young people of mixed race may see themselves as constituting a third group, rather than identifying themselves as either white or black.

In general, the black girls in my research did not seem to experience any greater degree of restriction on their lives than the white girls, or to put it another way, all the girls regardless of ethnic background experienced considerable constraints. In fact, the black girls felt less pressure than the white girls in terms of getting a boyfriend, and enjoyed staying in with their girlfriends without feeling it was second best.

School as a context for female friendships

In this study, the school formed both the initial base for the research, and the context for many of the friendships. School provided both an enabling and a constraining context for girls' friendships; sometimes both elements were present simultaneously, and were hard to disentangle.

On the enabling side, school is a place where girls can meet and make friends; it provides a greater number of potential friends than, for example, the road where each girl lives or the local youth club. As well as giving young women the opportunity to get together, school also provides the means of reinforcing friendships, because of the daily contact both in and out of lessons. Parts of the daily routine, such as walking to and from school, become important rituals in strengthening friendships.

Whatever girls' ability or attitude to school as a place for learning, school is an important arena for young women's social lives. As Ian Birksted (1976) also found in his study of boys, lessons at Barnsdale High seemed to be fitted into the structure of girls' social interaction rather than the other way round. Even in the most formal of lessons, some kind of interaction between friends was maintained, albeit in a muted or covert form. However, although some degree of interaction between friends was managed in most lessons, and there were various ways in which girls offered accommodation or resistance to school, there was a considerable contrast between girls' behaviour in lessons and outside, for instance, in form time or at break. This was particularly noticeable among the big group in G2 who were lively and assertive during registration and out of lessons; whereas in lessons their behaviour was muted because they wanted to maintain a good reputation with the teachers (Stanley 1993).

It is hardly surprising that, for many of the girls, subjects which allowed a comfortable, largely uninterrupted social interaction between friends to continue, such as Needlework, were favoured over subjects where girls were in the minority, such as Technical Studies. Getting away from boys' abuse may have been an important part in this too. I would suggest that this may be as much of a factor in girls' decisions about options as any interest in the subject or attitude towards 'girls' or 'boys' subjects. If this is the case, then it may not be enough for schools to urge pupils not to choose subjects just because their friends are doing it, as Barnsdale did; the implications for how lessons are conducted and the forms of interaction allowed within them are obviously important. The strength and support which girls can give each other need to be capitalised on rather than undermined and fragmented.

There are other ways in which school can be seen as a constraining and limiting factor on girls' friendships. In contrast to girls' out of school experience, school organisation, that is division by age, effectively prevents girls from making or continuing friendships with girls outside their year. The pressure to same sex friendships is also strong, even in mixed-sex schools such as Barnsdale; this is so common an occurrence as to be taken for granted by most teachers. In one way, of course, this strengthens female friendships. However, at Barnsdale, it did also create a tension which the older girls reported, by preventing friendships with boys unless they were boyfriends, which led in some cases to girls having to choose between their girlfriends or their boyfriend. I speculated earlier that perhaps female friendships flourish better in such polarised situations, where gender divisions are strong, as opposed to an atmosphere where mixed-sex friendships are encouraged, such as a college. Research in a sixth form college compared to a sixth form in a school would be interesting in order to compare the kinds of friendship patterns and gender interaction in each.

Other aspects of school organisation can also have an effect. At Barnsdale, the tutor group system, whilst providing a secure reference point within the school, did make it harder for girls to make close friends in other classes. Most of the close-knit groups were totally, or at least partially, school class-based, and loyalty to the tutor group was strong. As they got older and were divided into sets for more subjects, this effect was diminished, and girls were more likely to have at least some lessons with friends from other classes. On the other hand, this made it harder for friends within the same class or tutor group to keep together during the day; temporary interaction sets were then more

179

likely to form. I was not able to observe whether the increase in setting higher up the school brought about more differentiation by ability among the girls. Certainly, among the younger classes, differentiation by perceived ability was not strong. On balance, as far as I could tell, there seemed to be both advantages and disadvantages in the organisational system in terms of friendships.

Since I undertook the research at Barnsdale, much positive action has been undertaken in schools, arising from a concern about girls' previous underachievement and a greater realisation of the detrimental effects of gender divisions in school (Whyld 1983, Whyte et al 1985, Measor & Sikes 1992, Wrigley 1992). In particular, teachers have begun to take account of the inhibiting effect which boys' participation in lessons may have on girls, and to be encouraging towards girls so that they participate more freely and with less fear of ridicule. The implications for school organisation have also been taken on board. Many schools are now realising the importance of creating some girls-only space in school or lesson time; single-sex sets are being tried, particularly in subjects where girls have traditionally been seen as weaker than boys, such as maths and science (Whyld 1983, Smail 1984, Smith 1986). Whether any of these girl-friendly initiatives can be seen to have had a direct causal effect, recent examination results in both Great Britain and the USA (Mickelson 1992, Grant 1995) have shown a gradual increase in girls' attainment, so that girls are now taking and passing more subjects than boys, and achieving higher results, at both GCSE and A-level,

The dual nature of friendships: falling out

Like the romantic friendships of previous centuries (Faderman 1981), close relationships between young women can be turbulent and stormy. 'Falling out' sometimes occurs between close friends and can have a strong emotional impact on the girls. Betrayal of trust is often mentioned as either a reason for falling out or one manifestation of a quarrel. Many studies have indicated this duality in friendships between girls (McRobbie 1978a, Griffin 1985a, Aapola 1992, Thorne 1993), that is, that emotional intensity can often be accompanied by tensions and quarrels, but this has not to my knowledge been investigated in such detail before.

Among the 13-14 year-olds in this research, falling out sometimes arose out of jealousy because one girl was forming a new friendship with another girl, but at this age rarely occurred over boys. Indeed,

180

the intensity of the girls' friendships was in marked contrast to the superficial and temporary relationships with boys at this age. Among the 15-16 year-olds, tensions were more likely to develop when one girl started seeing a lot of her boyfriend and less of her girlfriend. However, I only found one case equivalent to Griffin's 'deffing out' (1985a), and this was relatively shortlived. I also noted a tension between a growing wish for independence, and the young women's need for closeness and support (Aapola 1992), which sometimes led to friction and falling out.

Quarrels between the girls were not always dramatic or long-lasting. A distinction was observed between more serious falling out and everyday 'tiff taff' which often resulted from the frequency of contact between friends. In most cases, particularly taken over the long term, falling out was not permanent but resulted in the friends making up again. Falling out also needs to be seen in the context of adolescence as a time of transition, when physical or emotional changes are likely to be accompanied by changes in friendships. The transition from school to work is also a time when changes of friendship are more likely to occur, but does not necessarily mark the end of friendships between young women.

Continuity of friendships

The question of the continuity of girls' friendships is a complex one. There is general agreement that girls' friendships are strong in early adolescence (Ward 1976, Meyenn 1980), but most previous studies (McRobbie 1978a, Leonard 1980, Griffin 1985a) indicate that girls gradually drop their girlfriends as they start to go out with boys. In my research, I found that girls continued to have strong female friendships both at school and after they had left, whether they had regular boyfriends or not.

This is not to say that girls' friendships always remain the same. As I have noted, there may be a considerable amount of falling out between younger girls, most of which are manoeuvres within the friendships and only lead to temporary changes. At Barnsdale, more permanent changes apparently resulted from girls who were at different stages in the transition to adolescence making new friends; however, even these, when looked at over a longer period, sometimes reverted to former friendships as they got older. This raises the important point about the time span of an ethnographic study of this kind. Certainly a study of only a few months would produce an inadequate or misleading account; even a year or eighteen months does not seem enough to obtain a full picture of developments and changes in friendship patterns. I was only able to obtain more long term information because I kept in touch after the official end of fieldwork, but this information was limited and did not cover all the girls concerned.

As the girls got older, it was boys rather than girls who posed a threat to friendships. However, in the Barnsdale study, continuity of friendships between 15-16 year-old girls generally occurred, even when they were 'going steady' with boys. Only in one case (Marje) had a boyfriend taken precedence over girlfriends. This is contrary to previous findings (Ward 1976, McRobbie 1978a, Llewellyn 1980), although some earlier studies (Leonard 1980, Griffin 1985a) stress the resistance girls make to the break up of their friendships. Throughout the stages of adolescence I looked at, the girls certainly found ways of resisting the breakup of their friendship groups and maintaining their female friendships alongside relationships with boys. I was particularly interested in the idea which the girls raised about 'girls' times' and 'boys' times'.

More recent research (Beuret & Makings 1987, Naber 1992) indicates the complexity of this process; Pauline Naber stresses that there is no straightforward or irreversible transition to boyfriends and that young women's friendships continue to be important, even if the context changes, which is certainly what I found myself. As with the question of falling out among younger girls, I might have obtained a misleading impression if I had only talked to the older girls at one stage. Because I met them again after they had left school, the young women were able to put their school experiences in perspective and give me a more complete account. For example, the tensions brought about by Tricia and her close relationship with a boy might have been seen as undermining Tricia's friendship group at the time, but in retrospect I heard how these tensions were resolved and the girls' friendships reestablished.

Nine months after leaving school, some previously strong friendship groups were dissolving, largely because of the lack of daily contact. Where young women lived close to each other, this contact could still be maintained. Pairs of friends also found it easier to keep in touch than larger groups. However, young women at work or at college were forming new female friendships, and these were seen as important. Definite times were often allocated in the evenings to see girlfriends, even when young women had steady boyfriends. This is in line with other research on friendships between young women (Pollert 1981, Westwood 1984, Beuret & Makings 1987).

Positive emphasis

Earlier in the book, I discussed in some detail the ethical issues and other tensions which arose whilst carrying out the research, and how I tried to resolve these in a feminist way. One of my main concerns has been to keep a sense of the young women as unique individuals with whom I built up a close, affectionate relationship, rather than as objects of research. Hence the importance of letting the girls speak for themselves, and giving their voice a prominent position alongside my own. At the same time, I hope that by documenting one small part of their lives, I will enlarge the picture of young women's friendships in general.

These two aspects have informed my analysis and the presentation of my findings throughout. My interpretation is grounded in the data, using a reflexive process. However, I have also taken into account previous research, and compared my findings with my own experience as an adolescent. The latter has been a particularly rewarding part of the research process. In both this and my previous research (Griffiths 1986), the girls enjoyed the special attention which I was able to give them. Although consciousness-raising was not a central aim, I would suggest that an important offshoot of the research was an increase in the young women's feeling of self-worth, judging from the warmth of feeling with which some of them still recall the project.

Two further points which give the research a certain symmetry. Firstly, just as I was focusing on friendships between the girls, so in the course of doing this I formed friendships with the young women myself, albeit rather 'lop-sided' ones (Brain 1977) owing to the difference in age, status and class. Secondly, just as talking formed a central part of the young women's friendships, so the talking which they and I engaged in as part of the research - the sharing of experience and mutual theorising - formed the basis of the theory generated by the research. In these ways 'research' and 'theory' ceased to be separate, abstracted entities, but very much part of everyday experience.

Overall, the emphasis of my research findings is more positive than much previous research on friendships between young women. Forms of resistance or finding their own space have been noted elsewhere

(McRobbie 1978a, Griffin 1985a, Lees 1986), but these tend to have been muted by the stress on women's subordination. I would suggest several possible reasons for this difference. Firstly, the experience of young women may actually have changed since the earliest studies of adolescent girls took place. The impact of the women's movement has been considerable, even though changes are slow and may apparently be reversed at times. The example of girls' current educational achievement mentioned earlier is one clear example of such changes.

Secondly, there seems to be a different emphasis generally in more recent feminist research, which can be characterised by a move away from the (all-important) documentation of women's oppression, towards a greater celebration of women's strengths, a re-evaluation of the roles women have already filled in society, and an affirmation of the ways in which women are finding new roles. In the field of gender and education, this move can be summed up by looking at the change in book titles, for example, from *Learning to Lose* (Spender & Sarah 1980), to *Girl Friendly Schooling* (Whyte et al 1985). This shift could lead to a different interpretation of the same data, or a closer focus on certain elements, which could result in rather different overall conclusions. With reference to my own research, I suspect that a mixture of these two factors is involved. Certainly, the more recent studies I have cited, particularly the non-British research (Aapola 1992, Wernersson 1992, Naber 1992, Thorne 1993), shows this kind of positive celebratory approach.

Other factors may be also important in explaining differences between studies. In reviewing the literature on girls' interaction at school, I suggested that the particular age of the girls concerned could be important, as well as the school organisation. Race, class and region are also important factors in the social construction of friendships. All these factors will interact to produce a unique configuration in each study, which makes straight comparisons difficult and could also account for some of the differences in findings. Having said this, I have been surprised by the similarity between the young women's friendships in this study and my own experience as a Southern, middle class adolescent girl in the 1960s. Although the social and political context is in many ways hugely different, the research has enabled me to reassess aspects of my own adolescent friendships alongside the current experiences of the girls in this study, and to identify similar features and strengths. As Barrie Thorne writes:

Solidarity among women, not just as background chorus for heterosexual romance, but as a primary form of bonding, has been crucial to women's struggles for equality with men....I believe that bonding among girls, when enacted out of shared respect and a spirit of support, can be a powerful force not only for surviving within but also, potentially, for challenging conventional gender arrangements and female subordination. (Thorne 1993 p.171)

One of the main aims of this book has been to demonstrate, by detailed reference to actual daily practices and interactions between young women in the different contexts of school and leisure, that they do indeed constitute just such a 'powerful force' (ibid.). The many positive ways in which they provide mutual support and solidarity are evidence of the active way in which girls take control over their lives against at times enormous odds. The particular young women with whom I worked so closely at Barnsdale have voiced their experiences and feelings powerfully, and it is only apt that the last words should remain with them:

Jackie   Well me and Lynn think - think alike you see....Me and her get on really really well.

June   We've shared all our secrets together haven't we? She's told me loads of secrets and I've never told anybody.

Jenny   We always find summat good to do.... we have a laugh don't we?

Bibliography

Aapola, S. (1992), 'Best Friends or Many Friends? New Patterns in Young Girls' Friendships', paper presented at *Alice in Wonderland : Girls and Girlhood* conference, Amsterdam.

Acker, J., Barry, K. & Esseveld, J. (1983), 'Objectivity and truth: problems in doing feminist research', *Women's Studies International Forum*, 6:4, 423-435.

Allan, G.A. (1979), *A Sociology of Friendship and Kinship*, London: George Allan & Unwin.

Amos, V. & Parmar, P. (1981), 'Resistances and Responses: The Experiences of Black Girls in Britain', in A. McRobbie & T. McCabe (eds.), *Feminism for Girls: An Adventure Story*, London: Routledge & Kegan Paul.

Anderson, C. (1994), *A Go-Ahead Schoolgirl: a Discussion of the Early School Stories of Angela Brazil and Her Contemporaries , 1906-29,* Unpublished MA dissertation, University of Sussex.

Anyon, J. (1983), 'Intersections of Gender and Class: Accommodation and Resistance by Working Class and Affluent Females to Contradictory Sex-role Ideologies', in L. Barton & S. Walker (eds.), *Gender, Class and Education,* London: Falmer Press.

Arnot, M. (1983), 'A cloud over co-education: an analysis of the forms of transmission of class and gender relations', in S. Walker & L. Barton (eds.), *Gender, Class and Education,* London: Falmer Press.

Atwood, M. (1988), *Cat's Eye*, London: Bloomsbury.

Avgitidou, S. (1994), *Children's Friendships in Early Schooling,* unpublished D.Phil. thesis, University of Sussex.

Ball, S. J. (1981), *Beachside Comprehensive: A Case Study of Secondary Schooling*, Cambridge: Cambridge University Press.

Ball, S. J. (1985), 'Participant Observation with Pupils', in R.G. Burgess (ed.), *Strategies of Educational Research: Qualitative Methods*, London: Falmer Press.

Barnes, J.A. (1977), *The Ethics of Inquiry in Social Sciences*, Milton Keynes: Open University Press.

Becker, H. S. (1971), 'Comment', in M. Wax, S. Diamond & F.O. Gearing (eds.), *Anthropological Perspectives on Education*, New York: Basic Books.

Bernard, J. (1973), 'My Four Revolutions: An Autobiographical History of the A.S.A.', in J. Huber (ed.), *Changing Women in a Changing Society*, Chicago: University of Chicago Press.

Bernstein, B. (1975), *Class, Codes and Control*, London: Routledge & Kegan Paul.

Best, R. (1983), *We've All Got Scars: What Boys and Girls Learn in Elementary School*, Bloomington: Indiana University Press.

Beuret, K. & Makings, L. (1987), '"I've got used to being independent now": Women and Courtship in a Recession', in P. Allatt, T. Keil, A. Bryman & B. Bytheway (eds.), *Women and the Life Cycle: Transitions and Turning-Points*, London: Macmillan.

Beynon, J. (1983), 'Ways In and Staying In: Fieldwork as Problem-solving', in M. Hammersley (ed.), *The Ethnography of Schooling*, Driffield: Nafferton.

Birksted, I. (1976), 'School performance: viewed from the boys', *Sociological Review*, 24:1, 63–77.

Bjerrum Nielsen, H. & Rudberg, M. (1992), 'Class and Gender in the Classroom', paper presented at *Alice in Wonderland : Girls and Girlhood* conference, Amsterdam.

Brah, A. & Minhas, R. (1985), 'Structural Racism or Cultural Difference: Schooling for Asian Girls', in G. Weiner (ed.), *Just a Bunch of Girls: Feminist Approaches to Schooling*, Milton Keynes, Open University Press.

Brain, R. (1977), *Friends and Lovers*, London: Paladin.

Bulmer, M. (ed.) (1982), *The Uses of Social Research*, London: Allen & Unwin.

Burgess, R. G. (1984), *In the Field: An Introduction to Field Research*, London: George Allen & Unwin.

Burgess, R. G. (1985), 'In the Company of Teachers: Key Informants and the Study of a Comprehensive School', in R.G. Burgess (ed.), *Strategies of Educational Research: Qualitative Methods*, London: Falmer Press.

Button, L. (1974) *Developmental Group Work With Adolescents*, University of London Press.

Cameron, D. (1985), *Feminism and Linguistic Theory*, London: Macmillan.

Campbell, A. (1984), *The Girls in the Gang*, London: Basil Blackwell.

Campbell, A. (1992), 'Girls at the Crossroad: The Construction of a Social Identity', paper presented at *Alice in Wonderland : Girls and Girlhood* conference, Amsterdam.

Canaan, J. (1987), 'A Comparative Analysis of American Suburban Middle Class , Middle School and High School Teenage Cliques', in G. & L. Spindler (eds.), *Interpretive Ethnography of Education*, N.J.: Lawrence Erlbaum.

Clarke, J. (1978), 'The Fan and the Game', in R. Ingham (ed.), *Football Hooliganism*, London: Interaction.

Connell, R.W. (1987), *Gender and Power*, Stanford: Stanford University Press.

Cooper, D. (1989), 'Positive Images in Haringey: A Struggle for Identity', in C. Jones & P. Mahony (eds.), *Learning Our Lines: Sexuality and Social Control in Education*, London: Women's Press.

Cowie, C. & Lees, S. (1981), 'Slags or drags', *Feminist Review*, No.9, 17-31.

Davies, B. (1982), *Life in the Classroom and Playground: The Accounts of Primary School Children*, London: Routledge & Kegan Paul.

Davies, B. (1989), *Frogs and Snails and Feminist Tales: Preschool Children and Gender*, Boston: Allen & Unwin.

Davies, L. (1984), *Pupil Power: Deviance and Gender in School*, London: Falmer Press.

Davies, L. (1985), 'Ethnography and Status: Focussing on Gender in Educational Research', in R.G.Burgess (ed.), *Field Methods in the Study of Education*, London: Falmer Press.

de Beauvoir, S. (1952), *The Second Sex*, New York: Vintage.

Deem, R. (1984), *Co-Education Reconsidered*, Milton Keynes: Open University Press.

Deem, R. (1986), *All Work and No Play: The Sociology of Women and Leisure*, Milton Keynes: Open University Press.

Delamont, S. (1976), 'The girls most likely to: cultural reproduction and Scottish elites', *Scottish Journal of Sociology*, 1:1, 29-43.

Delamont, S. (1980), *Sex Roles and the School*, London: Methuen.

Delamont, S. (1981), 'All too familiar? A decade of classroom research', *Educational Analysis*, 3:1, 69-83.

Denscombe, M. (1983), 'Interviews, Accounts and Ethnographic Research on Teachers', in M. Hammersley (ed.), *The Ethnography of Schooling: Methodological Issues*, Driffield: Nafferton.

Dixon, J., Salvat, G. & Skeates, J. (1989), 'North London Young Lesbian Group: Specialist Work Within the Youth Service', in C. Jones & P. Mahony (eds.), *Learning Our Lines: Sexuality and Social Control in Education*, London: Women's Press.

Douvan, E. & Adelson, J. (1966), *The Adolescent Experience*, New York: John Wiley.

Duck, S. (1983), *Friends for Life: the Psychology of Close Relationships*, London: The Harvester Press.

Ellis, H. (1913), *Sexual Inversion*, Philadelphia: F.A. Davis.

Faderman, L. (1981), *Surpassing the Love of Men: Romantic Friendship and Love Between Women from the Renaissance to the Present*, New York: William Morrow.

Faraday, A. (1989), 'Lessoning Lesbians: Girls' Schools, Coeducation and Anti-lesbianism Between the Wars', in C. Jones & P. Mahony (eds.), *Learning Our Lines: Sexuality and Social Control in Education*, London: Women's Press.

Farran, D. (1990), 'Seeking Susan: Producing Statistical Infomation on Young People's Leisure', in L. Stanley (ed.), *Feminist Praxis*, London: Routledge.

Finch, J. (1984), '"It's great to have someone to talk to": The Ethics and Politics of Interviewing Women', in C. Bell & H. Roberts (eds.), *Social Researching: Politics, Problems, Practice*, London: Routledge & Kegan Paul.

Fine, G.A. & Glassner, B. (1989), 'Participant observation with children: promise and problems', *Urban Life* 8, 153-174.

Frith, S. (1978), *The Sociology of Rock*, London: Constable.

Fuller, M. (1980), 'Black Girls in a London Comprehensive School', in R. Deem (ed.), *Schooling for Women's Work*, Routledge & Kegan Paul.

Furlong, V. (1976), 'Interaction Sets in the Classroom', in M. Stubbs & S. Delamont (eds.), *Explorations in Classroom Observation*, London: John Wiley.

Gardner, S., Dean, C. & McKaig, D. (1992), 'Responding to Differences in the Classroom: The Politics of Knowledge, Class and Sexuality', in J. Wrigley (ed.), *Education and Gender Equality*, London: Falmer Press.

Goodwin, M.H. (1991), *He-Said-She-Said: Talk as Social Organisation Among Black Children*, Bloomington: Indiana University Press.

Graham, H. (1982), 'Building a Feminist Methodology: The Case of the Survey Method', paper presented at B.S.A. conference, University of Manchester.

Graham, P. (1995), 'Girls' Camp', paper presented in *Queory* series, University of Sussex.

Grant, L. (1992), 'Race and the Schooling of Young Girls', in J. Wrigley (ed.), *Education and Gender Equality*, London: Falmer Press.

Grant, L. (1994),'First among equals',*The Guardian Weekend*, Oct. 22.

Griffin, C. (1980),'Feminist Ethnography', stencilled paper, Centre for Contemporary Cultural Studies, University of Birmingham.

Griffin, C. (1981), 'Cultures of Femininity: Romance Revisited', stencilled paper, Centre for Contemporary Cultural Studies, University of Birmingham.

Griffin, C. (1985a), *Typical Girls? Young women from School to the Job Market*, London: Routledge & Kegan Paul.

Griffin, C. (1985b), 'Qualitative Methods and Cultural Analysis: Young Women and the Transition from School to Un/employment', in R.G. Burgess (ed.), *Field Methods in the Study of Education*, London: Falmer Press.

Griffin, C. (1987), 'Broken Transitions: From School to the Scrap Heap', in P. Allatt, T. Keil, A. Bryman & B. Bytheway (eds.),*Women and the Life Cycle: Transitions and Turning Points*, London: Macmillan.

Griffin, C., Hobson D., McIntosh, S. & McCabe, T.(1982), 'Women and Leisure', in J. Hargreaves (ed.), *Sport, Culture and Ideology*, London: Routledge & Kegan Paul.

Griffiths, V. (1982), *Adolescent Girls and Attitudes to Gender: a Preliminary Investigation Using Drama*, unpublished M.A. thesis, University of Manchester.

Griffiths, V. (1984), 'Feminist research and the use of drama', *Women's Studies International Forum*, 7:6, 511-519.

Griffiths, V. (1986), 'Using drama to get at gender', *Studies in Sexual Politics 9*, Manchester: University of Manchester, Sociology Department.

Griffiths, V. (1988), 'Stepping Out: The Importance of Dancing for Young Women', in E. Wimbush & M. Talbot (eds.), *Relative Freedoms: Women and Leisure*, Milton Keynes: Open University Press.

Griffiths, V. (1989), *Adolescent Girls and Their Friends: A Feminist Ethnography*, unpublished Ph.D. thesis, University of Manchester.

Griffiths, V. (1990), 'Using Drama to get at Gender', in L. Stanley (ed.), *Feminist Praxis*, London: Routledge.

Griffiths, V. (1991), 'Doing Feminist Ethnography on Friendship', in J. Alridge, V. Griffiths & A. Williams, *Rethinking: Feminist Research Processes Reconsidered, Feminist Praxis*, Manchester: Manchester University, Sociology Department.

Hargreaves, D.H. (1967), *Social Relations in a Secondary School*, London: Routledge & Kegan Paul.

Hebdige, D. (1979), *Subculture: The Meaning of Style*, London: Methuen.

Hobson, D. (1980), 'Young Women at Home and Leisure', paper given at *Leisure and Social Control* Conference, Centre for Contemporary Cultural Studies, University of Birmingham.

Holly, L. (1989), *Girls and Sexuality: Teaching and Learning*, Milton Keynes: Open University Press.

Ingham, M. (1981), *Now We Are Thirty: Women of the Breakthrough Generation*, London: Methuen.

Jamdagni, L. (1980), *Hamari Rangily Zindagi: Our Colourful Lives*, Leicester: National Association of Youth Clubs.

Jayaratne, T. (1981), 'The Value of Quantitative Methodology for Feminist Research', in G. Bowles & R. Duelli-Klein (eds.), *Theories of Women's Studies II*, Berkely: UCLA.

Johnson, F. L. & Aries, E.J. (1983), 'The talk of women friends', *Women's Studies International Forum*, 6:4, 353-361.

Jones, C. (1985), 'Sexual Tyranny: Male Violence in a Mixed Secondary School', in G. Weiner (ed.), *Just a Bunch of Girls: Feminist Approaches to Schooling*, Milton Keynes, Open University Press.

Jones, C. & Mahony. P. (eds.), (1989), *Learning Our Lines: Sexuality and Social Control in Education*, London: Women's Press.

Kelly, A. (1978), 'Feminism and research', *Women's Studies International Quarterly*, 1:3, 225-232.

Kutnick, P.J. (1988), *Relationships in the Primary School Classroom*, London: Paul Chapman.

Lacey, C. (1970), *Hightown Grammar*, Manchester University Press.

Lambart, A. M. (1976), 'The Sisterhood', in M. Hammersley & P.Woods (eds.), *The Process of Schooling: a Sociological Reader*, London: Routledge & Kegan Paul/ Open University Press.

Lees, S. (1986), *Losing Out: Sexuality and Adolescent Girls*, London: Hutchinson.

Lees, S. (1993), *Sugar and Spice: Sexuality and Adolescent Girls*, Harmondsworth: Penguin.

Leonard, D. (1980), *Sex and Generation: A Study of Courtship and Weddings*, London: Tavistock.

Llewellyn, M. (1980), 'Studying Girls at School: The Implications of Confusion', in R. Deem (ed.), *Schooling for Women's Work*, London: Routledge & Kegan Paul.

Mac an Ghaill, M. (1988), *Young, Gifted and Black*, Milton Keynes: Open University Press.

McCabe, T. (1980), 'Girls and Leisure', paper given at *Leisure and Social Control* Conference, Centre for Contemporary Cultural Studies, University of Birmingham.

McRobbie, A. (1977), *Working Class Girls and the Culture of Femininity*, unpublished M.A. thesis, Centre for Contemporary Cultural Studies, University of Birmingham.

McRobbie, A. (1978a), 'Working Class Girls and the Culture of Femininity', in Women's Studies Group (eds.), *Women Take Issue: Aspects of Women's Subordination*, London: Hutchinson.

McRobbie, A. (1978b), '*Jackie*, an Ideology of Adolescent Femininity', stencilled paper, Centre for Contemporary Cultural Studies, University of Birmingham.

McRobbie, A. (1979), 'Settling accounts with subcultures: a feminist critique', *Screen Education*, 34, 37-47.

McRobbie, A. (1981), 'Just Like a *Jackie* Story', in A. McRobbie & T. McCabe (eds.), *Feminism for Girls: an Adventure Story*, London: Routledge, Kegan & Paul.

McRobbie, A. (1982), 'The politics of feminist research: between talk, text and action', *Feminist Review*, no.12, 46-57.

McRobbie, A. (1984), 'Dance and Social Fantasy', in A. McRobbie & M. Nava (eds.), *Gender and Generation*, London: Macmillan.

McRobbie, A. (1991), *Feminism and Youth Culture from Jackie to Just Seventeen*, London: Macmillan.

McRobbie, A. & Garber, J. (1976), 'Girls and Subcultures: an Exploration', in S. Hall & T. Jefferson (eds.), *Resistance Through Rituals*, London: Hutchinson.

Maccoby, E. & Jacklin, C. (1974), *The Psychology of Sex Differences*, Stanford: Stanford University Press.

Mahony, P. (1985), *Schools for the Boys? Co-education Reassessed*, London: Hutchinson/The Explorations in Feminism Collective.

Mandell, N. (1988), 'The least-adult role in studying children', *Journal of Contemporary Ethnography*, 16, 433-467.

Measor, L. (1985), 'Interviewing: a Strategy in Qualitative Research', in R.G. Burgess (ed.), *Strategies of Educational Research: Qualitative Methods*, London: Falmer Press.

Measor, L. & Sikes, P. (1992), *Gender and Schools*, London: Cassell.

Measor, L. & Woods, P. (1984), *Changing Schools*, Milton Keynes: Open University Press.

Meyenn, R. (1980), 'School Girls' Peer Groups', in P. Woods (ed.), *Pupil Strategies*, London: Croom Helm.

Mickelson, R.A. (1992), 'Why Does Jane Read and Write so Well? The Anomaly of Women's Achievement', in J. Wrigley (ed.), *Education and Gender Equality*, London: Falmer Press.

Morgan, D. (1981), 'Men, Masculinity and the Process of Sociological Enquiry', in H. Roberts (ed.), *Doing Feminist Research*, London: Routledge & Kegan Paul.

Mungham, G. (1976), 'Youth in Pursuit of Itself', in G. Mungham & G. Pearson (eds.), *Working Class Youth Culture*, London: Routledge & Kegan Paul.

Mungham, G. & Pearson, G. (eds.) (1976), *Working Class Youth Culture*, London: Routledge & Kegan Paul.

Naber, P. (1992), 'Friendship Between Young Women', paper presented at *Alice in Wonderland: Girls and Girlhood* conference, Amsterdam.

Nava, M. (1984), 'Youth Service Provision, Social Order and the Question of Girls', in A. McRobbie & M. Nava (eds.), *Gender and Generation*, London: Macmillan.

Nilan, P, (1991), 'Exclusion, inclusion and moral ordering in two girls' friendship groups', *Gender and Education*, 3 (2).

Oakley, A, (1974), *The Sociology of Housework*, London: Martin Robertson.

Oakley, A. (1981), 'Interviewing Women: A Contradiction in Terms', in H. Roberts (ed.), *Doing Feminist Research*, London: Routledge & Kegan Paul.

O'Connor, P. (1992), *Friendships Between Women*, N.Y.: Harvester Wheatsheaf.

Opie, I. & Opie, P. (1959), *The Lore and Language of Schoolchildren*, Oxford: Oxford University Press.

Orbach, S. & Eichenbaum, L. (1987), *Bittersweet*, London: Arrow.

Parmar, P. & Mirza, N. (1981), 'Youth work with Asian girls', *Working With Girls Newsletter*, No.2, 8-9.

Phoenix, A. (1992), 'Race, Social Class and Gender in Girls' Friendships', paper presented at *Alice in Wonderland: Girls and Girlhood* conference, Amsterdam.

Piercy, M. (1982), *Braided Lives*, Harmonsdworth: Penguin.

Poland, F. (1987), 'Making a Tape-slide from Biographies of the Elderly: Educational Resource or Objectification?' in V. Griffiths, M. Humm, R. O'Rourke & J. Batsleer, F. Poland & S. Wise (eds.), *Writing Feminist Biography 2: Using Life Histories, Studies in Sexual Politics* No.19, Sociology Department, University of Manchester.

Pollard, A. (1984), 'Goodies, Jokers and Gangs', in M. Hammersley & P. Woods (eds.), *Life in School: the Sociology of Pupil Culture*, Milton Keynes: Open University Press.

Pollert, A. (1981), *Girls, Wives, Factory Lives*, London: Macmillan.

Rich, A. (1981), 'Compulsory heterosexuality and lesbian existence', *Signs* 5, 198-210.

Riley, K. (1985), 'Black Girls Speak for Themselves', in G. Weiner (ed.), *Just a Bunch of Girls: Feminist Approaches to Schooling,* Milton Keyens: Open University Press.

Sanders, S. & Spraggs, G. (1989), 'Section 28 and Education', in C. Jones & P. Mahony (eds.), *Learning Our Lines: Sexuality and Social Control in Education,* London: Women's Press.

Schofield, J.W. (1992), *Black and White in School,* New York: Praeger.

Seiden, Anne & Bart, Pauline (1975), 'Woman to Woman: is Sisterhood Powerful?' in N. Glazer-Malbin (ed.), *Old Family/New Family,* New York: Van Nostrand.

Simons, H. (1981), 'Conversation Piece: The Practice of Interviewing in Case Study Research', in C. Adelman (ed.), *Uttering, Muttering,* London: Grant McIntyre.

Smail, B. (1984), *Girl Friendly Science: Avoiding Sex Bias in the Curriculum,* London: Longman/Schools Council.

Smith, D. (1974), 'Women's perspective as a radical critique of sociology', *Sociological Inquiry,* 44:1, 7-13.

Smith, D. (1977), 'Some Implications of a Sociology for Women', in N. Glazer & H.Y. Waehrer (eds.), *Woman in a Man-Made World,* Chicago: Rand McNally.

Smith, D. (1979), 'A Sociology for Women', in J. Sherman & E. Peck (eds.), *The Prison of Sex: Essays in the Sociology of Knowledge,* Wisconsin: University of Wisconsin Press.

Smith, Lesley S. (1978), 'Sexist Assumptions and Female Delinquency: an Empirical Investigation', in C.Smart & B. Smart (eds.), *Women, Sexuality and Social Control,* London: Routledge & Kegan Paul.

Smith, S. (1986), *Separate Tables? An Investigation into Single-Sex Setting in Mathematics,* Equal Opportunities Commission Research Series, London: HMSO.

Spender, D. (1978), 'Educational Research and the Feminist Perspective', paper presented at the B.E.R.A. conference, University of Leicester.

Spender, D. (1980), *Man-Made Language,* London: Routledge & Kegan Paul.

Spender, D. (1982), *Invisible Women: The Schooling Scandal,* London: Writers and Readers Publishing Cooperative.

Spender, D. & Sarah, E. (eds.), (1980), *Learning to Lose: Sexism and Education,* London: The Women's Press.

Stanley, J. (1993), 'Sex and the Quiet Schoolgirl', in P. Woods & M. Hammersley (eds.), *Gender and Ethnicity in Schools: Ethnographic Accounts*, London: Routledge/ Open University.

Stanley, L. & Wise, S. (1983), *Breaking Out: Feminist Consciousness and Feminist Research*, London: Routledge & Kegan Paul.

Stanley, L. (1988), 'Historical Sources for Studying Work and Leisure in Women's Lives', in E. Wimbush & M. Talbot (eds.), *Relative Freedoms: Women and Leisure*, Milton Keynes: Open University Press.

Stanworth, M. (1981), *Gender and Schooling: A Study of Sexual Divisions in the Classroom*, Explorations in Feminism, London: Women's Research and Resources Centre.

Tannen, D. (1991), *You Just Don't Understand,: Women and Men in Conversation*, New York: Morrow.

Thorne, B. (1993), *Gender Play: Girls and Boys in School*, Buckingham: Open University Press.

Walker, S. & Barton, L. (eds.) (1983), *Gender, Class and Education*, London: Falmer Press.

Walkerdine, V. (1990), *Schoolgirl Fictions*, New York: Verso.

Ward, J. (1976), *Social Reality for the Adolescent Girl*, Swansea: University College of Swansea, Faculty of Education.

Wernersson, I. (1992), 'Gender Differences in Social Interaction in the Classroom Setting: Alternative Explanations', paper presented at *Alice in Wonderland: Girls and Girlhood* conference, Amsterdam.

Westwood, S. (1984), *All Day Every Day: Factory and Family in the Making of Women's Lives*, London: Pluto.

Whitehead, A. (1976), 'Sexual Antagonisms in Herefordshire', in D.L. Barker & S. Allen (eds.), *Dependence and Exploitation in Work and Marriage*, London: Longman.

Whyld, J. (ed.), (1983), *Sexism in the Secondary Curriculum*, London: Harper & Row.

Whyte, J. (1986) *Girls into Science and Technology*, London: Routledge & Kegan Paul.

Whyte, J. Deem, R, Kant, L. & Cruickshank, M. (eds.), (1985), *Girl Friendly Schooling*, London: Methuen.

Williams, A. (1977), 'Reading Feminism in Fieldnotes', in Feminist Research Seminar (eds.), *Feminist Research Processes, Studies in Sexual Politics* No.16, Sociology Department, University of Manchester.

Willis, P. (1977), *Learning to Labour: How Working Class Kids Get Working Class Jobs*, Farnborough: Saxon House.

Willis, P. (1980), 'Notes on Method', in S. Hall, D. Hobson, A. Lowe & P. Willis (eds.), *Culture, Media, Language*, Centre for Contemporary Cultural Studies: University of Birmingham.

Wilson, D. (1978), 'Sexual Codes and Conduct', in C. Smart & B. Smart (eds.), *Women, Sexuality and Social Control*, London: Routledge & Kegan Paul.

Wimbush, E. & Talbot, M. (eds.) (1988), *Relative Freedoms: Women and Leisure*, Milton Keyens: Open University Press.

Wise, S. (1987), 'A Framework for Discussing Ethical Issues in Feminist Research: a Review of the Literature', in V. Griffiths et al (eds.), *Writing Feminist Biography 2:Using Life Histories, Studies in Sexual Politics* No.19, Sociology Department, University of Manchester.

Wolcott, H. (1975), 'Criteria for an ethnographic approach to research in schools', *Human Organisation*, 34, 2, 111-127.

Wolpe, A. (1988), *Within School Walls: The Role of Discipline, Sexuality and the Curriculum*, London: Routledge.

Woods P. (1986), *Inside Schools: Ethnography in Educational Research*, London: Routledge & Kegan Paul.

Woolf, V. (1938), *Three Guineas*, Harmondsworth: Penguin.

Wright, C. (1993), 'School Processes: an Ethnographic Study', in P. Woods & M. Hammersley (eds.), *Gender and Ethnicity in Schools: Ethnographic Accounts*, London: Routledge/Open University.

Wrigley, J. (ed.) (1992), *Education and Gender Equality*, London: Falmer Press.

Wulff, H. (1988), *Twenty Girls Growing Up: Ethnicity and Excitement in a London Microculture*, Stockholm: Univeristy of Stockholm.

Youth Work Unit (1981), *Working With Girls: A Reader's Route Map*, Leicester: National Youth Bureau.

HAVERING COLLEGE OF F & H E

144729